There is much to ponder on in this book. We live in difficult yet exciting days. God is longing to stir up his church to reach every community with the gospel. If we follow the leading of the Spirit, we can certainly become radiant and resolute in our faith and our witness.

Debra Green, founder of Redeeming Our Communities

This book is a 'must read'. In the midst of thought-provoking but readily accessible insights into end-time thinking, William Porter has set out a picture of the church that I am convinced everyone needs to grasp and work towards. It's of a church that is both overcoming and glorious – radiant and resolute. As I reached the sentence, 'God is asking the church in the coming years to step into its calling . . . Yet it starts with a "yes"', I found myself shouting 'YES, YES, YES' as loudly as I could. But I'd be thrilled if my 'YES' got lost in the deafeningly affirmative chorus that I'm sure will rise from congregations, ministries and leaders that this book will inspire. Thank you, William, for such a focus.

Hugh Osgood, past president of Churches Together in England

William Porter's book is an urgent call to be alert and to be faithful. He inspires us with the reality that God is in control of all things and that God can be trusted, even as the world seems to teeter on the brink of so much chaos. His careful and faithful exposition of Scripture points us to the reality that God will build his church and that we can be confident in the purposes and plans of God. As a result of this, we are inspired to be faithful. William reminds us that good eschatology is a motivation for faith, and for faithfulness. He reminds us that Christ will come for his bride, and that we, the Church Militant, can be confident, clear, courteous and courageous in our witness to Jesus, because one day we will join the Church Triumphant and we will reign and rule with our Saviour. This is a book about our times, for our times. It reminds us that we stand until the end of time and go to the ends of the earth proclaiming the eschaton, the gospel and the goodness of God.

Revd Malcolm J. Duncan F.R.S.A., F.I.P.T., senior minister at Kensington Temple London City Church, chair of Elim's Public Theology, Justice and Pastoral Ethics Task Force

This is a profound, provocative and very timely book taking us on a journey to look afresh at God's ultimate plan for his bride in this season of acceleration and shaking. With so much negative press about what the 'now' church is and isn't, William Porter's four-part book looks biblically and unashamedly at the end times; takes a long gaze at Jesus' teaching and the mindset of the 'early' church; peeps into seven marks of the 'emerging end-time' church and concludes with powerful chapters on how to prepare as the 'now' church – as leaders, as congregations and as individuals. The very insightful 'Pause for Thought' sections interspersed throughout help us to begin to engage with this in our own context. This book has deeply challenged me to want to be fully alert, on my watch, praying and working so as to play my little part in enabling a radiant and resolute church to welcome Jesus.

Jane Holloway, national prayer director of World Prayer Centre

Radiant and Resolute

Exploring the marks of the church before Jesus returns

William Porter

Copyright © 2025 William Porter

First published 2025 by Paternoster
Paternoster is an imprint of Authentic Media Limited,
PO Box 6326, Bletchley, Milton Keynes, MK1 9GG.
authenticmedia.co.uk

The right of William Porter to be identified as the Author of this Work
has been asserted in accordance with the
Copyright, Designs and Patents Act 1988.

All rights reserved.
No part of this publication may be reproduced, stored
in a retrieval system, or transmitted in any form or by any means,
electronic, mechanical, photocopying, recording or otherwise, without
the prior permission of the publisher or a licence permitting restricted
copying. In the UK such licences are issued by the Copyright Licensing
Agency, 5th Floor, Shackleton House, 4 Battle Bridge Lane, London SE1 2HX.

British Library Cataloguing in Publication Data
A catalogue record for this book is available from the British Library.
ISBN: 978-1-78893-296-7
978-1-78893-297-4 (e-book)

Unless otherwise stated, Scripture quotations are taken from
The Holy Bible, New International Version Anglicised
Copyright © 1979, 1984, 2011 Biblica
Used by permission of Hodder & Stoughton Ltd, an Hachette UK company.
All rights reserved.
'NIV' is a registered trademark of Biblica
UK trademark number 1448790.

Scripture quotations marked AMPC are taken from the Amplified Bible,
Copyright © 1987 by The Lockman Foundation. Used by permission.

Scripture quotations marked ESV are from the ESV® Bible (The Holy Bible, English
Standard Version®), copyright © 2001 by Crossway, a publishing ministry of Good News
Publishers. Used by permission. All rights reserved. The ESV text may not be quoted in any
publication made available to the public by a Creative Commons license. The ESV may not
be translated in whole or in part into any other language.

Scripture quotations marked KJV are from The Authorized (King James) Version. Rights
in the Authorized Version in the United Kingdom are vested in the Crown. Reproduced by
permission of the Crown's patentee, Cambridge University Press.

The Scriptures quoted marked NET are from the NET Bible® https://netbible.com copyright
©1996, 2019 used with permission from Biblical Studies Press, L.L.C. All rights reserved.

Cover design by S4Carslisle Publishing Services

To my friends in our End Times discussion group: Peter, Michael, Nick, Robin and Jim. The shared wisdom and insight when we meet is deeply encouraging. May this book inspire many such collectives of people searching the Scriptures and looking at the signs of the times.

Contents

	Foreword	xi
	Acknowledgments	xiii
	Introduction	xv
	Prologue: Calling Out the Church	xix
Part One	**An End-Times Context**	**1**
1	The Coming End Times	3
2	God Has Got a Plan	25
3	Great Revival, Great Turbulence	46
4	Keeping Our Eyes on the Lord's Return	78
Part Two	**The Bride Has Made Herself Ready**	**103**
5	A Fresh Look at the Church	105
6	Radiant: Journey into Intimacy in the Song of Songs	122
7	Resolute: Glimpses into the End-Time Church in the Book of Revelation	133
8	God Will Finish What He Has Started: The Book of Acts and the End-Time Church	151

Contents

Part Three	**The Unexplored Country of End-Time Ministry**	**165**
	Introduction to Part Three: Marks of the Emerging End-Time Church	167
9	**First Mark:** Known for the Numinous Presence of the Lord (the Overshadowed Community)	171
10	**Second Mark:** Devoted in Love for the Lord and for Each Other (the Fervent Community)	179
11	**Third Mark:** Spreading the Gospel in Word and Spirit (the Anointed Community)	188
12	**Fourth Mark:** Expressing God's Heart for the Poor and Broken (the Outpoured Community)	201
13	**Fifth Mark:** Refined by Persecution and Falling Away (the Cruciform Community)	210
14	**Sixth Mark:** Mature in Development, Growth, Influence and Prayer (the Grown-Up Community)	220
15	**Seventh Mark:** Creating First Fruits of the Coming Eschaton (the Transfiguring Community)	231
	Summing Up of Part Three	245
Part Four	**How Shall We Prepare?**	**249**
	Introduction to Part Four	251
16	Preparing as the Whole Church	254
17	Preparing as Leaders	270

Contents   ix

18   The Personal Challenge   285

Coda: Three Visions of the Bride of
Christ in the Age to Come (Rev. 19 – 22)   298

        Notes   310
        Bibliography   319

Foreword

We are living at a time in which, more than ever, it takes courage to be a true Christian. I think a symptom of our lack of courage is that we are afraid to talk seriously about eschatology – especially if we make certain claims regarding our being in the last days. Not only that; so many in the past have made such ridiculous and speculative statements about the present and future that it has put many off entirely from dealing with this matter.

When I began preaching seventy years ago, I was enamoured with the study of end-time prophecy. I had it all figured out! I thought I understood the book of Revelation – all because I had read one book on the subject and because my pastor when I was a teenager backed up that book. When my father heard me preach on prophecy when I was 19 years old, he reminded me of a word from Dr R.T. Williams, the man I was named after: 'Young men, stay away from the subject of prophecy. Let the older men deal with that. That way they won't be around to see their mistakes.'

I salute Dr William Porter for having the courage to stick his neck out and not only suggest that we are living in the end times but also dare to suggest what these times will be like. I find this encouraging. But this book will not leave the author embarrassed if it turns out he has got it wrong. He writes confidently but cautiously. He has done considerable research and demonstrates admirable learning.

Like the author, I believe we are in the last days. I have written some books on this too. But I tell myself that Jonathan Edwards (1703–58) also believed he was living in the latter-day glory. He got it wrong. But it is only a matter of time before *somebody* gets it right! How do I know this? It is because the Bible clearly teaches that there *will be a time of the end*. It teaches that one day the earth will be filled with the glory of the Lord as the waters cover the sea (Hab. 2:14).

In my old age I have taught that (1) things will get worse and worse in the world and (2) things will get better and better in the church, but also (3) the next thing to happen on God's calendar is not the second coming but the genuine and unmistakable awakening of the church just before the end (Matt. 25:6). Dr Porter would not have to agree with all I have written, but I believe he has got it generally right. The church in the end will be radiant and resolute. There will be great blessing ahead that will remind us of the book of Acts. But there will also be persecution that will remind us of the book of Acts.

I hope this book will be read by all Christians.

R.T. Kendall
Minister, Westminster Chapel (1977–2002)

Acknowledgments

I am indebted to R.T. Kendall for his gracious words in the foreword and for his prophetic teaching ministry over the years. I am grateful, too, to Donna, Roxanne, Mollie, Rachel and all the Authentic team for helping me get this book completed, and for their skills in pushing it through to publication. I want to also acknowledge the small audiences on whom I tried some of the early ideas of this book during conferences and seminars. Thanks to the community at the Beacon house of prayer, with whom I have been blessed to share a rich prayer journey. Thanks most of all to my immediate family – Karen, Joshua and Sarah – who love and believe in me, and were patient, particularly as I wrote the initial draft during the first difficult months of Covid lockdown in our home.

Introduction

Books about the future of the church tend to be instructive manuals and exhorting guides as to how to be more . . . something. More effective, more outreaching, more visionary, more biblical, more kingdom-oriented. This is not that kind of book.

I am looking at the church from a biblical end-times perspective. What does the Bible say the church is like at the end, the time when Jesus returns, and how does she become like that? What are the conditions of life on earth in the time leading to his return and how does that shape the life of the church? From Scripture I see a church that will emerge – through difficulty and through the work of the Spirit – as something very special. There are so many things we could find wrong with the church. We are certainly not the best advert for Jesus or for the wonderful reality of our faith. Yet God seems committed to his people through thick and thin. He seems determined to make a beautiful bride for his Son.

And so I am writing a book about our emergence, our becoming, a work that becomes clearer the further into the biblical end times we travel.

Books on the end times are not particularly prominent on the British scene. Neither did I ever think I would be a writer on these subjects. My turning point in taking eschatology seriously happened a few years ago now. I had been interested for years in revival, from a historical and contemporary viewpoint. I was on twin tracks of research and prayer – research into the work of the Spirit at the heart of revival movements, and prayer pilgrimages to places where God was moving in renewal and revival power. In February 2007, the month I was submitting my PhD research, we went as a family to the International House of Prayer, in Kansas City, USA, as an exploratory trip to understand how to start a house of prayer. While we were there, God spoke profoundly to me, one of the half-dozen times in my life when his word altered the direction of my life. I felt quite clearly from the Lord that all my research into revivals, and all my God-chasing to experience revival in my generation, was not just about any revival but about the last great awakening before Jesus returns. My hopes had been to be part of a move of God to help us through a season of decline in the church. God's whisper to me was as loud as the whisper to Elijah in the cave at Carmel: 'You are praying and preparing for the end-time move of my Spirit before the return of my Son.' That word reframed my life and ministry, and I have not been able to get away from this realization that eschatology is the radical edge of Christian thinking and the most relevant theme for faith discipleship in these days.

So I am writing from a committed perspective, but one that I hope is generous and open. I am passionate that the whole church should engage with the times we are living in. When we speak of a 'new normal' regarding life after the Covid-19 pandemic, I keep feeling that we have little understanding of how critical the times we are living in actually are. In what has been described as an age of panic, the Bible offers the clearest guidance about life and the future. And the church is such a key element in God's plans for our world.

This book is in four parts. In Part One we will look at a general understanding of eschatology and the end times, and what we find in Scripture concerning trends in the last days. We will consider God's salvation plans in the end times and how they affect the world and the church. We will look at the concepts of future revival and global trouble, and take a long gaze at the promise of Jesus' second coming and what happens afterwards.

In the second part, we will look at the church within the particular imagery of the bride of Christ. We will see how a bridal reading of Scripture enhances our understanding of the church, especially through three books: the Song of Songs, Revelation and the Acts of the Apostles.

In Part Three we will attempt to explore some of the marks of the emerging end-time church, noting a close correlation with the dynamics of the early church – namely becoming overshadowed, fervent, anointed, outpoured, cruciform, grown-up and transfiguring.

The fourth and final part of the book asks what this means for the church here and now, and what, if anything, we can do to prepare for the future.

I wrote the first draft of this book in the first few weeks of the Covid lockdown in the UK. The themes had been brewing in my mind for a few years, but the substance came together in that intense period we all went through when normal life was shut down and no one knew what the future would look like. At the time, I felt the weight of God's inspiration as I wrote, but I leave these themes with you for your weighing and discernment.

I hope that this book will be relevant for any reader interested in exploring what the Bible says about the end times. It will be particularly relevant for those either leading churches or watching and praying over the signs of the times. It will paint, I believe, a dramatic picture of the coming decades on planet earth, yet also a hopeful vision of what the Lord is helping us to become as his people, his church and his bride.

William Porter

Prologue: Calling Out the Church

The atmosphere was charged; great anticipation sparked in the air. The heavenly throng were watching and waiting. They had long perceived the movements of history, the fall and redemption story played out over so many generations in so many places. The swirling fog and rising smoke could be clearly seen over the circumference of the earth, obscuring contours and landmarks, and diminishing any detailed sight of battles raging on the planet. The angels were praising, certainty growing as they affirmed again and again the great plans of God Almighty for his creation. The saints above were gazing down and praying, praying for what must surely come. There had been critical days, moments of uncertainty when it seemed as if things had swung against the kingdom of the Lord and his Christ. Hell's schemes and devilish hordes had been wreaking havoc on communities, fires of conflict were sparking in random places, godlessness was rampant, hopelessness hung like a pall over nations. And the church on earth had been . . . quiet. Not inactive, not retreating, but unsure of herself, her confidence slipping, her strength sapping, her sense of destiny unclear. All those watching in heaven knew a moment had come, a critical juncture that could profoundly swing the spiritual balance. Great calm emanated from the throne; then suddenly, pulsating light, beauty, power, awesome splendour enveloped all the celestial hosts. As waves of grace and love streamed out across the universe, there was a moment of silence, and then a roar from the angels as the voice that called all things into being rang out like thunder over the redeemed on the earth: 'Arise and shine, for your light has come, and the glory of the Lord rises upon you! See, darkness covers the earth and thick darkness is over the peoples. But the Lord rises upon you and his glory appears over you!'[1]

Part One

An End-Times Context

But I know, somehow, that only when it is dark enough can you see the stars.
Martin Luther King Jr

1

The Coming End Times

Exploring the End Times

Future thinking

Humanity is fascinated about the future. In our personal worlds, people listen to clairvoyants and fortune-tellers with a nervous giggle, we dream endlessly of our retirements, we fantasize about how winning the lottery would change our lives, we wring our hands with anxieties and fears about things that could go wrong in the future yet rarely do. Collectively, we create cultures based not on what we want now but what could be useful in the coming years; revolutions are fuelled by projecting a more desirable future; we value foresight in creating huge visionary projects; we anticipate, we dream, we make fantasy films, we constantly look forward rather than back.

Psychologists are discovering that this trait is actually hard-wired into our brains as human beings. The authors of a book called *Homo Prospectus* argue that we are misnamed as a species. Whereas *Homo sapiens* ('wise man') is an aspiration, the capacity to anticipate and evaluate future possibilities, in guiding thoughts and actions, is actually the unique mark of human success: 'we believe that the unrivaled human ability to be guided by imagining alternatives stretching into the future – "prospection" – uniquely describes *Homo sapiens*. Prospection is the actual ability that, at its best, makes the aspiration of wisdom a reality. Hence, we are better named *Homo prospectus*.'[1] As 2020 dawned, people were bombarded with exhortations to have vision for the 2020s and beyond. What could this new decade be? What tremendous changes might we see on the horizon? Life seemed normal, certainly for those living in relatively peaceful democratic countries. We were full of vision. Within a few months, the global Covid-19 pandemic hit; as the virus broke out, 'normal' was redefined. Life was put on hold as nations battened down the hatches to get through a health emergency. Emerging from this storm, people found themselves, not in an easier place, but in a time of greater global instability, major European and Middle Eastern conflicts, rising social divisions and mass migration of people. The economic uncertainty and international tensions have caused many to worry and wonder where our world's future is going. Nobody would doubt that we are living in extraordinary and serious times, even possibly the biblical 'end times'. Our *Homo prospectus* tendency is facing quite a knocking.

This is a book about the end times, written to help us navigate this uncertain context. Our times may be changing on a bigger scale than we think. Many in the body of Christ felt that this decade would mark a major spiritual shift, but could it also mark a shift on the earth in heaven's countdown to Christ's return? It is just possible that we are moving towards an extraordinary timeframe of life on planet earth. To Christians reading their Bibles, this should not be a surprise, because there are many prophecies speaking of life in the 'last days', just before the return of the Lord. Yet we often forget to tune into our *Homo prospectus* ability to look to the spiritual horizon and find out what God tells us is ahead of us.

The Coming End Times

It is an interesting fact that, even though Brits love to talk about the weather, we don't often look to the horizon as weather watchers. Maybe it's because we are used to wet days or grey skies and slowly moving weather patterns. This is not true for many parts of the world. When I was on holiday in Florida with my family a few years back, we were warned to watch the horizon for thunderstorms. Now that was a surprise to us! We had expected the weather in the summer in Florida to be hot, dry and beautiful. Yet we soon learned to look over the flat landscape towards the horizon; for often in the afternoon, the heads of thunderclouds would form ominously. Within minutes, torrential rain could fall, and half an hour later, the atmosphere would clear again and the rain and puddles dry up in the balmy heat.

Jesus remonstrated with the religious teachers of his day for not looking to the spiritual horizon to see what God was doing: 'You know how to interpret the appearance of the sky, but you cannot interpret the signs of the times' (Matt. 16:3). Their inability to read the signs of the times left them unprepared to recognize the presence of the Messiah in their midst and what his ministry meant. Prophets should be watching the spiritual horizon, sensing what God is saying and doing. They should be looking ahead to what is coming, what it is on horizon level that God's people need to be aware of now.

Could we be near or even in the end-times timeframe which Scripture points to so clearly? Many prophetic people believe that a profound era of spiritual revival and great turmoil is on the horizon. We could well be entering a time when human society will experience more of what Scripture calls the *revealing of the glory of the Lord* and the *shaking of heaven and earth* – intense spiritual and social dynamics on a global scale.

Now globally intense spiritual and social dynamics are not part of normal life, and reading about the end times takes a big readjustment of spiritual expectation. The sweep of church history shows peaks and troughs of church growth and fruitful mission, ebbs and flows of the work of the Spirit through different generations; we tend to think of the kingdom of God coming gradually in our world. Apart from episodes of historic revival, to experience a dramatic increase in the experience of God's glory and his manifest presence in the midst of ordinary life would not be normal for us. Similarly, times of war, poverty, disasters and threats to social life have always been a factor in human history, but often sporadically and not in a way that is disruptive to the future of the planet. To experience a complex sequence of ever-increasing levels of global shaking in multiple spheres would also not be normal for us. Human society will one day soon enter a new context of life on earth – the increase of the glory of God and the increase of global shaking as part of the end times. This is what we shall examine at the outset of this book.

The end times as chronological

The subject of the end times is not just an evangelical fringe interest, or a plotline for a sensational Hollywood blockbuster; it is a major theme in the Bible. Just as Scripture teaches us about the beginning of our created world, it also speaks of the end of the world as we know it. The theological branch of study called *eschatology* concentrates on understanding the things described in Scripture as happening either at or after the end of human history – themes such as Christ's return, the judgment, the resurrection of the dead, a new heaven and earth. The end times are the climax of biblical history. So the first thing to say about the end times is that they are *chronological*; they speak of a sequence of events that will occur at some point in the future, events with great spiritual meaning.

In terms of chronology, Scripture speaks clearly about the end times. There are many diverse chapters of the Bible which include prophecies about the times surrounding Jesus' second coming and afterwards. They are more numerous than those which prophesy his first coming.

In the Old Testament, the prophets primarily refer to the end times as the 'Day of the Lord' or 'that day'. They agree that it will be three things:

- a time of turmoil and trouble when God judges the world: 'Alas for that day! For the day of the LORD is near; it will come like destruction from the Almighty' (Joel 1:15);
- a time when God demonstrates the power of his name and his kingdom: 'The eyes of the arrogant will be humbled and human pride brought low; the LORD alone will be exalted in that day' (Isa. 2:11);
- a time when the righteous are saved and vindicated for their faith: '"Then you will trample on the wicked; they will be ashes under the soles of your feet on the day when I act," says the LORD Almighty' (Mal. 4:3).[2]

In the New Testament, end-time themes are reframed around the return of Christ and the trouble that precedes that time. Mark chapter 13 is a good example: 'But in those days, following that distress, "the sun will be darkened, and the moon will not give its light; the stars will fall from the sky, and the heavenly bodies will be shaken." At that time people will see the Son of Man coming in clouds with great power and glory' (Mark 13:24–26).

Other New Testament writers make more explicit mention of a time of tribulation connected with the rise of a ruler known as the Antichrist before the Lord's return: 'that day will not come until the rebellion occurs and the man of lawlessness is revealed' (2 Thess. 2:3).[3]

There has been much popular Christian fascination with the events foretold in the Bible that indicate the coming end of the world as we know it. On one hand, the apocalyptic visions in the books of Daniel and Revelation have become the source of intense debate and 'doomsdaying', for example the rising of a beast-like empire (Dan. 7:7) and the releasing of the Four Horsemen of the Apocalypse (Rev. 6:1–8).

On the other hand, there are some very positive indications of the impact of God's kingdom before Christ's return, for example the gospel message going throughout the world (Matt. 24:14), a great harvest of people coming to faith (Rev. 14:15–16), and God's people living righteous lives and waiting for him (Titus 2:11–13).

So there seems to be a recognized sequence of events that people refer to when they speak of the end times. End-time prophecies may be scattered among or intermingled with other scriptures, but they are clearly there, an eclectic mix but also a coherent narrative in both Old and New Testaments.

It is interesting that people often turn to the book of Revelation to understand the end-time drama. This tumultuous vision of cosmic conflict between good and evil, and God's certain triumph, was actually given to encourage believers suffering for their faith in the here and now. Yet it simultaneously contains specific prophetic visions that count down to the end, so to speak, and show how the last days will play out in our world, for both good and evil.

The Coming End Times

Let me sketch out a few of the biblical signs Christians often think of that seem to directly precede and follow the second coming of the Christ. The biblical prophecy that we read between Revelation chapters 6 and 19, amplified by other scriptures, foretells a time of a global order of short-lived peace (1 Thess. 5:3) with an Antichrist ruler in place (Rev. 13:3). His rule becomes repressive as he proclaims himself divine (2 Thess. 2:4) and increases persecution against all who refuse to submit to his tyranny (Rev. 13:15–16). This blatant display of evil results in judgments from heaven on the sinful ways of humanity and the misuse of power (Rev. 9:20; 15:1). This forms the context for a period known as the Great Tribulation (Matt. 24:21) – trouble for those who follow Christ (Rev. 12:12,17) and turmoil for all who live through this chaotic time when creation is groaning (Luke 21:26). At the height of this, with a battle raging around Jerusalem (Luke 21:20), Jesus appears in glory (Matt. 24:30), splitting the heavens in the company of angels and resurrected saints. After a procession across the skies, Jesus defeats Satan's forces on earth (Rev. 19:13–16) and comes to reign from Jerusalem (Luke 13:35). From that place he completes the fulfilment of a prophecy in Psalm 110, whereby he rules (Rev. 20:6) until he has put all his enemies under his feet (1 Cor. 15:24–25). Then comes the great final judgment before God (Rev. 20:11) and the revealing of the new heaven and earth (Rev. 21:1 – 22:5).

Pause for Thought

- What Bible passages do I turn to when I think about the end times?

Glory and shaking

The end-times drama leading up to Jesus' return could be summed up as times of glory and shaking – times when the glory of God is visibly displayed in the world, and God allows tremendous shaking of all the things people put their trust in. Both glory and shaking are clear eschatological signs in a handful of places in Scripture. They are indicators of the nearness of the Lord's return. Habakkuk prophesied about a time in the future when people would collectively become more aware of God's activity and presence:

> the earth will be filled with the knowledge of the glory of the Lord
>   as the waters cover the sea.
>
> *Hab. 2:14*

The prophet Isaiah in his day spoke of a time far ahead when there would be troubling conditions on earth, close to the day of God's judgment:

> They will flee to caverns in the rocks
>   and to the overhanging crags
> from the fearful presence of the Lord
>   and the splendour of his majesty,
> when he rises to shake the earth.
>
> *Isa. 2:21*

I would say that the biblical view of the end times before Christ returns is one of increasing glory and shaking on a global scale. And soberingly, not one or the other but both together.

The Coming End Times

To confirm this end-time combination, in a later part of Isaiah's prophecy, God summons his people to stand in a new reality:

> Arise, shine, for your light has come,
>   and the glory of the Lord rises upon you.
> See, darkness covers the earth
>   and thick darkness is over the peoples,
> but the Lord rises upon you
>   and his glory appears over you.
>
> Isa. 60:1–2

Similarly, in the book of Haggai, the prophet gives both warnings and promises concerning the scenario in the last days: '"In a little while I will once more shake the heavens and the earth, the sea and the dry land. I will shake all nations, and what is desired by all nations will come, and I will fill this house with glory," says the Lord Almighty' (Hag. 2:6–7).

Neither Isaiah nor Haggai were speaking directly to the church of the twenty-first century; they were addressing the Israelites of their day. Yet the scale and tenor of their prophetic words went way beyond their local context into more apocalyptic imagery. The fulfilment of their prophecies has not yet occurred, but many believe it will occur in a dramatic way that will include the people of God in the end times.

What do these scriptures tell us? The increase of the revealed glory of God will come *in the midst of* darkness; the global shaking will occur *at the same time as* the filling of God's house with his glory. So glory and shaking are the twin themes of the end times in the decades and generation just before Jesus comes again in power.

Why people think we are living in biblical end times

Why do so many Christians perceive that we are in these times today? Well, there are a number of reasons based on biblical end-time markers. The fact that Israel is back in her promised land finally gives prophetic end-time relevance to the land and a gathered people in that place (see for example Ezek. 11:17 and 36:24, describing a reforming of Israel from many regions of the world, and Joel 3:1–3 linking this to an end-time battle in the Middle East). The miracle of Israel in the promised land is hugely significant. Also, the Great Commission to take the gospel around the whole world (Matt. 28:18–20) is nearly fulfilled, and possibly will be achieved within our current lifetime; Jesus indicated that this would happen before he returned (Matt. 24:14). Christianity is now a global phenomenon and, in a new digital age, the sharing of the gospel with all people could be done quickly. Waves of Holy Spirit renewal and revival continue globally, causing massive indigenous church growth in hitherto inaccessible cultures and bringing in a spiritual harvest among unreached people-groups. Yet the instability of the planet, the threat of societal collapse, and the persecution of Christians all looks very much like the picture Jesus paints in the time before the Tribulation in Matthew 24, Mark 13 and Luke 21.

People may say, 'Doesn't every generation of the church believe they are in the end times?' Certainly, there have been voices in times of turmoil in the past, or at epoch-making moments, saying that Christ's return is near. Yet there have never been as many people looking at their Bibles and making connections to signs of the end times around them, and with good reasons. Let's look at these negative and positive signs a little more closely.

The negative

In negative terms, we are facing the possible collapse of our global civilization like never before. In times past, empires and cultures would implode or be overtaken by others, yet always this was with regional effect. Today, we have a global civilization in which our technology, supply chains, economies and media influences are all interconnected. If this civilization goes down, would this be the end of the human race? Joshua Fields, CEO of Consciousness Hacking, writes about mechanisms that point to societal collapse: environmental degradation (a society that has come out of alignment with its ecosystems); excess complexity (where exponential complexity is uncoupled from linear competence, leading to a lack of sense-making); and gross inequality in the world. These have led to societal collapse in the past. There are catastrophic risks endemic when societies severely damage their environment, when they lose the ability to understand their technology, and when they tip into gross inequality. This sounds very like our current reality. Fields suggests that together these factors lead to an eventual destabilizing of a civilization: 'We have accelerating complexity with diminishing competence, a materialistic, narcissistic value system, we have never been wealthier or safer, and elite overproduction is at an all time high. On top of that, we're highly, highly fragile.'[4]

In his book *Metanoia*, Alan Hirsch, an American missiologist, speaks of the time we are living in as apocalyptic. By this he is not specifically meaning an end-times framework, rather that it is one of those 'revelatory moments [God] puts before us and to which we are called to faithfully respond'.[5] This response involves a profound turning (the meaning of the Greek word *metanoia*) towards God. Hirsch then draws from the social sciences to illustrate this profound moment of crisis: 'The social sciences also propose some compelling lenses which highlight the need for radical metanoia change. For instance, a well-developed sociological framework is expressed in the acronym VUCA, which describes the world as volatile, uncertain, complex and ambiguous. These terms accurately portray the situation of constant, unpredictable change that is increasingly the norm throughout all societies, cultures, and economies in the world.'[6]

In general, we have never before lived under such an existential threat to the human race as we are living under now. Irreversible climate change, the threats of a nuclear holocaust, and the overconsumption of the planet's resources have put us on a path to a time-limited future on earth. Theologian Jürgen Moltmann, in his book on eschatology, wrote this about the end times of human history: 'Hiroshima 1945 fundamentally changed the quality of human history: our time has become time with a time-limit. The age in which we exist is the last age of humanity, for we are living at a time when the end of humanity can be brought about at any minute.'[7] How true this is proving to be! Because you cannot un-invent either the atomic bomb or biological warfare; neither can you put the artificial intelligence genie back in the bottle.

The positive

Yet, from a positive viewpoint, many Christians are feeling a sense of spiritual expectancy because of this moment; it is a time in which God is stirring his people afresh. Lana Vawser, an Australian prophetic speaker, wrote at the start of the pandemic about stepping into a new era:

there is an invitation from God to step into greater realms and manifestations of your destiny and the plans God has for you in ways you never thought, imagined, or dreamed of. This is an era of acceleration, and there are opportunities, doors, and territories that are completely new awaiting His people. This is an exciting time to be alive. These are the days when the Spirit of God is heralding Isaiah 43:19 (ESV), 'Behold, I am doing a new thing . . . do you not perceive it?'[8]

Moreover, there has never been a time when the church is more able to share the gospel in every culture and language. Churches are being planted at a rate never seen before; Bible translations are being planned for nearly every unreached people-group. There are unprecedented moves of the Spirit happening in some of the world's major religions, as the light of Jesus' love is penetrating hitherto closed societies. Jesus' promise that his church would be a witness to the ends of the earth is happening before our eyes.

The belief that mission is leading to the culmination of the kingdom is foundational for the life of God's people. As missiologist Christopher Rowland states: 'The church's mission is rooted in the conviction that the presence of the eschatological Spirit enables those in Christ to bear witness to the ultimate fulfilment of the divine purpose in the coming reign of God.'[9] This conviction is increasing among the leaders of evangelical mission agencies, who are planning for a global saturation of the gospel in the power of the Spirit. Their sincere faith in doing so is that, as the Great Commission is completed, Christ will return.

The biblical picture is that the negative and positive aspects of end-time features will be mixed; great revelation of God's glory and severe measures of global shaking will be entwined. The revealing of the glory of the Lord will be wonderful, and will be great news for a church often downtrodden and marginalized. As global shaking increases, people will feel the need to seek God, cling to him and find hope in him. God's experienced presence will be the treasure that billions will discover in the midst of troubling times to come.

It can't be denied that the biblical end times will be profoundly disturbing to live through. The hope in Scripture is that the world will not be destroyed through shaking, but rather that the turmoil will have a destabilizing effect on people's lives and cause a growing lack of confidence in the things of the world that we trust in. In Christian apocalyptic thinking, the 'end of the world' is not just gloom and doom, but coincides with the decisive revealing of God's new world. The writer to the Hebrews gave a prophetic comment on the Haggai passage about shaking in the world:

> At that time [God's] voice shook the earth, but now he has promised, 'Once more I will shake not only the earth but also the heavens.' The words 'once more' indicate the removing of what can be shaken – that is, created things – so that what cannot be shaken may remain. Therefore, since we are receiving a kingdom that cannot be shaken, let us be thankful, and so worship God acceptably with reverence and awe, for our 'God is a consuming fire.'
>
> *Heb. 12:26–29*

God's heartfelt desire, through end-time shaking, is to unveil the reality of his unshakeable kingdom, and thus to reinforce his promise of a new heaven and earth, drawing people to have faith in him and find in him the only powerful and solid reality during that time. As his glory is revealed in the middle of global shaking and crises, the choice will be clear for people: run to the Lord for salvation and security, or try to survive by your own wits and human strength. God's coming glory is like the dawning sun that reveals his plans for the renewal of our world under the majestic kingship of his Son, Jesus. Eschatological glory and shaking are on the increase, and we need to get ready to live through extraordinary times in the future.

Pause for Thought

- Which current signs of the times make me think about the glory of God?
- Which signs make me think about the shaking of all things?

The Church Needs to Be Prepared

Jesus' guidance to an end-time generation of believers

Let us look at the clearest teaching on the end times in the New Testament – Jesus' eschatological discourse in the synoptic gospels. Placed in the middle of the Holy Week narratives, Jesus' teaching in Matthew 24, Mark 13 and Luke 21 is both dramatic and eye-opening. As the disciples sat on the Mount of Olives looking out over the walls of Jerusalem and the beautiful temple, Jesus spoke to them about coming times of judgment and tribulation. Most Bible commentators agree that there are two layers of prophetic meaning in these passages. The immediate application was the fall of Jerusalem at the hands of the

Roman Empire in AD 70. The future application was for an end-time framework preceding Christ's second coming. The uncertainty surrounds the question of which part of the discourse refers to which timeframe. Commentators such as R.T. France consider everything in Matthew 24 before verse 29 to refer to the sequence of events before the fall of the temple: 'Thus one event (the destruction of the temple) falls within defined and predictable history, and those who know what to look for can see it coming, while the other (the *parousia*) cannot be tied down to a time frame, and even Jesus does not know when it will be and so will offer no "sign."'[10]

In her remarks about the highly similar Markan account (Mark 13), another commentator, Morna Hooker, takes a different view as she comments on the tightly interlinked timeframes of the immediate and the far off: 'It is true that the discourse moves beyond the destruction of Jerusalem to the parousia and the End of all things but it is clear that these events are understood to belong together, so that one heralds the other.'[11]

From my reading of text and historical context, I take the view that the words of Jesus are prophetically double-layered. One can read the first part of his discourse as a historical warning about the destruction of the temple, the great cataclysmic event in Jewish understanding, and also read it as end-time training in what to expect in the years before the Great Tribulation. I am aware that apocalyptic language was used in Jesus' time to depict real, political events, and that cosmic imagery was deployed in narratives of near-time scenarios. Yet the weight of Jesus' words and the sweep of his prophetic outlook, for me and many others down the centuries, point to the larger movement of end-time events leading to the Tribulation and his return in glory.

The Coming End Times

Jesus spoke far into the future, covering centuries of dynasties and the trajectory of human history. While his prediction would be a sobering read for Christians in any age of the church, it would have a startling relevance for those Christians alive as part of the last-days generation. They would read it, not as a general warning, but as an urgent training manual for how to stand well in the troubled times of the Tribulation.

Let us focus on the account in Matthew 24. Much of Jesus' prophetic teaching is plainly relevant and clear. It is not cloaked in mysterious prophetic imagery, but lays out a future end-time scenario. In particular, Jesus prepares a future generation for the dynamics of navigating six things: truth versus deception; normal troubles versus end-time birth pains; persecution and harvest; faith and pressure to give in; Tribulation intensity and turbulence; and excitement and dread.

Truth versus deception

Jesus tells us to 'watch out'. There will be deceiving voices confusing people as to what they should believe, and tempting them to follow false messiahs (Matt. 24:4–5). What kind of voices will there be? Certainly, there will be false prophets turning people from spiritual truth (v. 11); leaders confusing their followers with false hope of deliverance from persecution and trouble (v. 23); and possibly even demonic counterfeits of apostolic ministry encouraging believers to give allegiance to the Antichrist empire (v. 24). The gift of discernment and unwavering gospel conviction will be needed. In the end times we will find clarity through the Spirit of truth, who will convict, guide and convince us of truthful paths. Knowing biblical truth from error, holding on to belief in the gospel, discerning the signs of the times, and distinguishing between godly and ungodly spirits – all these will be essential qualities for Christians in the coming years. Jesus here calls us to a close and discerning walk with the Lord.

Normal troubles versus end-time birth pains

Jesus says, 'See to it that you are not alarmed.' Wars, conflicts, troubles and disasters in isolation are not proof of the end times (Matt. 24:6–7). It is the intensification, combination and escalation of them that are indications of end-time birth pains (v. 8). Jesus clearly wanted his people not to be unduly alarmed by localized or time-limited crises in their day; yet he also wanted them to watch the signs of the times to be alert for the dramatic escalation that marks or prefigures the coming Tribulation. The implication of this passage is that it will gradually become obvious when localized troubles are moving into global shaking. Again, prophetic discernment, trust and wisdom are the qualities Jesus is calling for in his church. Spiritual sensitivity to the Lord and to what is happening globally is vital for sensing whether the birth pains are increasing. Wide-eyed prophetic wisdom comes from the place of prayer – and that is why Jesus calls his followers to always watch and pray (Luke 21:36).

Persecution and harvest

Jesus says, 'You will be hated', and also predicts that 'the gospel of the kingdom will be preached' (Matt. 24:9,14). He prophesies a time of increased persecution for his followers during the Tribulation. What kind of persecution? The turning of the tide of public opinion against followers of Jesus, the pressure of nations to clamp down on Christian activities, and eventually the hostile targeting of Christians by the Antichrist regime will be features of the last-days persecution (v. 9), more than at any other time in history. Parallel to, or just preceding this, will be the completion of the Great Commission in the context of a great mission push and possible revival harvest, with the gospel reaching every tribe and people (v. 14). This assumes that God's people will be vibrant witnesses to Jesus in the power of the Spirit in these closing years. The gospel harvest might peak in the intensity of the Antichrist empire and global shaking just before Jesus returns, but still, masses of people will turn to the Lord as the light and darkness increase in the end times. We might prefer to see a billion-soul harvest in times that are simply peaceful and glorious, but Jesus shows us that the harvest of people turning to the Lord will occur in the confusing mix of both dramatic trouble and revival. Courage and the empowering of the Spirit will be needed by God's people in coming years to enable them to witness bravely and not turn from their faith.

Faith and pressure to give in

Jesus calls on each of us to be 'one who stands firm' (Matt. 24:13). End-time events will not just be alarming; they will also be confusing for all people, including Christians. Jesus foresees a time (v. 12) when persecution, confusion and the spirit of the age will cause the faith of many to fold. The pressure to conform to the Antichrist world system will be intense. From the book of Revelation we know that there will be economic and personal freedom implications for those who do not support the global dictatorship. We can envisage a time when many Christians will give up their faith, and others may become informants, betraying friends in the global underground church during the Antichrist regime (v. 10). The hostility towards Christians who are on fire in their faith, alongside demonic oppression and evil at the level of national and international leadership, will cause many people – of all faiths – to compromise their convictions (v. 12); this could allude to a future one-world religious system under the Antichrist, mentioned in Revelation 13. Jesus calls for his people to be prepared for these conditions, and to stand firm through them, fearlessly witnessing and persevering in faith. This is the overcoming church, and she will be heroic in her day.

Tribulation intensity and turbulence

Jesus speaks of a time when there will appear an 'abomination that causes desolation' (Matt. 24:15). On one hand, Jesus here describes the desecration of the temple in AD 70, yet on the other hand, he simultaneously foretells the unmasking of the Antichrist's anti-God intentions part-way through the Tribulation time. This 'great distress', as described by Jesus (v. 21), will involve the greatest global shaking yet seen. Not only will human society and global systems be in trouble, but natural disasters and cosmic disturbances will cause people to live in great fear (v. 29). This could refer to the releasing of God's judgment on the Antichrist empire spoken of in the 'trumpets and bowls' depictions in Revelation. Christians will know that God's permitting of this shaking and turmoil will not lead to the total destruction of the world. They will need to trust him in a deep way, and share hope in Jesus with others, as life on earth becomes critically unstable. An unshakeable bedrock of faith and hope will be required as things get really tough.

Excitement and dread

Jesus tells us, 'Then will appear the sign of the Son of Man'. The climax to this end-time drama is the visible return of Jesus to earth in glory (Matt. 24:30). The contrast between faithful believers – elated to welcome Jesus and to be liberated from this Tribulation time – and others on earth – who aligned themselves with the world's systems and now dread Jesus' arrival to judge and rule – could not be greater. They will mourn while believers rejoice (vv. 30–31). The great sense of expectancy of Christians in that day will be fully vindicated if they stay true to Jesus. They will be the only ones to know what is about to happen, and they will be rewarded with the great gathering of the saints to join the Lord as he returns.

Can you see how Jesus is preparing his people for the end-time events that will happen in the future? He doesn't want us to be shocked or blindsided by these days. The relevance of his words will become increasingly clear, the closer we get to Tribulation times. The word of God is living and active, and full of prophetic insight. God's people will find themselves mining these passages of Scripture again and again for the Lord's insight into how to navigate discipleship in those troubling last days. A future generation of God's people will be led by the Lord through this time, and will come through profoundly tested, yet victorious in their faith and witness.

And so, as our global context gets closer to end-time realities, we need to ask ourselves: How prepared and discerning will we be? How trusting and unshakeable in our faith will we be? How persevering and witnessing will we be? From the gospel accounts, it is clear: Jesus wants his church to be prepared for the end times.

Pause for Thought

- How prepared do I feel for a more testing time of discipleship in the years to come?
- How would Jesus encourage me today?

2

God Has Got a Plan

The End Times as Teleological

We tend to think of the end times as a timeline; we understand that certain things will happen before, during and after the Lord returns. As such, yes, eschatology is chronological. Yet there is another way of looking at this, one which asserts eschatology as *teleological*, that is, purposeful.

My wife and I used to say to our children when they were young, 'God has got a plan'; in fact, we used to tap each finger of one hand as we said the five words together. One day, our 3-year-old daughter must have thought we were selling her short, because she turned round to her mother and, counting on the fingers of both hands, declared: 'God has got a . . . very, very, very, very, very good plan!' How true.

One of the cornerstones of Christian theology is of course God's sovereignty. God is fully in control and without equal. As creator and sustainer of our world, and as a divine being outside the constraints of time and space, God is able to lovingly bring about his salvation plans through the twists and turns of human history. This God has sovereign and loving purposes for our world, set in motion with the coming of Jesus.

The end times are therefore the culmination of God's purposes; the end is not just a chronological concept but also a teleological one. Teleology has to do with purpose, goal, primary function. In Scripture we are invited to step back to see the bigger arc of salvation history, one that started in eternity in the heart of the Trinity. Out of this overflowing love the universe and all created life were brought into being. Within the fallenness of humankind, election and covenant drew the people of Israel into relationship with God. When the time was fully right, the divine Word of God became flesh, as the fulfilment of promise. Jesus lived, died and rose again to reconcile us fully to God, and ascended again into glory. In all this, we see a cosmic plan in operation.

Of course, that is not the end of the story, because the drama has not yet had its climax. Despite the saving acts of God in Christ, and the presence of the church as a sign of the kingdom, human life is currently still flawed and tragic, sin is not fully overcome, and heaven and earth are not united. It is important therefore that Scripture points to the purposeful plans of God implemented through future end-time events, in an arc that stretches beyond our human history. Christ returns in glory to usher in the fullness of the kingdom and to herald the cosmic triumph of God's love. His coming brings about the resurrection of the dead, the marriage supper of the Lamb, a millennial rule, a great judgment, a joining of heaven to earth, an eternal dwelling of God with his creation, and the catching up of the redeemed into the great union of the Trinity.

It is therefore right to say that eschatology is teleological. The end of this age will come, not when we either destroy ourselves or make ourselves like God, nor when Satan in his rage tries to annihilate us, but when God determines in his sovereign plans. These are what Jesus called 'the times [and] dates the Father has set by his own authority' (Acts 1:7).

This is important for our Christian worldview. Without thinking about the end of God's plans, we can easily lose hope and perspective. The Bible reminds us that we are not just writing our best projected story, but awaiting God's completing of the divine narrative for our world. His plans to save people, to defeat evil, to complete his kingdom rule, to join heaven and earth, will come about in line with his loving and wise purposes. This is certain. Because we hold out for the return of Christ, the drama is not yet over. As God's people, we engage with the world on the way to the fullness of the kingdom, because we know that God has got a very, very good plan.

God's endgame plan

The philosopher Blaise Pascal once described the game of chess as the 'gymnasium of the mind'. This deceptively simple two-player strategy game, involving thirty-two pieces on a chequered board, is played by millions of people at vastly different levels of competence. I bought a beautiful set of carved medieval chess pieces once on holiday, yet have only played occasionally with my family, and poorly at that. Good chess players will work on a strategy, while constantly trying to think what their opponent's next few moves might be, so that they are not outmanoeuvred. Great chess players know how to move through stages of the game. Importantly, they know that the endgame (the finally stage of a match) is fundamentally different from the opening or middle section of the game; they are aware that rapid evaluation of changing strategies is needed and that most points are won or lost in the closing part of the match. An endgame can be spectacularly swift and dramatic. These expert players study avidly to develop endgame thinking.

Endgame thinking is not restricted to board games. An endgame plan can involve clever plans in progress where the overarching goal is not obvious. Another way of expressing an endgame plan is this: 'an extended process or course of events, especially with the implication of the imminent realization of a masterful strategy or plan' (Wiktionary definition).

When you read the Bible, you see that God has an endgame plan. He has a masterful kingdom-strategy which he has been putting into place throughout human history. In fact, we know that God put his salvation plan into place *before* human history – Jesus is 'the Lamb who was slain from the creation of the world' (Rev. 13:8).

Moreover, these plans are building towards a climax: 'He made known to us the mystery of his will according to his good pleasure, which he purposed in Christ, to be put into effect when the times reach their fulfilment – to bring unity to all things in heaven and on earth under Christ' (Eph. 1:9–10). This is a plan that unfolded through all the great saving acts of God in Christ, from the incarnation to the passion, resurrection and ascension, and it will come to a head at the *parousia* (a Greek word used for Jesus' second coming) and in the life of the age to come.

God's endgame plan is partly hidden and partly revealed. It is hidden in that the timing of end-time events is under his sovereign control; Jesus told us that no one knows the day or hour of his return except the Father (Matt. 24:36). In John's vision in the book of Revelation, there is a mystery in the timing of heaven's countdown as Jesus receives a special scroll symbolizing authority from God and starts to assume his rightful leadership of planet earth (see Rev. 5:7–9). We remember too that Satan does not know the timing or surprises of God's endgame plan. And yet elements of this plan in the end times have been clearly revealed. The rising up of the church as a prepared bride is indisputable. The bringing in of a final revival harvest of souls is certain. The climactic judging of satanic influence, and cleansing the earth of sin, are spelt out. That is not to say that we are walking like programmed robots through an end-time scenario. There are real choices for every person on the earth, and the devil is free to throw all he can in his rage against God and God's people. Yet the Lord has a brilliant and masterful strategy that will not be thwarted.

Pause for Thought

- How do I feel when I think about God having an overarching purpose for history?

The Church at the Centre of God's Plans

> The wedding of the Lamb has come,
> and his bride has made herself ready.
>
> *Rev. 19:7*

I have titled this book *Radiant and Resolute* and have not yet unpacked what I mean by this phrase, although it may well be obvious by now. I think that Christians have generally been quite agnostic about what the state of the church will be like in the end times, especially during the Great Tribulation. Some believers think that we will be snatched away before that terrible time of trouble in an event known as the Rapture – a neat way of circumventing the difficulties for Christian discipleship during the Tribulation. Others think that it will be a dire time of intense persecution and falling away, and that the church will come through the Tribulation by the skin of her teeth, nearly decimated and mostly martyred. There is another alternative. Many Christians are coming to the realization that the end times will be both the greatest and the most difficult time for the church, but that she will rise to the challenge of the hour with immense courage and fervour. I share the historic premillennial view of the church down the centuries – that God's people don't get taken out of the turbulent times but that they overcome the troubles of the last days. In addition, I hold with others that the end-time church will be both glorious and victorious in this hour. These could well become the greatest days of the church. Why? Because at the centre of God's plan is the creation of a radiant and resolute church ready to meet his Son as he returns.

Reading Scripture with a teleological lens, we can see that God could be powerfully at work among his people in the end times. How? The Father may give us both a deep revelation of Jesus in his beauty and his love for us, and a great anointing of the Holy Spirit for our life and witness. The deep work of the Spirit may bring about both of these dynamics in equal measure amid the intensity of the end times. In this way, we will become *radiant* because of our love for Jesus; worship and prayer will become pre-eminent and revelatory in the last days. So much dross, sin, compromise and unbelief will fall away as we behold Jesus in his beauty and majesty and are wholly undone by his transforming gaze of love towards us. In the same way, we will also become *resolute* in our determination to live wholly for him, whatever the cost of discipleship. The Holy Spirit may use the pressure of global shaking and religious persecution to both empower our witness and sanctify our Christian walk in the midst of difficulty. There may still be church division and a confusing mixture of false doctrine and lukewarmness in parts of the body of Christ, yet it is possible that millions of Christians will rise up with a resolute spirit to live in abandonment to Jesus and embody a glorious, authentic witness to him in every nation before he returns.

Pause for Thought

- Can I see signs of the radiant church in my nation right now?
- Can I see elements of the resoluteness of the church?

Recognizing a global shift in the body of Christ

'My, how you've changed!' When have you heard these words? Perhaps when meeting up with a friend who hasn't seen you in years? Or when people comment on your anniversary or birthday posts on social media? When a growth spurt happened in your adolescent years? Our personal experience of growth and change is incremental, but, over the years, the difference and changes are marked. For my wife and myself, looking back recently on wedding pictures taken thirty years ago, we could see ourselves as we were and are now, how life events and seasons and ageing have made their mark on us. Yet we could also comment on the growth in experience, our children, the fruitfulness of our partnership and love, and beautiful things that have transpired since the 'I do' spoken all those years ago.

And my, how the church has changed in recent generations! Would a Victorian or Edwardian observer of the church in their day even recognize much of the body of Christ in the twenty-first-century world? Let me remind you of ten profound shifts in the church over the last three generations (since the turn of the twentieth century). As a church, we have moved:

1. *From first world to majority world.* The centre of gravity of church representation has shifted dramatically from the first world to the majority world; non-western Christians comprised just 20% of the church in 1900, yet now make up 70%. So now, out of the 2.1 billion Christians in the world, the Christian communities in Latin America and Africa number 1 billion and Asian Christians number 400 million.
2. *From top down to bottom up.* Hierarchical denominational ways of life are being radically rethought. From liberation theologies in Latin America, where grassroots Christian communities challenge injustice in their society, to the holistic partnering of evangelism and social action in local churches in Asia, the shift from dependence on top-down national leadership to engagement in bottom-up mission and ministry in the church is important. Even among Catholics, there is the emergence of a new decentralized and interdependent way of being in the Catholic communion.
3. *From clergy to laity.* The spiritual renewal across historic denominational churches has brought a fresh understanding of the whole people of God living out their faith 24/7, the clergy as facilitators and team leaders, and the laity changing from being attenders at Sunday gatherings to being full-time ministers of the gospel.
4. *From rigid denominations to dynamic movements.* As the weight of the numbers of Christians has shifted to Africa, Asia and South America, it is significant that the majority of these Christians are Pentecostal or charismatic. This

has led to a great shift from maintenance to mission, with church-planting movements increasing in influence across the Asian and African continents, and disciple-making movements growing in secret underground churches.

5. *From old to young.* Although today's young adults are statistically adhering less than other generations to a specific religion, young people are leading the way in church planting and mission movements across the growing churches, especially in the southern hemisphere.
6. *From locally isolated to globally connected.* The old 'local parish' pastoral model that flourished in the centuries of Christendom has been replaced by an interconnected sense of streams and informal affiliations. Particularly among younger people, the digital revolution has produced a high-speed, always-connected cyber world, which is ripe fruit for Christian mission and for rethinking ways of 'being church' in a shrinking world.
7. *From maintenance to mission.* Even though the overall global percentage of Christians has remained about one-third of the global population in the last 120 years, the spread is vastly different. Christian mission has made massive inroads into every culture; there is no nation in which you cannot find a viable indigenous church. Christianity has become a worldwide religious force.[1]
8. *From prayer liturgies to prayer explosion.* The stirring of the church to pray is a global phenomenon unique to the present generation. National and international prayer movements, intercessory gatherings, stadium worship-events, prayer strategies, prayer rooms and houses of prayer have arisen faster than can be tracked. Especially among young people, the desire to worship and pray with a missionary focus is startling.[2]

9. *From dominant to persecuted.* In those areas where Christianity is growing the fastest, such as in China, Nigeria, Indonesia and India, the level of persecution against Christians is also highest. Hostility from Islamic extremism and ethnic nationalism is causing a backlash against the church in many nations.
10. *From gospel periphery to gospel-centred.* The western church has struggled to adjust to the end of Christendom and its place of privilege in society. Although this is a confusing scenario, it has forced churches to become less ecclesially self-centred and more gospel-centred, less concerned with denominational self-preservation and more involved with impacting their communities with gospel witness and service.

It is important to recognize these changes because we can see the church's response to changing cultures and also God's work in renewal and mission through his people. It reminds us that the church is not a static organization, but rather a dynamic movement. The vector of this book, however, is to point prophetically to even more radical change in the church across the world as we enter into end times of glory and shaking. The Lord is intentional about refining, reforming and empowering his people to rise and shine in these coming days. It is our privilege to bring in the final harvest, to shed past cultural and religious baggage, and emerge through trouble and revival as a transformed, resilient, gospel-bearing church in which every Christian from every nation plays their part as a witness for Jesus in the last-days drama.

God is preparing a globally connected, bottom-up, youth- and lay-led, mission-focused and movement-oriented, praying, gospel-centred, persecution-hardened church which will be well placed to ride the waves of revival and withstand the shaking that will happen in the coming years.

> **Pause for Thought**
>
> - Can I see God's hand in the changes that are happening in the church globally?

The Acceleration of God's Purposes

When divine purposes come to a head

We have spoken about endgame plans. What we can also glimpse in Scripture is that there will be an acceleration of God's purposes that will unfold before our eyes, an acceleration that denotes that God's endgame plan is coming into place at a globally critical time. That is an incredible thought to get our heads around. To aid us, let us look at a handful of times in the story of God's people in the Bible when God's purposes came to a sudden climax.

In the book of Exodus, after the time of Joseph, the Israelites were enslaved and mistreated for four hundred years before Moses' time. Yet in the thirteenth century BC, in one generation, there was a sudden acceleration of God's purposes to bring deliverance. After years of seeming divine inactivity, God was stirred to act. He told Moses at his commissioning at the burning bush: 'And now the cry of the Israelites has reached me, and I have seen the way the Egyptians are oppressing them. So now, go. I am sending you to Pharaoh to bring my people the Israelites out of Egypt' (Exod. 3:9–10).

Generations later, after cycle upon cycle of apostasy, God's people were overrun by their enemies and sent into exile away from their land. God's unending patience had seemingly run out. The author of the book of Chronicles narrates the climax of judgment – there was no longer any remedy for their waywardness:

> The LORD, the God of their ancestors, sent word to them through his messengers again and again, because he had pity on his people and on his dwelling-place. But they mocked God's messengers, despised his words and scoffed at his prophets until the wrath of the LORD was aroused against his people and there was no remedy. He brought up against them the king of the Babylonians, who killed their young men with the sword in the sanctuary, and did not spare young men or young women, the elderly or the infirm. God gave them all into the hands of Nebuchadnezzar.
>
> *2 Chr. 36:15–17*

Then again in the New Testament, halfway through the gospels, Jesus took his disciples aside to remind them about the privilege of the days they were living in, a time like no other when the kingdom of God had suddenly come near: 'But blessed are your eyes because they see, and your ears because they hear. For truly I tell you, many prophets and righteous people longed to see what you see but did not see it, and to hear what you hear but did not hear it' (Matt. 13:16–17). Indeed, Jesus' death as the central moment of God's salvation plan is itself described in Hebrews as the 'culmination of the ages' (Heb. 9:26).

As a final example, Jesus wept as he foretold the fall of Jerusalem in AD 70, within a generation of his ministry – the culmination of God's judgment on a people rejecting their

Messiah: 'And so upon you will come all the righteous blood that has been shed on earth, from the blood of righteous Abel to the blood of Zechariah son of Berekiah, whom you murdered between the temple and the altar. Truly I tell you, all this will come upon this generation' (Matt. 23:35–36).

The culmination of the ages – the moment when things reach their climax. This is what I mean about the acceleration of God's plans. Most of history falls under 'normal' in the economy of God's plans. The church lives and grows, history unfolds, nations fall and rise, the gospel spreads, the kingdom increases like mustard seed or yeast. Yet the end times mark a dramatic acceleration in God's purposes, as the previous examples have shown – a time when kingdom plans come to a head, when the consequences of sin reach a climax, when God says 'Now is the time'. Are we finding ourselves entering into God's endgame, the culmination of the ages? Peter used this same phrase in his New Testament letter: 'For the culmination of all things is near. So be self-controlled and sober-minded for the sake of prayer' (1 Pet. 4:7 NET).

Many people are starting to wonder, in the light of global uncertainty and turmoil: how close are we to the culmination of all things?

How to illustrate this sense of divine acceleration

I want to develop this argument about the acceleration of God's purposes. We notice that there are two things in Scripture which we should expect to illustrate this sense of acceleration. The first is the increasing labour pains of creation. The second is the acceleration of the work of the Spirit in Christian mission.

The groaning of creation is intensifying

Maternity wards are places of groaning. Women in labour and in the hours of painful childbirth are not usually silent. The contractions involved in the delivery of a child take up all of a woman's energy and focus; it is a messy, loud and exhausting process for the purpose of bringing forth life.

The groaning of creation is likewise seen in Scripture as taking place in the throes of a traumatic and purposeful process. In Romans 8, Paul uses a profound passage, in which he is speaking about the glorious life of the Spirit for Christians, to also paint a picture of cosmic liberation, renewal and glory. He follows traditional Old Testament thought, according to which the earth is under the curse of Adam, and all the created order is therefore subject to decay, suffering and death. The great hope of the universe, in Paul's language, is for the children of God to be revealed. This is not about Christians living out their faith here and now. No, the revealing of the children of God is part of the bundle of eschatological imagery that describes what occurs when Jesus returns in glory. It speaks of the glorification of the saints fully transformed into Jesus' likeness; it foretells Jesus' defeat of Satan and the renewal of creation; it denotes the start of the perfect age to come on earth. Paul uses the language of pregnancy and labour pains to graphically illustrate his argument:

> For the creation was subjected to frustration, not by its own choice, but by the will of the one who subjected it, in hope that the creation itself will be liberated from its bondage to decay and brought into the freedom and glory of the children of God. We know that the whole creation has been groaning as in the pains of childbirth right up to the present time.
>
> *Rom. 8:20–22*

One Bible scholar comments on these verses: 'The suffering of creation is like birth pangs leading to a glorious new world, rather than the death pangs of a dying creation.'[3] So Paul's apocalyptic vision, like many contemporary Jewish apocalypses of his day, is of Adam's curse reversed and a perfected world revealed, of God's triumph over sin, and the renewal of all things.

Now if the material world and the created order are tightly bound up with our human redemption story, then what does this say about the intense global shaking in the end times before Jesus' return? If Paul's 'labour pain' analogy is true, then we should expect an intensifying of the groaning of creation in the final push towards the climactic breaking in of God's kingdom to renew all things. That is exactly what James Dunn, a New Testament scholar, notes here: 'The metaphor of birth pain was a natural one to seize on for description of a period of turmoil and anguish likely to end in a new order of things; consequently, it is not surprising that it features quite often in passages where the anguish and prospects were seen to have strong eschatological overtones.'[4]

For Paul, writing in his letter to the Romans, the Spirit heightens the tension of travail and hope, both for believers and for all creation, animate and inanimate. Paul's 'present time' of Romans 8:22 shows that he was living in a 'now and not yet' age when God's kingdom was present yet not fully realized. God's people have been living in this tension for the last two thousand years. So, what should we expect in the closing generation before the Lord returns?

I think we should expect a sense of acceleration and intensification. The culmination of God's end-time purposes does not mean that everything is trouble-free now, or that the shaking stops the closer we come to the parousia. Rather, as God quickens his endgame plans, the earth is caught up in an intensified shaking, a period of painful contractions which look destructive but are actually creation anticipating its imminent liberation and glory, a shaking free from the curse of sin and death. Of course, a measure of shaking comes through the consequences of human sin and the increase of satanic evil, and God's judgment on these. Yet here is a real and vivid sense that God's accelerating purposes in coming years will involve increasing upheaval in the natural world. The whole of the cosmos is in the throes of final labour pains for the transformation that will occur when Christ returns!

Pause for Thought

- Do I agree with the quote 'The suffering of creation is like birth pangs leading to a glorious new world, rather than the death pangs of a dying creation'?
- How does this belief differ from contemporary cultural thought around us?

Mission in the power of the Spirit is quickening

You may remember the shockwaves in the news in 1998 when cosmologists revealed that the universe is expanding at an accelerated rate. Two independent teams of scientists (the Supernova Cosmology project and the High-Z Supernova search team) observed that the velocity at which distant galaxies recede from us is continuously increasing over time; they are racing away from the earth faster all the time! It was a seismic revelation. The scientific community's assumptions of constant laws governing the universe's size, age and movement have had to be reassessed in the years since those findings.

Scripture speaks of times when the pace of kingdom advance increases. The prophet Isaiah illustrates this well; in a highly charged eschatological passage about the Day of the Lord, he shows the energy and pace of God's saving and judging work in the world:

> From the west, people will fear the name of the LORD,
> and from the rising of the sun, they will revere his glory.
> For he will come like a pent-up flood
> that the breath of the LORD drives along.
>
> Isa. 59:19

Likewise, the miraculous rising of God's people and the return of the Jews to their land in the last days is seen as a rapid work:

> I am the LORD;
> in its time I will do this swiftly.
>
> Isa. 60:22

When we stand back and look at the history of spiritual revivals and times of renewal and reform, we see that there has been an increased pace of the life of the Holy Spirit flowing through the church in the last few generations. Jesus himself called his followers to be witnesses in the power of the Spirit, from the place where they were to the very ends of the earth (Acts 1:8). Let me walk briefly through part of the church's history. I can only speak clearly for streams of life within the Protestant Church of which I am a part, but the Catholic and Orthodox streams have parallel renewal and mission stories to tell. In the following historical sweep, please forgive the great simplification here but note the pattern.

A brief summary of mission in the Spirit

After the huge missionary expansion of the early church in the Roman world, and a Christianizing of mainland Europe in the early medieval age, the institutional church held sway for a thousand years in much of medieval Europe in various versions of Christendom. Fairly static and dominant religious hierarchies influenced many nations. It was the monastic and missional orders that kept alive a sense that the river of spiritual renewal was still flowing. Then in the 1500s there was massive reformation through the work of Martin Luther and John Calvin, bringing gospel correction and schism into a rigid and doctrinally impure church. Also around this time, the printed Bible became readily available to the 'common man', enabling people to further understand the gospel.

From the 1700s, the church in the West started to experience great moves of the Spirit and subsequent effective mission. History records the notable revivals of 'religious enthusiasm' in times of great awakening in America and Europe, with leading preachers such as John Wesley and George Whitefield. From that time and throughout the nineteenth century, during the Industrial Revolution and the era of colonial expansion, repeated waves of Holy Spirit revival occurred in random locations, often hand in hand with mission. It is sometimes said that the modern Christian evangelization of the world came through empire building and colonialism, but it also came through the missionary pulse of the Spirit, stirring a passive church into fulfilling the Great Commission of sharing the gospel in all parts of the world.

Since the start of the twentieth century there have been continual waves of Holy Spirit renewal across the globe, through Pentecostal and charismatic movements revitalizing churches in faith, worship and witness. From what was once a western missionary endeavour, the majority-world indigenous church has taken on the baton of mission, saturating continents with the gospel message, accompanied by miracles and compassion, and bathed in passionate prayer. And now, unreached people-groups and massive numbers of people of other faiths are experiencing divine encounters; and grassroots disciple-making Christian movements, sometimes operating underground because of persecution, are the result.

David Barrett, head of the global evangelization movement in the USA, has documented the impact of the Holy Spirit renewal movements, throughout the twentieth century until now, on the Christian task of evangelization. He concludes: 'We can sum up this extraordinary phenomenon as follows. With Pentecostals/charismatics/neo-charismatics now active in 80 percent of the world's 3,300 large metropolises, all in process of actively implementing, networking and cooperating with Great Commission Christians of all confessions, a new era in world missions would clearly appear to be under way.'[5]

Stand back and look at this picture. There is no doubt that there has been an acceleration of mission stirred up by the Holy Spirit in the cause of the kingdom of God. Where is God not at work right now in the world, in the growth of his kingdom and the mission of the gospel?

Through the vagaries of revival outbreaks, through the messiness of cross-cultural mission, through the myriad contextualized responses of churches in their nations to the needs of their day, the Holy Spirit is always working to draw individuals and societies into the coming rule of God. There is something in the quickening pace of both renewal and mission that reveals how the Spirit is sovereignly directing the people of God in an acceleration of both the witness and the dynamic life and growth of the church as we draw closer to the Lord's return. What has been happening in the last few hundred years through sporadic and increasing waves of Holy Spirit revival doesn't appear to be stopping. The Spirit is urging and coaxing us on towards completing our missionary task.

As I mentioned earlier in this book, the following prophecy from the book of Habakkuk remains an encouraging promise:

> the earth will be filled with the knowledge of the glory of the LORD
> as the waters cover the sea.
>
> *Hab. 2:14*

The whole earth is already filled with God's glory, according to Isaiah (6:3); most people are too spiritually unaware to see it most of the time. There is coming a time, however, when people's eyes will be opened like never before to the knowledge of the Lord's glory and reality. If that is God's intent, then it is likely to come through a great last wave of Holy Spirit revival, and a consequent last great missionary push by his people across the earth.

Summing Up

These twin dynamics – the sense of quickening of global revival and mission in the power of the Spirit, and the intensifying of the groaning of creation – I believe help to illustrate that God's endgame plan is moving into place. These things are not easily explained by chapter and verse in Scripture, although I have suggested that they are there.

An end-time understanding is gained in many ways: through patient rereading of particular scriptures, seeking the Lord for prophetic revelation concerning the present time, and a humble sharing with other believers for collective discernment, to name a few. However, some things are also felt by the spiritual senses. Can you feel the seismic changes taking place on the earth? Can you sense the spiritual reverberations of God's endgame plans taking shape?

And other things are understood by simply stepping back a little to see patterns. Like crop circles in fields, you need to see them from a height to understand the patterns. The pattern of the quickening pulse of the Spirit is appreciated when gauged from recent history. Look at the scale of what God is doing right now – the Christian faith more vibrant and relevant globally than ever before. Look at the weaving together of our interconnected global systems – and their fragility, meaning that the combined shaking of these systems could lead to global collapse. Observe both the yearning of people for spiritual reality, and the pain of our broken world. Look at both the groaning of creation and the quickening pulse of the Spirit, and let the Lord speak to you about the signs of the times and his accelerating plans. May we discern the teleological purposes of God! Our world may still be some way off the final end times, or we could be very close to them. The culmination of the ages could well be nearly upon us. If so, we must be ready.

Pause for Thought

- What spiritual 'patterns' do I discern worldwide that convince me of God's accelerating plans?

3

Great Revival, Great Turbulence

How Will God Prepare the Church?

In the previous chapter we considered God's end-time plans, his very good and perfect plans, to bring in his kingdom and reveal Jesus to the world at his coming. We also realized that we might expect to see an acceleration of God's activity the closer we get to Jesus' return. Moreover, we saw that at the centre of God's plans is his desire to do a great work in his church. The Bible indicates that the church will be standing strong for God at the end, and awaiting his coming:

> In that day they will say,
>
> > 'Surely this is our God;
> > we trusted in him, and he saved us.
> > This is the LORD, we trusted in him;
> > let us rejoice and be glad in his salvation.'
>
> Isa. 25:9

This is a great image of the people of God in the end times.

How will God create a radiant and resolute bride? How will he prepare us to meet his Son at his return? Will something dramatic happen in the closing generation of the church? Yes, I think it will.

The glory hole

Years ago, my wife and I visited an artisan craft fair, where skilled craftsmen and women were making and selling their work. The booth that most fascinated us was the woman demonstrating the ancient art of glass-blowing. She had molten glass waiting in a small furnace, where she inserted a blowpipe to form a globule of glass. The craftswoman spent a few minutes moulding this piece on a metal surface, then put it back into the intense heat. As we watched she took it out again and added other crushed glass pieces to create texture and colour. Then she blew through the pipe to create a delicate bubble of glass. Back into the furnace it went again to stop it cooling too quickly. A handful of times she repeated this process. To complete the work, the woman then twisted the bottom of the glass with tweezers, gave a sharp tap, and the piece of art was finished – a beautiful vase. Later, we found out that the furnace for glass-blowing is called the 'glory hole'!

Firing, moulding, blowing – these seem like biblical metaphors for God's work in his people in the last days, in a 'glory hole' context. The Father seems intent on bringing forth a beautiful jewel of a church in the last days. How? Through the fires of Holy Spirit revival and the pressure of trouble and persecution. The twin forces of Holy Spirit renewing power and the conditions of shaking will create a church that is severely tested and yet greatly blessed. In this 'glory hole', this crucible, the body of Christ rises as a glorious remnant into all she is meant to be, and a huge number of people come to Christ to fill out the church in the closing years before his return.

Exploring revival

Let us explore the term 'revival' a little more deeply. In the early 2000s I did some doctoral research into the combination of the human and divine dynamic in revivals. I coined a phrase: 'the pulse of the Spirit'. In explaining this, I gave a definition of how the Spirit is at work in revival movements: 'a vitalizing pulse of the Spirit, flowing from the missionary heart of the Trinity which, erupting within and mediated by historical human contexts, seeks intensively to reconstitute the church through crisis as an eschatological agent for mission, and extensively to draw individuals and the surrounding society and culture into the coming rule of God'.

That is quite a dense definition! I would argue that the intense surge of energy sensed in revivals can be likened to a pulse since it occurs time and again in church history. The first defining revival-pulse moment was, of course, the birth of the early church, described in the book of Acts. I suggested that revivals are due to an activity of the Spirit that is not qualitatively different from his normal empowering, teaching and sanctifying work, but rather they are the result of a greater degree, and a sharper focus, of the Spirit's energy. They are like an eruptive surge of kingdom life that is experienced both as a personal blessing and as an empowering for mission. One could use phrases such as 'Spirit life', 'revival surge', 'energy of the Spirit' and 'pulse of revival' in interchangeable ways with the term 'Spirit revival pulse'. To experience times of revival is like being in the middle of a great gust of power or caught by a mighty wave of outpoured love. This should not surprise us when the Holy Spirit is the source of life for the church and also the dynamic empowerer of mission. These great surges of forceful love from the heart of the Trinity break upon the seashores of the Christian community at unforeseen times.

Such surges of Spirit life are usually times of spiritual upheaval for Christian communities. They erupt unexpectedly, cause crises of faith, often cause new denominations to form, and bring new leadership and vision; and by such upheaval they create the church as an agent of mission, useful in God's work of calling people into the kingdom. Periods of revival often happen at the margins of church life, among those who are most open, most desperate, most ready for God to use them in a new way.

There is certainly a sense of desperation in the church of the West – a realization that what we are doing is not working any more, that we are not effective agents of mission. As denominations struggle to change institutionally, our need for openness to a new thing of the Spirit has never been clearer. Hirsch, in his book on metanoia and the radical transformation of churches from the inside out, remarks on this sense of crisis, particularly this side of the recent pandemic. He challenges the church:

> We are being tried and tested. We are told that judgment begins with the household of God (1 Pet. 4:17), and so we ought not to be surprised but rather seek to discern what God is saying. We must always respond by interrogating our systems and our roles within them: What is God saying to us in these portentous events? What is being revealed about us in this crisis? What must change? What specifically does God require of me/us?[1]

Major revival pulses of the Spirit, such as the eighteenth-century Great Awakening, and the twentieth-century Pentecostal movement, were times of great transnational disruption, yet they brought successive surges of spiritual life, new confidence in mission, and fresh ways of being church that were contextual for their communities in a form that brought many to faith.

What am I saying in all this? My point is that this 'revival pulse' of the Spirit, which can be seen in the book of Acts, is also seen at progressive points in the missionary push of the church. It can be noticed particularly in the middle of the global missionary expansion over the last three hundred years. We mediate this divine pulse in all our humanness, ingenuity, cultural peculiarities and weakness, yet through it the Spirit is moving us forward in God's mission. If I am right, then God still intends his church to move forward in spreading the gospel in pulses or waves of Holy Spirit power and grace. The closer we get to Jesus' return, the more the Spirit will use a context of global disruption to refine, renew and empower his people to live and witness well for him. In these last days, I believe the Spirit will reconstitute us as an eschatological agent for mission.

Yet it is not just the revival fires but also the pressure of the end-time shaking that will produce such strength in the church. Diamonds are formed deep under the surface of the earth when deposits of carbon are subjected to enormous heat and pressure. Persecution and pressure don't always bring out the best in people, but the Bible indicates that this will be the context for brave discipleship and bold witness:

> The one who stands firm to the end will be saved.
>
> *Matt. 24:13*

> They triumphed over him [i.e. the accuser, or Satan]
> by the blood of the lamb
> and the word of their testimony.
>
> *Rev. 12:11*

We are currently living in times of great pressure on the Christian faith. Both strident secular humanism in the West and militant groups within world religions such as Islam and Hinduism in the East are trying to stamp the life out of the church. Persecution of Christians is at an all-time high. Confusion as to which moral stances to take on major social issues such as same-sex marriage and transgenderism is threatening to tear denominations apart.

Moreover, we know that deception and persecution are only going to get worse the more deeply we move into the end times. When you add to this the universal pressure of global environmental instability and economic fragility, which is causing huge social anxiety, we can only conclude that the pressure in the closing years of history will be immense. And yet these pressures, amid the fiery life of the Holy Spirit within the church, in God's hands can be the cause of strengthening of our commitment to Christ, and a tremendous emboldening of our conviction in the gospel.

Pause for Thought

- Do I believe that huge change and renewal can come in the church through the 'glory hole' place of the fire of the Spirit and the pressure of global trouble?

The end-time prophecy of Joel 2

We are going to look at one particular prophetic passage in the Old Testament that combines both this revival dynamic and the pressure conditions we will find in the end times: the second chapter of the book of Joel.

Joel was a prophet-preacher at a time of crisis in his nation. His people faced twin problems: they were in a time of drought, and a locust swarm was devastating the country. He was looking to the horizon in prayer to see what God was doing and what the future would look like. God helped Joel to see a future beyond their crisis and a greater kingdom-horizon of what God was going to do for his people.

God called his people first to face the reality of a great time of trouble facing their world, and then to pray. The call was to blow a trumpet in Zion. The need was to intercede as a nation, in great seriousness and purpose, for God's mercy and help. Joel saw the need to blow a trumpet and gather everyone in prayer. Their cry was:

> Spare your people, LORD.
>   Do not make your inheritance an object of scorn,
>   a byword among the nations.
> Why should they say among the peoples,
>   'Where is their God?'
>
> *Joel 2:17*

God's answer to a heartfelt and wholehearted turning to him was, first, to bring a miracle of deliverance and a turning around of the nation's fortunes. It was then that the Lord revealed to Joel an even greater answer to the desperation of the times and the cries of his people. It was a vision of a great outpouring of the Holy Spirit.

This vision has become one of the most celebrated prophetic passages in the Old Testament:

> And afterwards,
>   I will pour out my Spirit on all people.
> Your sons and daughters will prophesy,
>   your old men will dream dreams,
>   your young men will see visions.
> Even on my servants, both men and women,
>   I will pour out my Spirit in those days.
> I will show wonders in the heavens
>   and on the earth,
>   blood and fire and billows of smoke.
> The sun will be turned to darkness
>   and the moon to blood
>   before the coming of the great and dreadful day of the LORD.
> And everyone who calls
>   on the name of the LORD will be saved;
> for on Mount Zion and in Jerusalem
>   there will be deliverance,
>   as the LORD has said,
> even among the survivors
>   whom the LORD calls.
>
> *Joel 2:28–32*

I don't think Joel was expecting to see and hear all that God showed him. Yet, because he was alert and praying, God showed him patterns of what would happen in the future. The hinge phrase in this passage is 'the Day of the Lord':

> The sun will be turned to darkness
>   and the moon to blood
>   before the coming of the great and dreadful day of the LORD.
>
> *Joel 2:31*

This is such a powerful phrase. As I mentioned earlier, the Day of the Lord in Scripture is the season when God breaks in, when he acts to right wrongs and bring salvation to his people. In short, the Day of the Lord became a great messianic hope for the people of God.

Although Christians agree that this passage refers initially to the day of Pentecost, many believe it has been only partially fulfilled – this prophecy also speaks of a future time. In fact, I believe the end of Joel 2 is a prophecy which bookends the life of the church age. It is most relevant for the early church and for the end-time-generation church. The outpouring of the Spirit described in Acts was a local occurrence that was experienced by 120 people in the city of Jerusalem. Its impact was huge because incipient in Pentecost was the overflowing life of the Spirit in the DNA of every church and the empowering of every mission endeavour in the name of Christ. Yet the scale of Joel's prophetic word was not local – it was worldwide; the vision was for a global outpouring on all people. And it was intrinsically linked to a time of great cosmic turbulence. This prophecy therefore speaks more of an end-time fulfilment than anything else. This is not surprising, for, as in much Old Testament prophecy, there are different peaks of fulfilment. It is like looking at distant hills, where you see the foothills and the much more distant mountain peaks. The early church experienced the initial foothills fulfilment (Joel chapter 2 was quoted by Peter in his first sermon in Acts 2), but there remains a fuller mountain-peak fulfilment just before Jesus comes back.

In fact a Bible commentator says about this passage: 'Pentecost triggers a series of powerful events which begin the birth of the church, expand in its world-wide mission . . . and move on step by step to God's final judgment of his enemies and his vindication of those who truly trust him.'[2] It is because of this 'distant hills' sense of Joel 2 that this passage continues to be a powerful future prophetic word for the end times, and very relevant for us as Jesus' return draws closer.

The 'great' and 'dreadful' Day of the Lord

The Day of the Lord is described as both 'great' and 'dreadful'. Why is that? It is because there will be amazing things that God will do – such as an outpouring of his Spirit – and also troubling things that God will bring about – wonders on the earth, blood, fire and billows of smoke. I would put these descriptions of the great and dreadful in the categories of glory and shaking that are described elsewhere in the Bible.

As one commentator states regarding the twin dynamics of the Day of the Lord in Old Testament understanding:

> This 'day', described in Isaiah 2:12–21, is one in which God will destroy everything that has exalted itself against him. It was expected that the covenant promises of God would be fulfilled in the day of his coming, that he would 'tend his flock like a shepherd' (Isaiah 40:11) and that Jerusalem's 'hard service' would be ended (Isaiah 40:2). At the same time there would be a fearsome rooting out of evil.[3]

So I believe that Joel speaks about what it will be like to live through coming end-time days, in an extraordinary timeframe and amid the accelerating purposes of God.

Marks of glory

Under the overarching theme of glory, Joel describes the following in chapter 2:28–29:

- global outpourings of the Spirit by God's gracious initiative ('I will pour');
- a dynamic, prophetic, witnessing generation of church ('will prophesy');
- his people experiencing great revelation of, close communion with, and deep knowledge of the things of God ('see visions' and 'dream dreams');
- whole communities of faith living with great anointing (reinforcing again 'I will pour');
- a great harvest of people coming to faith in turbulent times ('everyone who calls on the name of the LORD');
- the call for faith going out powerfully in the preaching of the gospel ('whom the LORD calls').

This encourages us to look with expectancy into the future to see more outpourings of the Spirit in the days that precede the Lord's return. What would it be like for Christians and churches to come fully alive in God, for there to be a massive harvest of salvation of both Gentiles and Jews, with people wide open to consider God's reality because of the dynamic life and witness of his people? The liberal giving of the Spirit was a sign to Israel, in those days, of God doing a new thing. Could this bookending of the church age see the same powerful outpourings of the Spirit and the unveiling of the glory of God that marked the early church?

Marks of shaking

Joel also speaks about shaking (2:30–31). He describes wonders and signs of turmoil: blood, fire and smoke. There is a prophesied shaking of things in heaven and on earth. Just as the giving of the Spirit was a sign for Israel, so 'wonders' such as the plagues in Egypt at the time of Moses (Exod. 4:21; 7–9) are a warning sign to the nations. These are portents, extraordinary phenomena – natural or supernatural, as the case might be – which arrest people's attention.

Commentator David Hubbard again remarks on this passage: 'Prophetic passages like this one from Joel and Isaiah 13:10 have made a distinct contribution to the language with which Christ's second coming is described in texts like Mark 13:24 and Revelation 6:12, but it is probably better to view them not as pictures of Messiah's advent but as dramatic descriptions of battle with smoke so thick it obscures the very lights of heaven.'[4] Such 'battle' pictures are tremendous metaphors of future global shaking. Joel prophesies a shaking of the natural world (vv. 30–31) – wars ('blood'), disasters and troubles ('fire'), and devastation or shaking of aspects of society ('billows of smoke' from ruined cities). He foresees that the people of the earth will feel great anxiety about the apparently constant things in which we trust ('the sun will be turned to darkness and the moon to blood') and a fearful uncertainty about the times in which we live. All this precedes the coming of the Day of the Lord.

We don't have to look far to see such uncertainty today. As an illustration, the Covid-19 pandemic caused panic and lockdowns. The floods, droughts and fires of increasing global warming are making many places difficult to live in. Recent conflicts between Russia and Ukraine and between Palestinian

Hamas and Israel have threatened to spill outside those borders. The fresh rise in jihadist terror attacks; a polarization of opinions and a weaponization of 'truth'; the Doomsday Clock turning the closest it ever has towards midnight – all in the opening years of a new decade. These things will increase, the closer we get to Jesus' return.

What is our response to the crises of our day? Our context is not the same as Joel's. It is a lot darker and more critical than a locust swarm and a drought. The world is facing escalating trouble, and nations are looking for solutions anywhere except to God. The countdown to the last of the last days is moving quickly. Our response should be the same as that of Joel's generation. The need for the church to pray and ask for God's mercy is greater than ever. A wholehearted turning to God by his people is the key that unlocks blessing and then revival outpourings of his Spirit.

Mike Bickle, pioneer of one of the 24/7 prayer movements in Kansas, USA, writes about this passage:

> When we come as a collective unit, corporately turning to Him with all our hearts (v12) by obeying the commands He has given us, then we enter into a new arena. Then we shift into the second half of Joel 2, in which the Lord responds to our prayers. Then we move into the wondrous things believers like to focus on: an end-times outpouring of the Holy Spirit that, like the one described in Acts 2, dramatically changes the world.[5]

We don't know why God will allow such shaking in future years. But Jesus told the parable of the wheat and the weeds, indicating that both would grow together until the harvest at the end of the age (Matt. 13:30). The light will get brighter and the darkness darker and, when both are at their peak, during the Great Tribulation, we will find ourselves in the timeframe called the Day of the Lord as described by Joel. The stage

Great Revival, Great Turbulence

will then be set for the biblical climax long prophesied – the time for Jesus to return, to come for his redeemed people, to restore devastated planet earth, and bring in the age to come.

If we read through to the end of the book of Joel, we see the climax of the vision – judgment of the nations, a trial, and a holy war in the Valley of Jehoshaphat (3:1–2,12–16). We see cosmic signs and the Lord thundering in judgment from Jerusalem (3:15–16), and the restoration of his people in a new messianic age (3:17–18). There are parallels here with the climax of John's vision in Revelation, with the last battle and Jesus' return in glory.

The end-time fulfilment of this global revival promise requires a sober assessment of our current time of shaking, and then great prayer and seeking after the Lord for his mercy. Past revivals have nearly always hinged on groups of people praying and interceding for the fresh breaking in of the Spirit. How much more significant is the time we are living in?

I hope that you can see why Joel's vision is such a powerful prophetic passage of Scripture. It faces desperate times, and calls for a response of prayer, which then opens up into awesome end-time events. The prophecy is hugely relevant, challenging and exciting in equal measure. I would encourage you to blow the dust off this Old Testament prophecy and pray it through on your knees and with others. See what God shows you and how he helps prepare you for the days we are coming into.

Pause for Thought

- Reread the passage from Joel 2:28–32.
- Ask yourself: what phrases particularly impact me and stir my faith and prayers?

Are We Right to Expect an End-Time Revival in Scripture?

We have to pause here and check whether there is enough general biblical evidence for believing in an end-time revival. Joel 2:28–32 is a key prophecy, both because it was used at the start of the church age and because of the aspects not yet fulfilled. We are awaiting the greater fulfilment of this prophecy. David Sliker, a teacher on biblical end-time prophecy, believes that Joel 2 is one continuous prophecy about a future worldwide event that impacts people on a global scale. He says:

> Imagine the phenomenal power of the Holy Spirit being poured out across the whole planet in every village, town and metropolis, on isolated farmsteads and in jungles, on board every ship and airplane – simultaneously. What would it look like to have a combination of the day of Pentecost, the First Great Awakening and the Azusa Street revival happening everywhere on earth at the same moment in time?[6]

One could argue that increasing waves of Holy Spirit revival are needed to bring in the harvest, as people are shaken out of their spiritual lethargy by global trouble and uncertainty. They are also needed to change a divided church into a united family of believers, to deal with the myriad compromises and the spiritual lethargy found in us as disciples, and bring us to the point where the global church lives for Christ alone.

Harvest is a key theme in another prophetic image of revival. In particular, the image of the 'latter rain' has been popularized in charismatic circles as a prophetic promise of a coming move of the Holy Spirit. The 'latter rain' in Israel was traditionally the springtime rain that ripened the harvest, coming after the early autumn rains a few months before. Both Joel and

Great Revival, Great Turbulence

Zechariah, in highly charged eschatological prophetic passages, speak of this 'latter rain':

> He sends you abundant showers,
> both autumn and spring rains, as before.
>
> *Joel 2:23*

> Ask the LORD for the rain in the springtime;
> it is the LORD who sends the thunderstorms.
>
> *Zech. 10:1*

James, in his New Testament letter, alludes to the nearness of the Lord's return in a passage about the sending of the latter rains: 'See how the farmer waits for the land to yield its valuable crop, patiently waiting for the autumn and spring rains. You too, be patient and stand firm, because the Lord's coming is near' (Jas 5:7–8).

These passages seem to indicate the reality of an initial pouring out of the Spirit and a future 'last days' revival. Although the particular group espousing a 'latter rain' movement within Pentecostalism in the 1950s was controversial, the hope of these Old Testament prophecies has been absorbed into many charismatic prayer streams.

In a wider way concerning end-time revival, some Old Testament prophecies speak of a global dimension of experiencing God's glory, in which not just regions or isolated communities but the whole world encounters a measure of God's manifested presence and power – such as we see in Habakkuk 2:14, Isaiah 40:3–5 and Joel 2:28–32 mentioned above. This has clearly not yet happened, but in our digitally connected global media culture, a move of the Spirit could conceivably touch every continent very quickly. There is also other eschatological language, used in Old Testament prophecies given to the Jewish exiles, which seems to go far beyond the context of a return from exile. Promises of God's blessings of great light, glory and inheritance seem to have a future relevance for global revival, along with a greater return of the Jews to their promised land; see, for example, Isaiah chapters 54 and 60. Indeed, the language of the end of Isaiah 60, describing how 'the LORD will be your everlasting light, and your God will be your glory' (v. 19), suggests in the words of commentator David Payne a 'look towards a more distant, unearthly future'.[7] In fact, the end of the prophecy contains a paradox: that 'God will not delay in the fulfilment of what He promises, and yet He will not act until "the fullness of time"'.[8] Perhaps the fullness of that time is the harvest in the last days.

In the New Testament, a great turning of Jews to the Lord is prophesied once the full number of Gentiles has come in (Rom. 11:25–26) – a double harvest, so to speak. Revelation 14:14–16 also prophesies about a great harvest at the end of the age before the world experiences the winepress of God's wrath. In our experience, the turning of large people-groups to the Lord is usually associated with times of revival and awakening. And in the story of the miracle of turning water into wine (John 2:1–11), we are told that Jesus has 'saved the best [wine] till now'. This parable has eschatological overtones beyond launching Jesus' kingdom ministry, as many Christians have felt. Has the Lord got it in mind to bring the best wine of his kingdom life late in the day of the church's life? Is there an extravagant season of 'new wine' outpourings of the Spirit before Jesus the 'bridegroom' returns?

Outpouring, rain, harvest, glory, new wine – all these are powerful images of the Holy Spirit's work. When these scriptures are combined with our church's historic experience of revival moves of the Spirit, they convince many that God intends to bring about a powerful spiritual awakening across the globe in the last few years before Jesus' return. In such a scenario, the word 'revival' seems too constricted. More appropriate terms are 'surges' or 'waves' of Spirit life, which could happen successively over a period of time on a global dimension in the midst of turmoil and darkness. Such an outpouring would fulfil a worldwide context for Isaiah's call to 'arise' and 'shine' (Isa. 60:1). These are wonderful promises, providing a powerful motivation to hope and pray for greater things than we have seen so far as believers.

Pause for Thought

- Do I think that revivals have finished?
- If not, which of the images of a last-days revival is most helpful for me?

The Great Turbulence

If the church is to become a beautiful jewel in God's hands, then it will be not just the fires of the Spirit which create the gemstone, but also the global pressure and difficulty experienced as a context of faith. Jesus' warnings of deception and falling away in the last days are to be taken seriously. We tend to like faith that comes in a neat, hopeful package; we prefer prophetic words given in meetings that paint rosy pictures of the near future. The end-times scenario appears to be much more complicated than that.

Yes, a final revival is a biblical promise, but so is a time of great falling away from the faith. What on earth would make so many sincere believers abandon their life of faith in Christ? Jesus names four things in his Olivet discourse in Matthew 24 that I alluded to earlier: persecution, betrayal, prophetic deception, and an increase of wickedness. The end times appear to be a mix: a glorious period of waves of Holy Spirit revival in the midst of and surrounded by growing turmoil and great confusion for the church in the world. Let us look more closely at what is meant by Jesus' warnings.

First, persecution. There are more Christian believers being persecuted for their faith today than at any other time, and that trend doesn't look likely to abate. The history of the church shows that religious persecution brings great conviction in some believers and a renouncing of faith by others. Jesus calls us to be 'faithful, even to the point of death' (Rev. 2:10). Apostasy is a hidden shame for the oppressed church in some anti-Christian countries today. Opposition and insistent persecution may truly prune the church in the end times, yet in the end will make her stronger. Persecution will be a turbulent test of faith.

Second, betrayal. In a last-days move of state-sponsored hostility towards the church, it is easy to see how people could turn other believers in to the authorities, as has happened in the harsh Communist regimes of Russia and China. Pressure to conform to anti-Christian laws and to inform on friends who don't toe the line could easily increase, even in the so-called liberal West. Micah prophesies about such times in the end:

> The day God visits you has come . . .
>   Now is the time of your confusion . . .
>   a man's enemies are the members of his own household.
>
> Mic. 7:4,6

Even today in our 'cancel culture', those with strong Christian convictions which are culturally unpopular could find that their brothers and sisters in the faith turn their backs on them. How far would the demonizing of the 'other' who disagrees with us go? Could believers misunderstand each other's faith stance to the extent of being disloyal to them? Betrayal will be a tough test of faith.

Third, prophetic deception. In Jesus' words this is not limited to a few blatant false messiahs leading misguided cults. That would be relatively easy to spot and avoid. Deception is, of course, subtle and easily missed; in some ways it is already working its way through the church as through the world. Fake truths and 'echo chamber' ideologies are seeping into Christian circles. In 2 Timothy 4:3 we read of a time when people 'will gather round them a great number of teachers to say what their itching ears want to hear'. Are people deceived because someone with a persuasive voice misleads them, or because they only want to listen to those who agree with them? It is becoming far too easy to take a stance on biblical guidance towards moral issues as one's *version* of the truth. Even the relativizing of Christian absolute claims in order to accommodate the wider culture can become the appropriate attitude of the day. To be told that a certain slant or reading of Scripture is the 'new relevant gospel', or to be encouraged by others not to rock the boat of the church in society by expressing unpopular truths – either of these can erode the certainty of faith. Deception will be a confusing test of faith.

Fourth, wickedness. Although there are always evil forces at play in our world, the sense of the biblical end times is that evil becomes so prevailing that it leads many to despair, to lose hope; and in so doing, faith grows cold. As Psalm 11:3 says:

> When the foundations are being destroyed,
>   what can the righteous do?

The increase in lawlessness, the blatant celebrating of and fascination with evil and the occult, growing violence, and the flaunting of any value that disregards a God to whom we give account of our lives – this despairing mix, in the vortex also of global shaking, may well pull a significant number of sincere believers away from a white-hot, passionate faith in Christ. Wickedness will be a suffocating test of faith.

Therefore, part of God's plan to bring forth a jewel of a church ready for the Lord's return will clearly be to allow his people to go through a crucible of testing and a refining process of faith. God will use difficulty to sift people, to purify the church, and to bring great heart-searching about our human weakness and temptation to compromise. This time of testing will also come like a tremendous wave. Many of God's people, particularly in the West, are not prepared for such testing times. It will certainly feel like a period of great turbulence if churches split over doctrine or political and moral stances. The Lord may choose to bring waves of revival to groups of believers who profoundly disagree with each other, or he may bypass some streams and denominations entirely. A situation where some believers are growing white-hot in faith and others are growing cold will create a huge tension in Christian communities. This mix of glory and shaking will undoubtedly reshape the church in a profound way. Churches in their nations may be profoundly splintered and unable to easily have fellowship with one another. Denominational rejection of a revival move of God might leave groups to shrivel and die. Personal refusal to walk closely with God or live under the truth of his word might lead many to shipwreck their faith. Global troubles may cause people to become confused about their beliefs and to lose their hope in the gospel.

If Jesus is serious in his words about the love of many growing cold, then the logic is that a righteous remnant will emerge, refined and uncompromising in faith. They may be young believers; they may be people who have gone through great testing. They will include a mix of people from every stream of Christian faith, not coasting on a prosperity gospel or an easy discipleship track, but having run a gauntlet of everything that could throw them off course in faith. If there is a billion-soul harvest in coming years, as different prophetic voices suggest, even if many fall away, those new Christians will still join maybe a billion or more believers – wiser, hardened, tested, ready to face the Tribulation time.

Pause for Thought

- Is there anything I can do to prepare myself and my Christian friends to navigate a confusing and disruptive time for the church?

Transitional Generations

Have you ever had a discussion with friends where you ask the question 'If you could enter a time machine and choose one time in history to go back to, what would it be?' People's answers are always fascinating, some wanting to have first-hand experience of an emerging civilization, others to witness a revolution, or a golden age of prosperity. I often think that I would like to go back to the times in the Bible when God's glory and purposes were so clearly on display. The most significant of those would have to be the time of Moses described in Exodus, and the time of the first disciples and early church in the gospels and book of Acts.

If we stand back and look at salvation history, there are three generations spoken about in Scripture which see the mighty acts of God in a widespread way. The generation of the Israelites during the time of Moses is the first. Collectively, these people experienced the mighty deliverance of Yahweh. They lived through the impact of the plagues in Egypt, the miracles of the Red Sea parting, supernatural provision of food in the form of manna and quail in the wilderness, and the giving of the covenant law combined with the awesome power of God displayed at Mount Sinai.

The second is the generation of the first disciples and the early church. They witnessed first-hand the awesome breaking in of the kingdom of God in the ministry of Jesus. They saw the shattering and amazing events of his cross and resurrection. As a whole group, they experienced the outpouring of the Spirit at Pentecost and the powerful dynamic of the presence of the Lord among them in the anointed growth of the young church, as the gospel touched the known Roman world with demonstrations of healing and miracles.

The third generation to see the mighty acts of God is a future generation who will be alive during the end times and witnessing Jesus' second coming. This has yet to happen, but it is prophesied in the Bible. That generation is described in Scripture as those who will undergo huge opposition and persecution and yet will arise and shine in the brilliant glory of God in their midst. They are a generation who will witness fearlessly to Jesus, even through martyrdom, and will bring in the last great harvest of souls. These are the people of God who will watch, resist and pray in the deep darkness of the

Antichrist regime, and then stand to welcome the return of Jesus on the clouds in glory.

How could we describe these three epochs and groups of people? They are *transitional generations*. This is an important term, because these seasons are so unusual in the Bible narrative and salvation history. A transitional generation is one in which the majority of the people alive witness God's glorious presence in unusual ways and walk together into a new part of God's salvation plan. The generation of Moses moved from slavery into freedom, into a covenant with the Lord and the inheritance of the promised land. The generation of the early church moved from old covenant to new covenant, the establishing of the church, and mission in the power of the Spirit. The generation of the end-time church will move from the end of the present age to the full dawning of the age to come, and from the kingdom 'now and not yet' to the kingdom fully established. These three transitional generations are remarkable and unique. What would it have been like to be one of the Israelites as you walked through the Red Sea or entered the promised land? What would it have felt like to experience the wind and fire of the Spirit in the upper room at Pentecost, and to be part of the anointed first wave of church planting across the Roman world? We could also ask: what will it be like to live through a time of unprecedented Holy Spirit activity and the revealing of the glory of God in the turbulent last days, and stand on the cusp of the visible return of the Lord?

There will be a last generation of believers

One thing is certain. The transitional generations referred to in Scripture concern real people living real lives, experiencing first-hand these cataclysmic and newsworthy events. Similarly, the logic about the end times is that there will be a generation of people of faith who will be alive, surviving the Tribulation times and ready to welcome Jesus' return in glory. Just stop and consider that for a moment. We often think or read about the end times in Scripture almost as if it's a dramatic novel. We read about it in the abstract, but forget that real people will live through these coming events.

If I am right about our being close to the end times, then you, or your children or grandchildren, and your friends will be history makers, simply by being alive in this frame of time. How we stay true to the Lord and live out our faith will of course be a result of our own crucial choices, but billions of people will experience end-time glory and shaking, revival and tribulation. And, if you can stretch your heart and imagination around these prophetic truths, if you are alive at that time, you will experience the promised transformation of a glorious new body, be caught up in the air to meet Jesus, and witness him coming on the clouds and returning to Jerusalem to rule and reign.

It is important to press this point, because the Bible foretells a real, living, breathing generation of church people, making history as saints, who happen to be alive and walking in God's dramatic purposes in their generation at the moment when Jesus returns. Would I like to be part of this end-time transitional generation? In fear and trembling, I would say 'yes'. Who would volunteer to undergo Tribulation times? Who would naturally ask for martyrdom? Yet who wouldn't want to be part of the greatest time of global revival? Or see Jesus' second coming at the sound of the angel's trumpet and be present in the triumphal procession as heaven comes to earth? Whether or not you would volunteer to be part of the end-time church, you might well be, simply because you would be alive on planet earth at that specific time to come.

Pause for Thought

- Do I ever think about being in the generation that sees the Lord return?

The Greatest Generation

American journalist Tom Brokaw has written a powerful book about the generation who fought in the Second World War. His inspiration came from making a documentary in 1984 celebrating the forty years since the 1944 Allied landings in Normandy. While walking along the French beaches and talking with veterans, Brokaw was moved to research and document the experiences of American men and women who exemplified the best of the virtues and sacrifices which were needed at that crucial time in history. This generation – who were born around 1920, came of age during the Great Depression of the 1930s, fought in the Second World War, and then came home to rebuild a postwar world and hand a legacy of freedom to the next generation – Brokaw calls the 'greatest generation':

> They faced great odds and a late start, but they did not protest. At a time in their lives when their days and nights should have been filled with innocent adventure, love, and the lessons of the workaday world, they were fighting, often hand to hand, in the most primitive conditions possible . . . they were in the air every day, in

skies filled with terror, and they went to sea on hostile waters far removed from the shores of their homeland . . . They were mature beyond their years, tempered by what they had been through, disciplined by their military training and sacrifices.[9]

In his book, Brokaw is keen to highlight that the heroic responses were a result of rising to the immense challenges. It was a collective test of character for that generation of American people and, of course, for the armed forces of all Allied countries. The greatness of that generation was discovered in the pressure of the days they had to navigate and the trials they faced and overcame.

I think that there is a parallel to be made here with the end-time generation of the church. They will be a unique generation, precisely because of the challenges they are called to face and the opportunities laid before them. A people who live to see the release of waves of revival and transformation on earth, to bring in a great harvest of faith through their bold and humble witness. A people who find the jewel of utter devotion to the Lord in the midst of deception, confusion and church division, and who have their characters tested in the greatest time of global turbulence, darkness and persecution ever known – that is the destiny of the last generation of the church. Not qualitatively different, but quantitatively heroic, rising up to shine in the midst of great glory and shaking. Perhaps they will be the 'greatest generation' of the church.

Pause for Thought

- How does thinking about the dynamics of the last generation encourage me to pray for the church around the world in the coming years?

Looking Ahead: Two Possible Timelines

How far off are we from this time of Tribulation and the biblical countdown to Christ's return? I think we could be very close. I think that the labour pains of the world are increasing. I think that the church is already starting to rise up into a fresh awareness of the glory of God. I think greater shaking is going to take us all by surprise. Yet of course, 'close' is a difficult word to understand in the economy of God. Many people felt that the return of the Jews to their promised land in 1948 would mark the return of the Lord within a generation. Well, more than seventy-five years have passed since that milestone. Also, many mission groups have set goals for the evangelization of the entire world, and those laudable aims have always had to be put back, as the task continues to be just out of our reach. And although the Doomsday Clock is periodically set nearer to the apocalyptic midnight of global destruction, threats could recede and more time be gained. Yet I still think we are soon to enter the end of the end times. I don't consider that we have another hundred years to run before Jesus comes back, let alone another thousand years. I hear some of my Christian friends speaking about reformation of the church and transformation of cities in terms of passing a legacy on to their grandchildren and beyond. I don't think we actually have that much time left. We, or our children, or certainly our grandchildren, could well be in the last unique generation alive on earth and ready to meet the Lord in his coming in glory. Let me sketch out a couple of possible scenarios.

Shorter term

The first scenario is one where the time is very short indeed. The economic and political effects of the recent pandemic and regional conflicts could very quickly destabilize our global society. Deep recessions, and social problems such as unemployment and people migration, could mark the end of our western consumer culture and lead to the breakdown of law and order. People could quickly start to adopt what is often called 'game B'-type alternative community living and economics, which then becomes a threat to existing governments. The current international alliances of G7 and G20 nations could crumble within a handful of years, and tensions would then grow with rogue nation terrorist threats and larger nations flexing their military muscle in land grabs. The lack of progress in combating climate change could bring an awareness that the planet is desperately unstable and spark widespread panic.

At the same time, the church could, within a decade, see revivals spread worldwide as they did during the global waves of Pentecostalism. The embracing of the glory of God in our midst would flood every church stream and be the main vibrant expression of Christianity. Persecution of bold preachers and witnesses to Holy Spirit power could arise. Great schisms could occur within denominations as people choose either to embrace easy nominalism or to stand strong in faith. The success of the gospel shared digitally and a new wave of missionaries could see the effective completion of the Great Commission. Remarkable touches of God in communities and spheres of city life could be the only bright hope in a quickly crumbling society. Everything could be in place across the nations for a galvanized last-ditch attempt at global order, and a fresh government might then emerge, superseding national powers, based on a unity of faiths and a fresh model of economic power.

This would be a pragmatic and benevolent cross-nation leadership given oversight of global issues. Yet, within the span of a governing term of office, one leader would surface, coasting on his astounding short-term success in dealing with societal issues, yet masking dictatorial aims. Everything would be in place for the Antichrist regime and Tribulation time. All of this could happen within fifteen or twenty years.

Longer term

The second possibility is a longer-term scenario. The times of shaking could come in waves over twenty or thirty years. The world would recover from each, with a short period of peace before the next one comes. The forms of shaking would be various. Solar flares could wipe out communication systems; extreme climate events such as floods, fires and drought could force millions to flee their communities. Outbreaks of war, even including a rogue nuclear strike, might create limited but dangerous local devastation. Economic inequality could continue to grow, and revolutions and regime changes might therefore be common in the coming generation. In the midst of shaking times, there could still be great technological, scientific and social advances to develop resilience to catastrophic threats.

The Christian church might go through a time of great turbulence, with some believers giving up on faith and others becoming more radical, and a thorough dismantling and reshaping of what church looks like. Institutional church organizations could totally break down and small, radical, networking communities of faith emerge as the dominant expression of Christianity. Compromise to social pressure might cause great numbers of Christians to walk away from their faith. Yet, as others choose an all-out Christianity, many could find themselves at the heart of wise breakthroughs to help communities and nations in need. There could be multigenerational, decentralized church movements, leading massive waves of church planting, helping in humanitarian crisis relief, and setting up transformational think-tanks; all this could be part of the growing influence of the Spirit-filled people of God. As the waves of shaking happen, so also various waves of revival and outpouring of the Spirit will increase, each one gathering in a harvest of people coming to faith. The waves will themselves further rock the church and cause splits; the rejection of the new moves of God will create a twin-branched church made up of more nominal groups and more renewal-based streams. Interfaith religious distrust will rise, yet every nation will be touched with the glory and power of God at work in homes and people groups. In contrast to expected international tensions, considerable work among governments could go into tackling global threats; if anything, international cooperation and resolve might increase, especially against rogue nations, radical terrorism and climate change.

After a generation of waves of both glory and shaking, and this cooperative climate, a gradual pressure would increasingly be exerted on people, over a couple of decades, to conform to the global government. The radical stance of the church would become a threat to social order, and Christians would find themselves at odds with a consensus of political, economic and religious systems. This global system of governance and trade would take a while to become fully established. Yet when it is clearly in place, with all nations signed up to a new world order, the stage will be set for the emergence of the Antichrist and the unleashing of the Tribulation time. This story could unfold over fifty or sixty years.

Two very different scenarios: one short term, one within a couple of generations. You could imagine other future pictures.

I am looking at the logic of what may need to change in the global context between this current time and the last few years of Tribulation. The church will need to be radically reshaped and be led by the Lord in a rising up in his glory and the Spirit's strength for a period of time before she is equipped to stand in the darkness of the Tribulation years. This period, either short or long, will be exhilarating and amazing, at the same time as troubling and perturbing. The church that responds well to Jesus will be riding twin crests; one will be the wave of revival, while the other will be the wave of persecution. God's people will be joyous in the river of the Spirit, living in the fullness of Jesus' calling on their lives, and walking in the clarity of gospel truth and life. At the same time, they will have to learn to endure the pressure of opposition, navigate the difficulty of global troubles, and live with uncertainty about what the cost of following Jesus will mean. This will be a necessary preparation for the end-time Tribulation that is coming on the earth. And even as the joy flowing from this great intimacy and divine love fills the church, the Lord will simultaneously bring a great focus and readiness to live wholly for him. God will put his people on a war footing, as the mobilization for mission, service and discipleship moves them into a new level of maturity. There will be a great contending for the gospel, a willingness to lay down their lives for the King, and a desire to bring every nation into its redemptive destiny in these closing years. What a high calling for the emerging church of the future!

Pause for Thought

- When I think about biblical end-time scenarios, how close or far off do I think they are from our world today?

4

Keeping Our Eyes on the Lord's Return

Expectancy about Christ's Return

So far, we have been considering God's end-time plans, and the church at the heart of his purposes – to prepare a radiant and resolute bride ready for his Son's return. The Bible indicates that in order for this to transpire, the church must walk through an intense time of experiencing the fire of Holy Spirit revival and the pressure of end-time trouble and persecution. This will happen in a way that mirrors the preparation of all people on earth for the age to come, in which everyone encounters both a measure of God's glory and the shaking of everything that can be shaken.

What will hold the church steady in the midst of this unprecedented time? It will be to keep our eyes and hope fixed on the Lord's imminent return in glory. Scripture shows that the Great Tribulation will culminate in cosmic disturbances, with the sun darkened and the moon turning to blood (Matt. 24:29). These will be the days when the church is looking with great anticipation for the sign of Jesus' return on the clouds. Yet it is not just the horrific closing days of Tribulation that bring the hope of the parousia. It is also the growing longing for Jesus to return for his bride that seems to mark the end-time church at the end of the book of Revelation, where John cries

Keeping Our Eyes on the Lord's Return 79

out: 'Amen. Come, Lord Jesus' (Rev. 22:20). At the end, we are waiting for the Lord in great anticipation.

I like airports. I love the buzz, the people milling around, these wonderful hubs of global transport. I particularly like the experience of waiting in the international arrivals hall. It is a place of pick-ups and reunions, friendly greetings and tearful hugs. It is therefore a great place for people-watching. Friends and loved ones are usually there, whatever the time of day, closely analysing the information screens and waiting to see who will come through the automatic doors. The flight may have arrived, but disembarkment and baggage collection may be taking a while. There is collective anticipation every time the doors open. Sure, there will be many business travellers in the mix, their greeter holding a card of recognition. Yet it is the families I enjoy watching – children fidgeting, adults checking watches, a nervous waiting; until the moment the loved one emerges, bags in hand, to be swept up quickly in multiple embraces, love and excited chatter. They have been greatly anticipated.

In a sober assessment of the worldwide church, more people may be wondering about the signs of the times than ever before, but, judging by our current behaviour, you would not conclude that the majority of Christians are excitedly expectant about Jesus' second coming. Even after a global pandemic, most leaders of church denominations and Christian events have wanted to focus simply on returning to normal, or to take an opportunity to think afresh about what church can be. That is not necessarily wrong in itself. In the return to normal, we are keen to learn more relevant ways of being church and more faithful ways of serving our world. In the desire to think afresh, we are trying to be faithful to our Christian mission. However, a realization that we are closer to the end of the end times has generally not yet gripped the body of Christ, nor has a great desire for Jesus' return yet overtaken us as his people. We are not exactly milling around in the arrivals hall of time, excitedly waiting for him to appear.

Throughout church history, people became more stirred in expectation of Jesus' return either during waves of revival or in great moments of transition. Moves of the Holy Spirit tended to spark new worship songs about the parousia; powerful outpourings often carried an electric eschatological atmosphere. Think of the early Pentecostals who, inspired by the baptism of the Spirit, were willing to sell everything they owned to become missionaries to the ends of the earth in the last gospel push before Jesus came back. Great moments of disjuncture, such as the turn of centuries, the collapse of civilizations, and great wars or plagues, have also concentrated attention on biblical prophecy and created a cry for Jesus to come quickly to his faithful people. So, if global revival and global shaking will mark the end times, this should jolt the worldwide church into much greater expectancy about the parousia.

The New Testament encourages such expectation, for the Christians at that time were living in days of eschatological fulfilment themselves. Jesus was an apocalyptic prophet. He clearly taught about his coming kingdom, breaking in now, and one day to fully be manifested. The tenor of his teaching was that the kingdom's arrival was imminent, and this has proved to be a source of embarrassment to some modern theologians, who have been caught on the fence of explaining that either Jesus was wrong or his teaching was misunderstood. Yet this sense of kingdom imminence caught on in the early church. The first disciples had their eyes fixed on the Lord's return. It fuelled their expectancy and their missionary purpose. Peter's second sermon called for a hope in God to send the Messiah, whom heaven had received 'until the time comes for God to restore everything' (Acts 3:21). Peter also called for faithfulness in trials that 'may result in praise, glory and honour when Jesus Christ is revealed' (1 Pet. 1:7). Paul encouraged his followers to see that their citizenship was in heaven and to 'eagerly await a Saviour from there, the Lord Jesus Christ' (Phil. 3:20). He believed that those in his generation 'who are still alive and are left will be caught up together . . . in the clouds to meet the Lord in the air' (1 Thess. 4:17). Jesus must have known that an uncertain period of waiting for his return would be a challenge to his followers, as he repeatedly called them to 'keep watch, because you do not know on what day your Lord will come' (Matt. 24:42).

The end times as the culmination of God's fidelity

I have already mentioned how eschatology is concerned with chronology (God's timing) and also with teleology (God's purposes). In addition, eschatology is concerned with fidelity, God's fulfilment of promise. The divine revelation in the Old Testament is so often linked to his promises – of a land, of descendants, of deliverance, of kingship, and of course, of a future Messiah. God is fidelious, always faithful. In the same way, eschatology is not just about prophetic events or a timeline, but also about our hope in God's faithfulness; he will fulfil all his promises to us. Paul says in 2 Corinthians 1:20: 'For no matter how many promises God has made, they are "Yes" in Christ.' God's promises to complete his redeeming work in your life (Phil. 1:6), to work all things for good for those who love him (Rom. 8:28), even to reconcile all things in heaven and earth through Christ's death on the cross (Col. 1:19) – all these promises are wrapped up in God's saving work through Jesus. There are clearly promises that God has made to his people in the Bible that await a future end and fulfilment.

By this logic, Jesus is eschatological not just in his message but also in his person. He always has been so. He came to proclaim and inaugurate a coming kingdom. The Messiah was the one to fulfil promise and hope. If that is true, then he was eschatological in his first coming, as well as in his second. The two are intrinsically linked. Just as God was faithful to his promise of sending his Son as the Saviour, so he will be faithful in sending him as the coming King. Christians must not let their hope in the future acts of God in Christ be eroded. Since the days of the early church, scoffers have often said: 'Where is this "coming" he promised?' (2 Pet. 3:4). Our Christian hope is founded not just on what God has done in Christ, but also on what he will fulfil and complete in Christ. As Paul puts it: 'we boast in the hope of the glory of God' (Rom. 5:2). Our Christian hope is linked to the coming of the kingdom of God. It is anchored in the faithfulness of God himself to his promises. So eschatology is about God's fidelity.

Theologically, therefore, the parousia is of vital significance to Christian belief. As theologian Larry Kreitzer explains:

> The Parousia is important in that it serves as an intersection of Christian understandings of christology, eschatology and soteriology: as the supreme moment of revelation of Jesus Christ as Lord for all the created order to see, as the culmination of God's eternal purposes as they are worked out in human affairs and as the time at which the world is judged and believers are granted resurrection existence and are ultimately united with their Lord.[1]

The Christian hope of the parousia becomes the pinnacle of faith in God as the great promise-keeper. He will not let us down.

Films often pick up on the great spiritual themes of promises kept. In the blockbuster movie *Avengers: Endgame*, the superheroes have forged an unbroken trust in standing together against evil forces. Yet the steady warrior Captain Rogers, also called Captain America, finds himself alone as the only hero left standing when the enemy Thanos destroys the protected Compound base. Facing imminent death from a hostile army, with little hope left, Captain Rogers then hears a crackled communication in his ear – and his fellow Avengers appear through different portals, alongside a collective of earth's armies, to rescue him and destroy the threatening evil. This is a favourite climax among fans of the Marvel adventures. The Avengers were faithful to their commitment to stand by their friend and to save their planet. In those movies, they always come through in the end!

Our fidelious God is the ultimate faithful promise-keeper. All that he has promised in Scripture he will fulfil. Our trust in his ability to save, deliver and bring his kingdom will be vindicated. The fidelity of God underpins the spiritual shift that will come as we walk more deeply into an end-times context for living. Christians who are caught up in waves of Holy Spirit awakening, and who are refined by persecution and turmoil, will find hope rising in them for the Lord to come to right all wrongs, save our planet from destruction, and become the rightful king of the earth. He will do it precisely because he promised to do so. The Spirit is the one who stirs the cries of '*Abba*, Father' and 'Jesus is Lord'. He also stirs the cry 'Come, Lord Jesus' in the global end-time church. We await the fulfilment of his promises to return and to usher in the age to come.

And so, back to the 'Come, Lord Jesus' prayer in Revelation 22. This prayer has become an unquenchable cry in the heart of the church by the end of the age. There is an internal stirring and reorientation of the heart of God's people in the closing chapter of history. As we worship him for his death and resurrection, so also we long for his appearing. The church will become radiant by finding fascination in the Lord who is her bridegroom. This is a trend that will increase exponentially the closer we get to his return. We will not just recite the creedal statement that 'he will come again in glory to judge the living and the dead'; we will long with intense desperation for this coming.

There is weight to all the events of the second coming as Scripture tells them; they are not fantasy stories. The second coming is not just a spiritual event, but an actual event. Jesus comes to be revealed, to save, to vindicate, to raise the dead, to be united with his church, to rule, to receive his inheritance, to judge, to usher in the age to come, and to prepare the earth for the new heaven and earth. He really is coming back. Our gospel message in the end times includes these future events. We proclaim the cross and the resurrection of Jesus, we proclaim him as the only hope for a world falling apart, and we proclaim the ever-nearer parousia and his coming kingdom rule on earth: 'There is a king coming!' We long to see him and we long for the great unveiling of the fullness of the kingdom of God. We affirm the cosmic triumph of God over every evil. And we invite people to share this faith in Christ as we call out 'Come, Lord, come!'

Pause for Thought

- Do I really believe that God will come through in the end and rescue our world from destruction?

Jesus Will Come to Receive the Rewards of His Suffering

We are called to always watch for Jesus to come. We speed his coming through every act of love and kingdom service. We share the gospel in the hope that, as the Great Commission is completed, it will pave the way for his return. We pray 'Your kingdom come' because we know that only God's decisive act through Jesus will one day fulfil all our hopes and dreams at his return.

I would like us to consider how our vision of Jesus the coming king will inspire the worship and witness of the radical church in these last days. We say in our Christian songs that Jesus is worthy of our praise. In what way do we mean that? Well, that phrase comes from Revelation chapter 5, when the end-time drama in heaven reaches a tipping point. Jesus, standing in the centre of the heavenly throne-room with the Father, takes a scroll from God's hand and initiates heaven's countdown to the end of the age and his return. As he does so, those surrounding the throne of God fall down in worship and prayer and say:

> You are worthy to take the scroll
>   and to open its seals,
> because you were slain,
>   and with your blood you purchased for God
>   persons from every tribe and language and people and nation.
>
> *Rev. 5:9*

The angels then cry out:

> Worthy is the Lamb, who was slain,
>   to receive power and wealth and wisdom and strength
>   and honour and glory and praise!
>
> *Rev. 5:12*

Jesus' worthiness comes from his sacrifice on the cross as the unique Lamb of God, and therefore from his right to rule and reign and bring his kingdom to earth. The songs of heaven in this moment focus on God's saving actions through Christ in rescuing a people from sin and darkness into the kingdom of light and a righteous standing before him. This unveiling of the worthiness of Jesus to receive all praise and honour is so awesome and humbling that it touches our hearts every time we glimpse him in our Christian walk, every time we come to him in worship. Heaven thunders 'Worthy is the Lamb', and the same strains reverberate from God's people on earth in our praise that echoes around the world.

We are the redeemed; we are the ransomed ones. We would have no hope without Jesus, but because of him we have a glorious hope and an eternal destiny.

And then what happens in the narrative? In a moment of great drama, because of his worthiness as the rightful king of the earth, Jesus takes the scroll of unfolding history from the hand of the Father on the throne and initiates the end-time countdown. That connection between the 'worthy' chorus of heaven and the following Revelation events and countdown to his return is the key to understanding our worship and witness as the church in the last days. Jesus is the only one who can sort out the global chaos and tide of evil and suffering. He is the rightful king of the earth, precisely because he died and rose to redeem the world. No one else could do that, and no one else is worthy of our love and ultimate allegiance.

The fruit of his suffering

Living to honour the worthiness of the Lamb will be a key end-time motivation in our life and mission. The church will become more Christocentric in her identity and urgent sharing of the gospel, because we are preparing the way for Christ to return and receive his kingdom in fullness. There is an anecdotal story of the first Moravian missionaries, David Nitschmann and Johann Dober, who went as European evangelists to the West Indies in 1732. Inspired by the furnace of prayer and revival they had been a part of in Herrnhut, Germany, they prepared to leave family and friends behind to witness to the African slaves in the Caribbean. At the port of Copenhagen, these young men turned to say goodbye to their loved ones, raised their hands and shouted: 'May the Lamb receive the rewards of his suffering!' That phrase became a rallying cry for sacrificial Moravian mission around the world, and it stirs our hearts as we read it.

What did those two missionaries mean – the rewards of his suffering? In the passage about the Suffering Servant in Isaiah 53, the Amplified Version says: 'He shall see [the fruit] of the travail of His soul and be satisfied' (v. 11 AMPC). We know that Jesus didn't suffer needlessly on the cross. The paradox of the Christian gospel is that, in the insignificance of an unknown Jewish travelling rabbi being executed in an ancient Roman province, we believe the most significant event in human history transpired. History turned on that moment; salvation for the human race was won in that moment. And, as Isaiah says, after he has suffered he will see the fruit, or rewards, of his suffering.

Jesus is returning to earth one day to rule and reign; he is also coming to receive the rewards of his suffering. What are the rewards of Jesus' suffering? They encompass various things in Scripture.

One reward is a spiritual harvest for the Father. Jesus redeemed a portion of humanity for the Father, as described in Revelation 5:9. At the Lord's return, the saints on earth will be joined to the saints in heaven. Jesus will present to his Father a vast remnant of people from every tribe, language, and age of history. He will say in effect, 'This is the harvest we have laboured for; these are the people I have redeemed for you, *Abba*; this is the fruit of your salvation plans since the beginning of time.'

A second reward is a kingdom inheritance on earth. The ends of the earth will one day be Jesus' inheritance. Psalm 2 speaks of Jesus' glorified position at God's right hand and depicts the Father inviting him to bring his kingdom rule across the globe:

> Ask me,
>   and I will make the nations your inheritance,
>   the ends of the earth your possession.
>
> *Ps. 2:8*

Jesus' reward from the Father will be the kingly rule he brings to the nations of the world as he returns in glory and brings his perfect kingdom of truth and justice to all people in the Millennium.

A third aspect of Jesus' reward is a people who are set apart for him. Psalm 110, another prophetic messianic psalm, foretells how the church will be ready to partner with him in end-time ministry as his return draws near:

> Your troops will be willing
>   on your day of battle.
> Arrayed in holy splendour,
>   your young men will come to you
>   like dew from the morning's womb.
>
> *Ps. 110:3*

This powerful poetic passage speaks of the devotion, readiness and sacrificial service offered by the saints on earth in the coming last days – a willing, anointed, shining army of the Lord, marching with him as his dedicated followers. There is a devoted army of Christ-lovers and gospel witnesses arising even as you read this.

A fourth way we can see Jesus receiving the rewards of his suffering is in the unique place of honour he has in heaven forever. As the early Christian hymn in Philippians 2 shows, because of his deep humility and sacrifice, Jesus now receives a name and regal position higher than anyone, other than the Father:

> Therefore God exalted him to the highest place
>   and gave him the name that is above every name,
> that at the name of Jesus every knee should bow,
>   in heaven and on earth and under the earth,
> and every tongue acknowledge that Jesus Christ is Lord,
>   to the glory of God the Father.
>
> *Phil. 2:9–11*

The Father is determined that his Son will receive all due honour, praise and worship for his saving, redeeming work on the cross. Angels and archangels worshipped him at his glorious ascension to the Father's side. At Jesus' second coming, all human beings on earth will see him, and bow their knee, in either great love or great dread. As Revelation 1:7 says, 'Look, he is coming with the clouds', and 'every eye will see him, even those who pierced him'; and all the peoples of the earth 'will mourn because of him'. This will be the public moment when Jesus is fully vindicated for his saving work and revealed in his true glory. Redeemed saints, joyful angels in heaven and everything in creation will all alike hold Jesus in high honour throughout eternity. Jesus will be pre-eminent as the Lamb who is worthy to receive all power, wealth, wisdom and strength and honour and glory and praise . . . forever!

Pause for Thought

- Do I ever think about Jesus receiving the rewards of his suffering?
- How does this add to my understanding of Jesus?

Our love for Christ as the motivation for mission

If Jesus is worthy to receive these rewards – a spiritual harvest to present to his Father, a kingdom inheritance on earth, a people set apart for him, a unique place of honour in the cosmos – worthy because of his sacrifice and worthy because of his risen glory, then this surely becomes a prime motivation for the life of the bridal church in the last days. We don't just work for him as our Lord and Master; we love him as our beautiful bridegroom King. His longing to receive the rewards of his suffering becomes our longing. The church in the end times therefore becomes a co-labourer with Jesus. We become determined that our love and witness will contribute to Jesus' rewards. This is what motivated those two young Moravian missionaries as they set sail for the mission field.

The end-time church will be a church that co-labours with Jesus out of love and devotion. We can't do what he did in winning salvation for humankind. Rather, our co-labouring is like that of Paul in his apostolic ministry, which he describes in Colossians chapter 1. In his suffering for the kingdom, his unashamed spreading of the gospel among the Gentiles, and his discipling of others to bring them to a maturity of faith and love, he laboured strenuously with all the energy of Jesus in him (Col. 1:24–29). Paul becomes even more explicit to the church in Corinth when he writes: 'I am jealous for you with a godly jealousy. I promised you to one husband, to Christ, so that I might present you as a pure virgin to him' (2 Cor. 11:2).

I believe that the transformed church in the end times will be a church madly in love with Jesus because of his utter worthiness, and eager to do whatever will contribute to him receiving his rewards. Our love will motivate us in finishing the Great Commission, carrying the gospel in every way and to every place and whatever the cost, so that the full harvest can be reaped for him to present to his Father on that day. Our love will motivate our serving, working and blessing, as we endeavour to extend signs of his kingdom into every community and every sphere of life, even in the midst of darkness, anticipating his inheritance of the nations of the world when he returns.

Our love will motivate our living and discipleship as we call the church into maturity and holy set-apartness for Jesus, to be his willing troops on his end-time day of battle. Our love will motivate us to place praise and worship at the centre of our personal and corporate lives. There will be unfettered, uninhibited and extravagant worship in which more and more people on the earth see the magnificent worthiness of Jesus Christ and swell the earthly praise, ready to welcome his triumphal coming in glory. A people in love with their Saviour – that is our greatest motivation for mission.

He Will Come Again in Glory: The Second Coming

The hope of Jesus' return is fundamental to our faith and inscribed in our creeds. As the Nicene Creed declares: 'he will come again in glory to judge the living and dead, and his kingdom will have no end'. How tragic, then, that such a hope divides many believers in doctrine. When will Christ come again? As I have mentioned, Scripture points to Jesus returning at the darkest time in history – a time when the Antichrist is ruling, armies surround Jerusalem, the tragic consequences of sin are at their height, and Christians and Jews are being harshly persecuted, with many falling away from faith. And yet, paradoxically, it will also be a time when the church will be at her strongest – finishing the mission task, standing in the light of God's glory, and ministering in the overflow of the global outpourings of the Spirit.

Sadly, this central tenet of our faith, the parousia, has more recently become a divisive issue in some circles. Christian dispensationalism, which asserts that God works in various dispensations of salvation plans throughout history, has skewed the thinking of many evangelicals in their reading of Scripture. They have been taught to look for a secret rapture of the church before the Tribulation, and then a revival of Messianic Jewish faith to lead the kingdom witness before Jesus' triumphal return on the clouds. The main reasons to reject this teaching are, first, that one has to be taught a dispensational doctrine in order to see scriptures in that light. The main and plain reading of verses pertaining to the parousia shows that they speak of one return, public and visible, at the end of the last-days drama, not before. Second, this doctrine is based on a belief that God would not want the righteous to suffer in the Tribulation along with the rest of humanity. It ignores the reality that, in much of church history, God's people have been a suffering, persevering remnant; Jesus' call is to overcome, not to avoid, the distress of the earth.

Keeping Our Eyes on the Lord's Return

Once we have that clear in our minds, the hope of Jesus' glorious return is the bright light of our faith and the fulfilment of our longing. What will that moment be like? As preacher J.C. Ryle wrote:

> The second coming of Christ shall be utterly unlike the first. He came the first time in weakness, a tender infant, born of a poor woman in the manger at Bethlehem, unnoticed, unhonored, and scarcely known. He shall come the second time in royal dignity, with the armies of heaven around Him, to be known, recognized, and feared by all the tribes of the earth. He came the first time to suffer – to bear our sins – to be reckoned a curse – to be despised, rejected, unjustly condemned, and slain. He shall come the second time to reign – to put down every enemy beneath His feet – to take the kingdoms of this world for His inheritance – to rule them with righteousness – to judge all men, and to live for evermore.[2]

There is no doubt in Scripture that the return of Christ to earth will be public, dramatic and victorious. The sequence of events is described by various writers. He will come on the clouds of heaven (Matt. 24:30) to destroy the Antichrist regime by the breath of his mouth (2 Thess. 2:8). Angels will gather his faithful followers to join him in a triumphal procession (1 Thess. 4:17), alongside resurrected saints. He will come with the armies of heaven, marching across the Middle East (Isa. 63:1) towards Jerusalem, to rescue the Jews (Zech. 14:1–3) in the battle of Armageddon (Rev. 16:14–16). He will defeat the Antichrist forces (Rev. 19:19–21) and be welcomed by the Jewish people as their Messiah (Luke 13:35). Jesus will be recognized as true king and rightful ruler of the world (Zech.14:9), and all will submit in love or fear to his greatness (Phil. 2:10).

The waiting of the worshipping and witnessing church will be greatly expectant in the weeks and months before Jesus' return. As the biblical signs of prophecy are fulfilled before our eyes, through the global experience of Tribulation and the turmoil of shaking on multiple levels across the world, the faith and conviction of the church will burn more brightly. God's people will know that their redemption is drawing near. The devil's schemes will be laid bare, and the earth's inhabitants will have chosen their allegiances, either running to God in desperation, or cementing their hope in the Antichrist and the global ruling system. It is hard to adequately describe the dramatic context of that day, as even heavenly bodies are shaken, and tragic loss of life occurs through the oppression of the Antichrist and in the judgments of Revelation. Yet God's glory will rest on this witnessing martyr church, even in the great distress of those days. Faith in Christ as the only hope will still impact communities and even nations. It is in this turbulent process of events that the bride will have made herself fully ready for the Lord's return.

Pause for Thought

- What do I think Jesus' second coming will be like as a worldwide public phenomenon?

Preparing to Reign with Jesus: A Look at the Millennial Reign of Christ

We cannot finish this chapter without asking: what we are expecting as Jesus returns? This is a radical question and one that not many Christians give thought to. We have bought into an assumed theology in which Jesus comes to take us away to an ethereal heaven and we leave the ruined earth behind. Thinking like this unfortunately only adds to the escapist attitude in which our world is doomed and saving people from hell is the only worthwhile vocation. It also reinforces old dualistic mindsets in which physical matter is bad and spiritual reality is the only noble focus. Yet what if God does not want to annihilate his precious earth but to renew it perfectly? What if God's desire, revealed in Scripture, is instead to 'bring unity to all things in heaven and on earth under Christ' (Eph. 1:10)? What if the Lord's desire is to give his people a wonderful inheritance on earth at the 'renewal of all things' (Matt. 19:28–29)? This is the topic of the millennial rule of Christ.

Millennialism has been a hot potato of a topic throughout church history. Early church millennial expectation was strong, and Justin Martyr, a Church Father writing in the second century, is illustrative of the views of his time: 'I and others, who are right-minded Christians on all points, are assured that there will be a resurrection of the dead, and a thousand years in Jerusalem, which will then be built, adorned, and enlarged, as the prophets Ezekiel and Isaiah and others declare.'[3]

Hopes in a literal Millennium have varied since that time. Views have differed wildly, including:

- a militant millennialism, with people trying to force the coming of a Christian golden age;
- a postmillennial optimism about the Christianizing of culture;
- an amillennial status quo, which conceives the victorious reign of Christ as happening through history;
- a resurgence of literal premillennialism, based on prophetic scriptures, which advocates waiting for the return of the Lord, who then ushers in a golden age.[4]

I would argue for a re-engagement with the hopes for a literal millennial reign of Christ. The language of the prophetic and apocalyptic scriptures is shadowy and tentative about a millennial reign, but the doctrine is clearly there, distinct from a new heaven and earth that is still to be revealed. The description in Revelation 20 of Jesus ruling and reigning on earth for a thousand years cannot be unpicked from the narratives of the parousia beforehand and the great judgment afterwards without doing a disservice to the writer's intent and the integrity of the whole prophetic book. A combination of scriptures paints the following possible scenario.

There will be a literal or symbolic period of a thousand years in which saints rule with Jesus on the earth (Rev. 20:4). This will be a righteous reign from the 'mountain of the LORD' which draws all people on earth to walk in God's ways and be discipled in a kingdom culture (Isa. 2:2–5). There will be a great renewal project going on in the Millennium as the fury of war is stilled, nations learn to live in harmony, and communities find peace (Mic. 4:3–4). In this context, there will be a subduing of all evil powers as Jesus puts all enemies under his feet (1 Cor. 15:25). The Millennium will be an idyllic era of wholeness and fruitfulness across the whole of creation as the earth is filled with the knowledge of the Lord as waters cover the sea (Isa. 11:6–9). There will be global processions of worship to Jerusalem (Zech. 14:16). In some way, the heavenly and earthly realms can be seen as intermingling during the Millennium, but they are not yet fully joined until the final day of judgment (Rev. 20:11–15) and the revealing of the new heaven and earth (Rev. 21:1–4). The new Jerusalem is being prepared by the Father, even as the Son is preparing to present the earth back to the Father. The vision of the new Jerusalem is one that is coming down out of heaven, maybe hovering over the earth, during the millennial rule. Jesus' throne is in both the temple in Jerusalem and in the new Jerusalem; his is a cosmic governmental rule (Isa. 66:1). There is an intermingling of heavenly and earthly realms, every place filled with God's glorious presence (Isa. 11:9); maybe even a glory corridor will join these realms, a heavenly canopy extending from the new Jerusalem to the literal Jerusalem (Isa. 4:5), awaiting full perfection in the Father's timing.

The scope of this book does not allow me to move through into discussion of the great day of judgment and the new heaven and earth, although they are the most weighty and ultimate realities. However, the theme of millennialism is an important hinge between the present age and the age to come, and since it has implications for living our lives now, it is worth consideration here.

The relevance of millennialism today

Why is it important theologically to consider an eschatological Millennium? Principally, it is about the element of transition – transition between this current age and the age to come. Transitions usually take a while. Think about the idyllic long summers you experienced after stressful school exams and before work or college started. Consider the period of a couple's engagement as they plan a wedding and look for a home. Or what about the couple expecting a child? They have a whole nine months of change and anticipation as they prepare for life to never be the same again! Transition time is not wasted time but purposeful and celebrated – a 'stage-on-the-way' time.

Renowned theologian Jürgen Moltmann highlights two essential areas of transition between this age and the age to come.

One is the messianic kingdom, which will be a kingdom of Jews and Christians living under the theocracy of Jesus in this world together. The Millennium here will be a realization of the 'one new humanity' of Ephesians 2:15, redeemed by Jesus' death and living in his resurrection life. As Moltmann states: 'Israel's resurrection and redemption belong to the great process of giving life to this mortal world, and the new creation of all things, a process which has begun with Christ's resurrection from the dead.'[5] Such a sign of reconciled humanity would allow the realizing of all prophetic hopes from Scripture, both Old and New Testament.

The second area of transition concerns that of time itself. Rather than viewing the parousia as bringing a total disruption of human history that gives way to the eternal new heaven and earth, Moltmann envisages from Scripture a time when we experience the necessary enjoyment of the fullness of the kingdom. The ages-long kingdom struggle for justice, salvation and peace is rightly fulfilled in the millennial span of the kingdom victory of Christ on earth. Again he suggests that 'the Millennarian expectation mediates between world history here, and the end of the world and the new world there. It makes the end as transition imaginable.'[6] Jesus' rule on earth would bring an important epoch of renewal for the world and a filling of the earth with the glory of God.

From what I have said above, we can reflect on these beautiful biblical hopes. God in his wisdom is true to his promises to people of both the old and the new covenant; he will bring the foretaste of unity of everything in heaven and earth through Gentiles and Jews fellowshipping as the full expression of the bride. Moreover, after the darkness of the Tribulation, when evil nearly triumphs, there is the enjoyment of the blessed reign of Christ. The saints in Revelation 20 are privileged to reign with Christ for a thousand years. While the fullness of the new heaven and earth is being prepared to be revealed by the Father, there is the full flourishing of God's kingdom on earth, so that heaven's reality is reflected here without the marring of sin or the darkness of evil. The day of final judgment is still coming for all who have lived on earth, as is the ultimate dwelling of God with creation, yet the full flowering of life in the kingdom of God is allowed expression in this millennial rule.

Perhaps, to use another analogy, the millennial rule of Christ will be rather like taming a wilderness. You may have watched those popular 'garden makeover' TV programmes where the designers take on a tired patch of fenced garden – overgrown, having seen better days – and undertake a great renewal project. Not everything is junked or uprooted, but rather the old and the new are melded together; in this way, great order and beauty are instilled into a plot of land, turning it into a little Eden. Jesus will undertake the greatest renewal project, bringing kingdom order into a broken world and releasing the potential of all life on earth, restoring and enhancing its original purpose and beauty. Only under Jesus' kingship can we see human society and the creative order flourishing under the wisdom of heavenly oversight, anticipating the day when the Father makes all things new.

Too often, we have set our sights too short in our end-time thinking. We have muddied the waters with pre- or mid-Tribulation secret raptures. We have spiritualized the parousia, turning it into a message of going to heaven to be married to Jesus. We have also been over-optimistic about our ability to bring the kingdom by our own efforts. The second coming has ceased to be an earthly hope of any true weight.

The biblical understanding of the fullness of the kingdom of God's rule is very much earthly. We receive a resurrection body as Jesus did. We are fully rescued, fully vindicated, fully restored after the ravages of sin and the horrors of the Tribulation. What could be better than attending the wedding feast of the Lamb described in Revelation 19:7 and Matthew 8:11? Being chosen to participate in the actual renewal of planet earth, and the filling of the earth with God's glory under Jesus' gracious rule – that would be even better. In the Millennium we don't just sit on clouds but live as priests and kings – ministering to the Lord in glorious worship, helping to rebuild communities, turning swords into ploughshares, and teaching the nations the ways of the Lord.

I want to challenge you to revisit familiar scriptures and consider the wonderful vocation in the age to come: we don't go to heaven to be married to Jesus, but stay on the earth to reign with him. That is the fulfilment of earthly hope – Gentile and Jewish Christian believers together as one new humanity, with the full representation of the body of Christ from every tribe and language, walking and serving by Jesus' side, in glorified bodies, assisted by angels. We will have stood before the judgment seat of Christ to receive our rewards (2 Cor. 5:10). Our citizenship will be in both the heavenly Jerusalem and the earthly one. With glorified bodies we will walk in a glorious realm of kingdom life, one that is earthed in a world that Jesus is filling with kingdom glory.

An earthly millennial hope is a powerful motivation for Christian living; it means that our signposts to the kingdom are not in vain, nor our attempts at personal and community transformation. Remember that all our work here is contributing to bringing the Lamb the rewards of his suffering, and fitting us for our destiny in the age to come.

Pause for Thought

- How does thinking about a millennial reign of Christ on earth deepen or challenge my faith?

Summary

We need to take the second coming of Jesus as serious biblical truth and pregnant hope. What motivated the early Christians in their mission needs to similarly motivate us as well. The church must grapple with biblical prophecies that anticipate the best and worst of times in the last days, and that don't duck out of the need for hard discipleship in the Tribulation, hoping for rescue from the coming days. Greater understanding of what Jesus' coming means and brings will help the church embrace the hope of the parousia.

Because popular end-time teaching often concentrates on the biblical prophecies about the Tribulation, a secret pre-Tribulation rapture, and the destruction of planet earth, evangelical eschatology has often been quite truncated and myopic. If we widen out our thinking to include Jesus' great appearing to save the world, redeem his people, and return as rightful king to reign, we start to become more earthly-minded – to be of more heavenly use. Our end-time thinking becomes much broader when we consider the fidelity of God, how he is the fulfiller of promise and hope, and how his second coming concludes his first coming. Jesus is the one who fascinates us, the mighty Son of God who inaugurated a new age in his incarnation, and who ushers in its fullness as he returns on the clouds in great glory to rule and reign with us. He is worthy of our praise and of our sacrificial living, and he is our glorious bridegroom and prize as the end-time body of Christ.

In Part Two of the book we will examine more closely this biblical picture of the emerging bride of Christ. In the end times, the church will be a bride both radiant and resolute. The transforming difference will be that a fresh revelation of the beauty of the Lord Jesus, and a fresh realization of our identity and destiny as his beloved people, will overwhelm the church. It is to this subject that we now turn.

Part Two

The Bride Has Made Herself Ready

*Being deeply loved by someone gives you strength,
while loving someone deeply gives you courage.*
Lao Tzu

5

A Fresh Look at the Church

Introduction: Reading Scripture in an End-Time Bridal Framework

In Part One of the book, we looked at an end-time context for living out the Christian faith – a context of glory and shaking, of a church moving in revival and refined by global troubles, waking up to an end-time awareness and anticipating Jesus' imminent return. In this second part, I want to lay out a general biblical framework for understanding the church as a bride. I will then focus particularly on two biblical books, the Song of Songs and the book of Revelation, to develop our thinking about the church being radiant and resolute as she prepares for Jesus' return. This reading of Scripture in an end-time bridal framework may help us gain new insights into how God will prepare his people in the last days. The journey of love in the Song of Songs is very relevant for Christians awaiting their bridegroom. The cosmic battle in the book of Revelation creates a ripe context for followers of Jesus to wise up to the darkening days in the future and grow strong and uncompromising in their faith. Moreover, a closer look at the book of Acts reveals a dynamic link between the early church and the end-time church that will then launch us into a consideration of the marks of the emerging church in the end times in Part Three of the book.

I find it fascinating when I approach Scripture in an end-time bridal framework. Who are these people whom God has redeemed – this peculiar, beautiful, compromised, set-apart, divided mix of people called 'the church', spanning two millennia? There is nothing special about them in one sense, and yet they are everything special in God's eyes. They are a people called into relationship with the Lord who redeems them. And what kind of relationship might that be? We are identified as children of God and as the bride of Christ. 'Children of God' denotes our spiritual identity in God's sight right now. The 'bride of Christ' brings into focus a special relationship between the redeemed and their Saviour, an intimate marriage relationship which will be revealed fully in the future. This is incredibly important for our understanding of the church, as we shall see in due course.

Images of the church

You are never on your own as a Christian. The moment you put your trust in Christ you joined a global community of believers, spanning the whole of history, and those believers on earth are mystically connected to the believers in heaven. Although sometimes your walk with the Lord may seem lonely, the very nature of church is togetherness, both with the Lord and with other Christians. Regardless of how big or small, trendy or boring, satisfying or dry your local congregational sense of belonging is, know that you are walking a walk of faith joined to billions of other believers. There are moments when we realize this and it transforms our view of church. Even persecuted followers of Christ, isolated and locked up in hostile nations for their faith, have testified to the sense of love and prayer from the worldwide church upholding them. This, alongside the nearness of the presence of the Lord, has sustained them in difficult times. Yes, people have been bruised and mistreated by Christians and churches, but that is an aberration; the flawed yet beautiful worldwide community of believers is still the most amazing context for living out our faith side by side.

As a child I had the privilege of experiencing what it was like to belong to church in a number of expressions. Growing up in a Christian home with both parents active in their faith, I was exposed to some different and rich experiences. The formality of a large town-centre Protestant church with box pews, choir and a high pulpit, and families in faithful worship together. Rustic village chapels, with oil-stove heating, a harmonium for accompanying hymns, and friendly old saints enjoying our presence as my lay-preacher father led services. Charismatic fellowship meetings in our lounge at home, where we were allowed to mingle for a while with adults living the fresh joy of the Spirit-filled life, before being shooed off to bed. Fervent prayer meetings ahead of a town-wide evangelistic mission, where I was a fascinated observer of the faithful crying out for the salvation of those who didn't know the Lord. A mercy mission of a small group of Christians from our town travelling across Europe to a hill town in Italy in the aftermath of an earthquake, towing caravans as a gift; the excitement of a journey of faith and trust in the Lord with strangers who quickly became like family. Being part of the people of God was always an important aspect of my early years of faith, and it prepared me for the greater richness of the church I have discovered in its flaws and beauty in the years since.

How does one describe the church? Well, the New Testament uses several important metaphors for the church. They help to describe facets of who we are as the people of God. Some of the many descriptive images in Scripture are: a field, a flock, a vine, a pilgrim people, a lampstand, the seed of the kingdom, kings and priests, a sign of the reign of God. These are all helpful, but the most important images are of the church as the following: God's building, God's family, Christ's body, God's army and Christ's bride.

Some of these are more static images, namely the ones that speak of us as God's building. We are described as God's house. A building has a foundation (Jesus), and it has a structure (leaders and systems): 'But Christ is faithful as the Son over God's house. And we are his house, if indeed we hold firmly to our confidence and the hope in which we glory' (Heb. 3:6). We are also encouraged to see ourselves as the Lord's temple. Not a magnificent building like the Old Testament temples, but a new living temple, where we are living stones with a priestly function, in which the Holy Spirit dwells in our midst, building a household of faith with special privilege: 'you also, like living stones, are being built into a spiritual house to be a holy priesthood, offering spiritual sacrifices acceptable to God through Jesus Christ' (1 Pet. 2:5).

Other metaphors are more dynamic. The most familiar are those about being a family and a body. Jesus encouraged his disciples to see God as their heavenly Father, and, as the church was established, the image of the family of God became important. Where there once was alienation, there is now a living relationship between God our Father and his children, and between ourselves as brothers and sisters. We love and care for each other, sharing the joys and sorrows of life as the Spirit creates community: 'Therefore, as we have opportunity, let us do good to all people, especially to those who belong to the family of believers' (Gal. 6:10).

A Fresh Look at the Church

The church as the body of Christ is also a powerful image, as it shows a living connectedness between Jesus our head and all of us as part of his body on earth. We have different functions and gifts, but a deep sense of belonging and spiritual purpose: 'we will grow to become in every respect the mature body of him who is the head, that is, Christ. From him the whole body, joined and held together by every supporting ligament, grows and builds itself up in love, as each part does its work' (Eph. 4:15–16).

Perhaps the most active metaphor of all is that of the church as the army of God. The idea of a gospel of peace does not sit easily with a military metaphor such as this, until we realize the extent to which Jesus expected us to live in conflict and tension because of our following after him. He warned that he did not come to bring peace but a sword (Matt. 10:34). The church is called to be on the offensive against the 'gates of hell' (Matt. 16:18 ESV). We fight the good fight of faith (1 Tim. 6:12); we pull down strongholds in the cause of gospel truth (2 Cor. 10:4). Corporately, we are a battalion of soldiers fighting alongside one another against the powers of darkness. As Paul tells us: 'Put on the full armour of God, so that you can take your stand against the devil's schemes. For our struggle is not against flesh and blood, but against the rulers, against the authorities, against the powers of this dark world and against the spiritual forces of evil in the heavenly realms' (Eph. 6:11–12).

The Church as Bride

The above metaphors are rich in symbolism and truth; they each have a facet describing some reality of our identity together as the people of God. Yet I want to focus in this chapter on one specific image: the church as the bride of Christ. This picture is of great importance as we think about the end times. Whereas the other images consider the present reality of our spiritual structure, our family relationships, our purposeful interconnectedness, or our strategic battle, the metaphor of the bride of Christ is both present *and* future-oriented. The bride is what we are in God's eyes now, yet also what we are becoming and how we will one day be revealed. It is a metaphor about love and about union.

I have conducted a number of weddings over the years in my role as a church minister. They are always wonderful occasions, times of celebration and joy, a culmination of hopes and love. Yet, in the midst of all the flurry of wedding cars and dresses, photographs and confetti, there is a holy moment in the middle of the church ceremony. It is the 'two into one' moment that always seems so profound. Everything seems to slow down for this moment of great solemnity. After the promises and vows, after the exchanging of rings, I find it moving to make the public declaration that these two individuals are now husband and wife. Although nothing has outwardly altered in the couple's love and commitment, everything has changed; what was two has now become one – a marriage.

The church will one day become fully the bride of Christ, a moment of marriage and union. When will this great reality be revealed before heaven and earth? It will happen when Jesus returns in glory! So it would make sense to understand more of what this powerful metaphor shows us about the church's identity.

Throughout church history, the church as the bride of Christ has not really been a central part of our ecclesial understanding. Early church theologians such as Tertullian and Irenaeus recognized the importance of this metaphor as it spoke into their context about the purity of the church and its eschatological

A Fresh Look at the Church

reality. Even the Reformers such as Luther realized that the church was simultaneously a blemished harlot and a spotless bride. Calvin described both a visible church to be led and discipled, and an invisible church of the elect as God sees it. Yet it was often the Christian mystics, such as Catherine of Siena and Teresa of Avila, or contemplatives like Bernard of Clairvaux, who developed a fuller bridal theology; they eschewed New Testament references to the church as bride and focused on the Song of Songs to reveal a mystical union between us as individual believers and Christ. Catherine recounted a vision in which Jesus appeared to her and declared his desire to make her his mystical bride, a marriage which included a wedding ring made of his own flesh. Teresa followed an intense spiritual path over many years, fixed on responding to a suffering saviour; eventually she experienced a 'transfixion', in which a cherub pierced her heart with an arrow, resulting in a burning desire for marriage with God. Bernard reflected on the Song of Songs as an expression of the contemplative soul who finds spiritual union with Christ through a prayerful ecstasy. Gregory the Great also focused on this image, in his commentary on the Song of Songs, but with more emphasis on the bride as teacher about the soul's union with Christ – again an individual journey, not a corporate one for the church.

The most obvious thread in our ecclesial self-understanding that connects to Jesus as our bridegroom is found in the celebration of communion, Eucharist or the Lord's Supper. Every Christian tradition would recognize that sharing in the bread and wine as an earthly community is a foretaste of the heavenly banquet. As the apostle Paul told his churches: 'For whenever you eat this bread and drink this cup, you proclaim the Lord's death until he comes' (1 Cor. 11:26). Through the long history of the church this thread of communion ties us into an anticipation of the eschaton, the age to come. It has backward significance, drawing us into the mystery of what Jesus did in his death, resurrection and giving of the Spirit, and forward significance as we anticipate the day when we will share in the feast of the kingdom as Jesus ushers in the fullness of the reign of God. The heavenly communion with the Lord, our reuniting with him, our joyous celebrating with him, our face-to-face intimacy with him, will occur as he returns in glory as our bridegroom King.

Brad Harper and Paul Metzger, in a book called *Exploring Ecclesiology: An Evangelical and Ecumenical Introduction*, attempt to create a theology of the church which counteracts the individualism at the heart of many evangelical churches – the fact that so many Christians are 'into' Jesus but not 'into' church. Drawing on the feminine images of church as mother and as bride (one spatio-temporal and one eschatological), they try to draw on the best of all church traditions to create a mosaic metaphor of the church as unity in diversity. Their reasoning is that they see an ecumenical reality where the various parts of the global historic body of Christ are in the process of becoming something remarkable together:

> The church – not this or that uniform movement or niche faction – is one body with many parts, created by the one God and Father for his Son as his bride, the only Lord, who gives his life for her redemption, a body gifted in a diversity of ways by the one Spirit who calls the church to unity (not uniformity), both to embody and to proclaim the one gospel of God's salvation. The mosaic will be complete on that day where the entire church sits down together at the marriage supper of the Lamb.[1]

It is this remarkable sense of 'becoming' which lies at the heart of the biblical images of God's people as bride, and which demands our understanding.

Pause for Thought

- Which images of the church have I been most drawn to in the past?
- How does the image of the church as the bride of Christ enhance my view of the church?

The Bridal Image in Old and New Testaments

I would like now to explore this bridal paradigm in Scripture. Although not traditionally a major part of our ecclesiology, many believe it is an important scriptural truth that God is highlighting to us as his people. The bridal metaphor tells us how Jesus sees us; it is an image of partnership, passion and intimacy. It speaks deeply of relationship and spiritual union, and brings fresh revelation about our collective identity in the last days.

In the Old Testament, the prophets reflected on how God saw his covenant with his people, namely like a marriage contract. Israel was married to God but was typified by the prophets as an unfaithful wife. The waywardness of Israel was likened to an adulterous wife. With the coming of the new covenant, the Lord, who is ever faithful, would restore a heart-to-heart relationship with his people. There are a number of scriptures which together build this picture:

> For your Maker is your husband –
>   the LORD Almighty is his name . . .
>
> *Isa. 54:5*

> 'But like a woman unfaithful to her husband,
> so you, Israel, have been unfaithful to me,'
> declares the LORD.
>
> *Jer. 3:20*

> 'The days are coming,' declares the LORD,
> 'when I will make a new covenant
> with the people of Israel
> and with the people of Judah.
> It will not be like the covenant
> I made with their ancestors
> when I took them by the hand
> to lead them out of Egypt,
> because they broke my covenant,
> though I was a husband to them,'
> declares the LORD.
>
> *Jer. 31:31–32*

> No longer will they call you Deserted,
> or name your land Desolate.
> But you will be called Hephzibah,
> and your land Beulah;
> for the LORD will take delight in you,
> and your land will be married.
> As a young man marries a young woman,
> so will your Builder marry you;
> as a bridegroom rejoices over his bride,
> so will your God rejoice over you.
>
> *Isa. 62:4–5*

So the promise in the Old Testament is of a new covenant, a new name given, and a rejoicing by God in our bridal identity

A Fresh Look at the Church 115

as his people. Some Christians would say that this image does not carry through into the New Testament. It is obvious that Jesus is depicted as a bridegroom in the gospels, yet the church is more clearly his body (part of who he is) rather than his bride (the one whom he is waiting to marry).

Peter Hocken, author and ecumenicalist, highlights the essential link between the Old and New Testaments in this regard:

> Between the Old Testament prophets and the teaching of Jesus, we see at least two important developments in the use of this marriage imagery. Whereas in the Old Testament God is the bridegroom, in the Gospels it is Jesus. Whereas in the Old Testament Israel is already the spouse of the Lord, in the Gospels the references to the marriage feast have a strong eschatological 'end-times' character. That is to say, though Jesus is already the bridegroom, the marriage feast takes place at the end and is associated with his second coming.[2]

Let's see if this is true.

Matthew's Gospel gives the clearest insight into Jesus' teaching about a bride and bridegroom. Jesus called his disciples 'guests of the bridegroom' (Matt. 9:15); the physical absence of Jesus causes his people to fast and long for his return. Jesus also told a parable about a wedding banquet where the Father is like a king preparing a marriage for his son (Matt. 22:1–14); Jesus' listeners are again invited as guests to the wedding feast. In Matthew 25:1–13, Jesus encouraged readiness for his coming by telling a story of ten young women waiting to accompany the bridegroom at a wedding: five were well prepared for the groom to appear; the other five allowed their oil lamps to burn out as they waited: 'But while they were on their way to buy [more] oil, the bridegroom arrived. The virgins who were ready went in with him to the wedding banquet. And the door was shut' (v. 10). Here the midnight cry to go and meet the bridegroom calls for a prepared people ready for his return and a banquet feast. Not all are ready and not all enjoy the banquet and wedding joy. It is true that the identity of the bride in Matthew's Gospel remains obscure, yet the bridegroom identity of Jesus is clearly portrayed. His followers are to have a close involvement with him in some future wedding celebration, but what that involvement entails is not quite clear.

The other place in Scripture where Jesus speaks of a future intimacy with his people akin to marriage union is in the Gospel of John during Jesus' 'high-priestly' prayer in the upper room. Jesus prays for us, those who will believe in him in the future, that we will be one, as he is one with the Father, and that we will be with him to see his glory and will love him as the Father loves him (John 17:22-26). This is Jesus our heavenly intercessor praying a high-priestly prayer for the whole church in an image of intimacy and glory akin to that of a marriage union.

The clearest New Testament passage speaking about the church as bride is in Ephesians chapter 5. The apostle Paul is giving pastoral instruction on how husbands and wives should treat each other. He uses a 'mystery' to illustrate this, namely how Jesus treats the church: 'Christ loved the church and gave himself up for her to make her holy, cleansing her by the washing with water through the word, and to present her to himself as a radiant church, without stain or wrinkle or any other blemish, but holy and blameless' (Eph. 5:25-26). Jesus is portrayed here labouring to present the church as a pure and radiant bride. The 'presenting' here is not to the Father, although Jesus did purchase a people for God through his death and resurrection, as Revelation 5:9 makes clear. No, this is a presenting of the church as a bride for himself. Is this in the present tense, as though Jesus has given us his robes of righteousness through his perfect sacrifice and now looks on us as though we are without stain or wrinkle? Actually, it seems more future tense, because the church is not yet pure and radiant. Our full radiancy will only be seen when he returns, when the saints rise in glory and are arrayed in white at the marriage supper of the Lamb (see 1 Cor. 15:51–52; Rev. 19:8).[3]

Let's pause for a moment. These are stunning images: of a people getting ready for the long-awaited arrival of the groom; the mystery of being drawn into the loving intimacy of the Godhead; the labouring of Jesus to have a bride for eternity.

Thus far, we can piece these parts of the New Testament marriage imagery together to see that there is a present identity of the church as bride, and also a future consummation, a future wedding celebration. We are not just the body of Jesus; we are also his bride. Jesus is a glorious bridegroom, and his people are invited to share with him, not just as honoured guests, but in union with him as his beloved bride. There is a present-tense reality in that we are given the righteousness of Christ; his sinlessness and right standing with God is imputed to us, and in that place of union with Jesus, the Father now looks on us as having the righteousness and holiness of Jesus. Yet there is a future-tense and greater reality to come, when the redeemed people of God are gathered before the Lord, and we are presented to Jesus as a glorious and mature bride, in holy union with him, a perfect match made in heaven!

There's Going to Be a Wedding: The Jewish Wedding as Bridal Metaphor in Scripture

When studying the Bible, we can sometimes miss the depth of an analogy because we don't appreciate the original context. This is especially true concerning ancient Jewish wedding celebrations. Many of the glimpses we get in the New Testament regarding the church as the bride of Christ come into amazing focus when we consider the parallel of a Jewish wedding at the time of Jesus.[4] Weddings in Israel at that time were elaborate celebrations with a series of steps or stages to them. When we look at these various stages, the end-time significance of the bridal metaphor suddenly becomes much clearer.

There were three parts to a typical ancient Jewish wedding:

- the *shiddukhin* (mutual commitment or covenant);
- the *erusin* (time of engagement or betrothal);
- the *nissuin* (the marriage).

The *shiddukhin* or *mutual commitment* stage involved the arranging of the marriage between the prospective groom and the bride's father, the contract (*ketubah*) drawn up by the man, its acceptance by the woman, a bridal price paid by the man, and a separate ceremonial act of washing in water for cleansing by both of them.

Then there immediately followed a time of *erusin* or *official engagement*. The couple came together before witnesses under a canopy (*chuppah*). They drank from a covenant cup shared between them, and exchanged vows. The couple were then legally husband and wife. They were therefore betrothed, and the bride wore a veil to show she was spoken for. The groom returned to his father's house for roughly a year with the task of preparing a place for his bride, often an extension of his family home. The couple had no physical union during this period. The bride spent this time preparing a wedding gown and also keeping herself pure. Both she and her bridesmaids lived in a state of expectation, for they did not know when her groom would return.

A Fresh Look at the Church

Eventually, the last stage of *nissuin* or *marriage celebration* took place with a dramatic flourish. When all preparations had been made, the father of the groom would announce the moment his son could leave to get his bride. The groom and his attendants would go at night and announce 'The bridegroom is here' with a blow on the shofar (a trumpet made from a ram's horn). The bride and her attendants would be ready for him with their lamps lit and wedding garments prepared, and he would then carry her off to the new home. There would follow a blessing and further vows under the canopy (*chuppah*), and then a time of private honeymoon, with the best friend of the bridegroom awaiting the announcement that the couple had consummated their love. The friends would start celebrating for seven days, and when the couple emerged from their canopy, a great feast would take place with many guests invited to share the happiness of the newly married couple.

You don't have to look too deeply at this Jewish wedding analogy to see the link between the physical and the spiritual. There is a profound picture here of the relationship between Jesus and the church in our salvation story. Without stretching the analogy too far, in Jesus' first coming we can see how he paid the price of dying on the cross for his bride. He immersed himself in the waters of baptism, and collectively we do the same as we identify with being church (Rom. 6:5). That *shiddukhin* is what Jesus has already instituted for us.

The second stage, *erusin*, is illustrated when Jesus told his friends that he was going to prepare a place for them in his Father's house (John 14:2). He gave a new covenant cup for us to share (Luke 22:20) as we remember his death and look forward to his return. We are sealed with the Holy Spirit (Eph. 1:14) to show we are 'spoken for' by Jesus, and we keep ourselves pure and ready for him and our future life together in eternity (Titus 2:12–13). Short or long time it may be, but we wait in anticipation for the coming of our bridegroom.

The last stage, *nissuin*, is the end-time culmination of this preparation and waiting time. No one knows the day or hour of this moment, except God the Father (Matt. 24:36). Jesus promised to return in the night with the blowing of the shofar and the cry 'Here's the bridegroom!' (Matt. 25:1–13). In the darkest hour of history, in the Tribulation, some will be sleeping, but the bride will be waiting expectantly with her lamp burning. As Jesus comes in glory, we are caught up together with him in the air, and joined too with all the resurrected faithful believers from down the years who have died in hope (1 Thess. 4:16–17). The heavenly wedding feast can then begin as we celebrate our wonderful union with the Lord after all the centuries of waiting (Matt. 22:8–10).

What a powerful analogy God has given us in the ancient Jewish wedding celebrations! Jesus often used contemporary illustrations taken from his culture, and the meaning of his parables and other New Testament reflections would not be lost on listeners of their day. As we rediscover the treasures of this rich picture of the stages of a wedding, it creates a fresh sense of the immediacy of Jesus' teaching and the importance of seeing ourselves as the bride and Jesus as our bridegroom.

Pause for Thought

- What do I see in the Jewish wedding analogy that most speaks to me about the relationship between Jesus and his church?
- Is there anything that surprises me?

Summary

What insights do we gain from this regarding the church in the end times? The church is clearly called to live with a sense of expectancy for the Lord's imminent return. That is relevant for any generation; how much more so when we sense the time drawing ever closer? We also have a call to live in a way that is set apart for God, demonstrating a collective life which is united and holy, with our priorities wholly for the Lord. There is an implication that these truths will be very pertinent for the last generation of the church, when the sense of expectancy will grow in the global body of Christ, and the pursuit of unity and a holy lifestyle will become all-pervasive for many. Yet not everyone will be ready for the midnight cry heralding the bridegroom's arrival. For those with ears to hear, our end-time interests as a church will not be so much in biblical time-charts of the future, nor in nit-picking over the relevance of various prophetic passages of Scripture, but in the surge of corporate awareness that the Lord is so very dear to us and his coming is so very near to us. Let it be so!

6

Radiant: Journey into Intimacy in the Song of Songs

The first place to explore an understanding of a bridal image of the church in Scripture is the Song of Songs in the Old Testament. It is the place in the Bible where we can see most clearly the growing radiance of God's people as his beloved.

Do you remember those tender moments when someone you knew fell deeply in love with a partner? The changes in attitude and demeanour were very cute: how the boy smartened up his appearance and suddenly grew up; how the girl enjoyed being fussed and treated specially; the long phone calls, the romantic gestures, and the brightening of the person's face when the loved one appeared or was even just mentioned. Love is remarkable for how it changes us – changes us to being more other-oriented and less selfish, changes us by making us realize that we are special and lovable just as we are.

The Song of Solomon is a love poem; both mysterious and beautiful, this short book has fascinated both Christian contemplatives and preachers. When looked at from a surface reading, it is often misunderstood and therefore passed over as an unusual part of the wisdom literature of the Hebrew Scriptures. Yet, when looked at in depth, it is a jewel of writing, revealing love at its most spiritual, passionate and sensual.

Radiant: Journey into Intimacy in the Song of Songs

St Bernard of Clairvaux, the twelfth-century monastic father, in one of his many sermons on the Song of Songs said:

> Only the touch of the Spirit can inspire a song like this, and only personal experience can unfold its meaning. Let those who are versed in the mystery revel in it; let all others burn with desire rather than to attain to this experience than merely to learn about it. For it is a melody that resounds abroad by the very music of the heart, not a trilling on the lips but an inward pulsing of delight, a harmony not of voices but of wills.[1]

Charles Spurgeon, the great nineteenth-century preacher, when making a comparison between reading the Scriptures and walking on a journey of discovery through the Jewish temple, said: 'The song of Solomon is the most holy place: the holy of holies, before which the veil still hangs to many an untaught believer.'[2]

We can read this love song on both a literal and an allegorical level. It is clearly a delightful journey of passion and romance between a young prince and a Shulammite shepherdess. The devoted love and sensuality between the couple is clearly affirmed here from God's word. And yet, more importantly for Christians, the Song is a holy insight into the awesome and intimate relationship between God and his people and, with a gospel understanding, between Jesus and his bride the church.

Brian and Candice Simmonds, authors of a book on the Song of Songs called *The Sacred Journey*, write about the personal relevance of the Song for believers today:

> Jesus is the King of Glory who is first seen in the book as a kind Shepherd. You are the Shulamite, beloved follower of Jesus Christ, for you are the one He sings His song over each and every day.

This may in fact be the song of the Lamb that will be heard in heaven, which is sung by a multitude of those who have conquered the 'beast' of our old life (Rev. 15:3).[3]

Pause for Thought

- Have I ever read the Song of Songs?
- Which specific verses have I read that have already helped me in my faith?

I would like to use the themes from the Song of Songs as a lens to view the end-time church as she becomes a more radiant lover of Jesus. This is because the journey in the text, a maturing and growing love between lover and beloved, is one that has a powerful message for how our faith commitment grows, the closer we get to Jesus' return. I have not the time here to make a full commentary on this beautiful book, but simply desire to highlight five things from the Song that speak to the identity of the church as Jesus' bride. These aspects result in greater radiance in our lives, the radiance of love found, commitment deepened and union fully expressed.[4]

The Awakening of Mature Love in the Bride

God will awaken his church to fervent passion and love in the last days. There is clearly a stirring of love in the young woman in the Song of Songs. From her initial desire to be loved and kissed, combined with a certain reticence in case she is seen as a rather weather-beaten shepherdess (Song 1:2,5), we see a beautiful development in the love relationship between her and her lover. The church is likewise being called to intimacy, and an active intimacy at that. Like the girl, we progress from having a shy love for Jesus to beginning to see ourselves as he sees us; we are like a rose in his eyes (2:1). We learn to feast at his banqueting table and rest in the orchard of his love (2:3–4). The church hears his call to come away with him (2:13); we receive his embraces and begin to pursue knowing him (3:2).

This active intimacy with Jesus is to know at our deepest level what God has freely given us. There is a transformation in our hearts to fulfil the great commandment to love God with all our heart, soul, mind and strength. Even in the so-called dark night of the soul, when we struggle through personal battles or outward persecution, like the young woman, our devotion to him grows (5:7–8). We mature in love to the point where we realize we belong to our beloved and that his desire is for us (7:10). Akin to the girl's longing, our desire is eventually to be the seal of love on the heart and arm of Jesus (8:6).

There is something very powerful here about the end-time church maturing in love for Jesus. The centuries of Christendom, the religious formalism of historic church streams, and the fractured life of newer denominations have been giving way to an amazing season of renewal and revival in recent generations of the church, and this will continue most powerfully in the coming generations. Our passion for Jesus can overcome the historic divisions in the body of Christ. It is love for our God that will motivate our prayer and discipleship. It is the fire in our heart for him which will keep us steady and loyal in the midst of difficulties and coming tribulation. In the midst of all the swirling troubles of this world, can the church stay strong in her identity as the beloved of God?

The Revelation of the Bridegroom

As the bride is changed by the revelation of her bridegroom, so the church will become captivated by Jesus in a new way. In the Song it is the glorious pursuit of the lover for the heart of his beloved that stands out. Like the young woman, we are gradually becoming convinced of Jesus' zealous love as he describes the beauty that he sees in us (Song 4:1–9). We become more and more fascinated by his magnificent character (5:10–16); we are undone by his tender mercy (2:5–6); we are learning to rejoice and be secure in his heart of gladness, for 'I am my beloved's and my beloved is mine' (6:2–3).

As the girl in the Song describes the attributes of her lover that make her adore him, so we see more and more of Jesus' glory. An allegorical understanding of the poetic descriptions of the couple's bodies has been perfectly acceptable in church history and invites our contemplation. As our spiritual eyes are opened to fresh revelation of the risen Lord, we can see, for example, in chapter 5: his golden head of leadership, his Nazirite hair of holy dedication, the purity of his gaze, his cheeks revealing deep emotions, his life-giving words, his arms of perfect power, the kingly compassion in his heart (body), his ways of wisdom founded on righteousness, his unrivalled excellency like the best panorama, and his intimate kiss and embrace of us as his cherished one (5:10–16). This is our beloved Jesus!

The bridal metaphor in Scripture is actually more about the revelation of Jesus as our bridegroom than it is about us as the church. In these end times, the beauty and majesty of Jesus will be revealed to the church in a fresh and dynamic way. As a flawed church, often dim in vision and beset by sin, we cannot change ourselves. It is the glory of encountering Jesus afresh, and becoming fascinated by his risen magnificence, which changes our heart and changes a generation of Christian followers. The revelation of Jesus coming as a bridegroom king to meet his bride is one of the most powerful messages for the last days. It is not about us; it is about Jesus and his overwhelming beauty. We become radiant in our passion for him. Are we in the church ready for a global revelation of Jesus our beautiful bridegroom?

The Preparation of a Bride Ready for Partnership

The bridal message is not just about love; it is also about partnership, and the church will be prepared for great partnership with the Lord in end-time ministry. As in every good marriage, the couple in the Song are starting to enter a life of togetherness, walking side by side in their joys and challenges. This relates to the church always, as Jesus is calling for a people who will not just be intimate with him but will also learn to share his heart and minister alongside him. As Jesus said to his disciples in the upper room, 'I have called you friends, for everything that I learned from my Father I have made known to you' (John 15:15). The young woman in the Song, once wooed by her lover to come away with him from her comfortable and safe life, in the end joins a dance akin to the image of resurrection life, calling to him now:

> Come away, my beloved,
>   and be like a gazelle
> or like a young stag
>   on the spice-laden mountains.

Song 8:14

In a similar way, the church in this song is becoming a willing bridal partner for the Lord. We undergo a process of being cleansed by the heart of Jesus from the things that would prevent our fruitfulness (2:15). His love gives us the strength to arise with him (2:10); we begin to follow the Lord up the hidden stairs on the mountain, into the ascended life of glory and resurrection power (2:14). We welcome the winds of the Spirit to blow on our garden so that we might be more fruitful (4:16). We learn to bless and encourage the whole body of Christ in his orchard (6:11); we move with him into the countryside of mission and harvest fields, and give him our love in the midst of sacrificial service (7:11–12).

In past church history, there have always been pockets of people who have risen up and co-laboured with the Lord in prayer, service and mission, carrying the gospel and extending the kingdom, even while many lived an immature life of nominal faith and religious ritual. I believe that in the coming last days, a great multitude of the church across the world will hear the voice of Jesus calling them to arise into the fullness of the life of the Spirit and to partner with him in end-time ministry. We are getting ready to rule and reign with him, even through sacrificial, loving service and costly yet Spirit-empowered discipleship. Can the church rise above the issues that would hold us back to partner with Jesus in his harvest fields of witness and justice?

The Journey from Selfish Pursuit to Wholehearted Loving Obedience

The church will come into a time of radical devotion for God in the end times. The young woman in the Song walks a journey of change and transformation of her heart. Yes, it is about love and passion and maturity; it is also about a move from selfishness to the giving of her life to follow her great lover. Her heart is stirred to offer herself to him in covenant relationship (8:6).

Likewise, as the church, we move from a simple desire for the Lord's blessing to learning to embrace the cross, his suffering, and the giving up of our fleshly ways (1:13). We see afresh that we are not our own institution but rather his possession, his garden to delight in (4:16). Like the beloved, we turn from satisfaction with our comfort to a holy pursuit of his calling on our lives, even when this is inconvenient to us (5:2–5). We persevere in trusting him in the darkness of his perceived absence and in times of difficulty (5:6–8). We are increasingly willing to publicly own our faith in and devotion to our King (8:1). We cry out that we want to be a seal of covenant love on his heart, burning with the fire of his transforming Spirit (8:6).

We are coming into years of amazing transformation in the end-time church. The whole body of Christ will become more consumed by a pursuit of God, whatever the cost. Our holy calling will resonate powerfully with our fellow Christians and congregations to follow Jesus wherever he would lead us. Believers will enter into deep unity with the Holy Spirit as we say and do what God is saying and doing in these days. Sacrificial love will mark the end-time church, and there will be an uprising of disciples who are filled with his Spirit and laying down their lives for the cause of the King and his coming kingdom. What would it be like for the church to live in sacrificial devotion to Jesus, whatever the cost?

The Life of Jesus Fully Expressed in the Bride

In the Song, we notice how the bride is becoming more like the bridegroom, not the other way round. The end-time church will reflect the life and heart of Jesus to the world in a wonderful way. The young woman is embracing his wild and romantic dance; she is seeing her beauty and potential as he sees her; she has fully opened her heart to him and is reflecting his mature commitment and passion back to him. The two are becoming one. This speaks powerfully to the church as we draw closer to Jesus' return. We will sit at peace under the tree of the cross, his finished work of righteousness, and rest in the shade of his grace and glory (Song 2:3). We will find our voice and the courage to own our love for Jesus before a watching world (2:14). We will walk on the high places with him, in spiritual authority and with God's eternal perspective on his purposes (4:8).

We will be the garden of the Lord, his inheritance for his delight; we will bear the spices and fruits of his heavenly land and will be a banqueting table for others to taste of his goodness. We will be seen in Tribulation times as a church shining like dawn light in a dark world, like the moon reflecting the glory of Jesus, like an awesome army of God (6:10). Like the young woman, we will come through the wilderness of testing and refining, leaning on our Lover, fully dependent on Jesus, our lives enmeshed in his glorious life (8:5).

Of course, the words of this song apply to every saint and have always encouraged sincere followers of Jesus in their personal walk with him. Yet there is going to be a bride-like church that radiantly reflects the glory and nature of Jesus to the world in the closing years of human history. This is the bride who is without blemish or wrinkle whom he will present to himself on that wedding day of his coming. How will the world respond to a church that truly reflects Jesus' overflowing life and heart and this sense of oneness?

Summary

These five things – an awakening of mature love for the Lord, a great revelation of Jesus our bridegroom, a readiness for partnership with him, a wholehearted set-apartness to him, and a deep reflection of his life in us – are the dynamics of the journey we can see in the Song of Songs, and they are deeply relevant for the last-days church. This reframes end-time issues – away from prophecies about the Tribulation and shaking elsewhere in Scripture regarding the end times, and towards the deep relationship being forged between bride and bridegroom. Its value is in highlighting the growing radiance of God's people in the last days. It is a poem with great prophetic resonance as it depicts the church as Jesus' bride in deep and wonderful language. It assures us that, in the very context of the noise of end-time battle, the dazzling of God's glory being revealed, and the confusion of global shaking, millions of believers will grow and blossom in a loving romance with the Lord. Radiance and maturity will mark the church in the last days. The main theme in the Song is that of a journey in a relationship, and how the Lord will bring about such transformation in coming years is known only to him. Perhaps the successive waves of Spirit outpourings and the ever-crashing waves of trouble and persecution will gradually refine and purify the end-time church until she is truly a jewel.

I agree with Charlie Cleverly, who wrote an extensive book on the Song of Songs, in how he describes this change:

> The whole Church worldwide has never been mature together at any one time. However, the Bible hints that before Christ returns, the Church will have substantial maturity. She will somehow 'make herself ready'. The Church will enter into the measure of

the stature that belongs to the fullness of Christ (Ephesians 4:13). We don't yet know what that will look like. But God will finish what he began. The gates of hell will not prevail against her; she will arise and become prepared.[5]

May this radiance increasingly mark our lives and Christian communities, as we fall deeper in love with our Lord, experiencing a powerful and irresistible romance at work by his Spirit in the church, even in the midst of global turmoil.

Pause for Thought

- Take a while to read through the Song of Songs again.
- Use some of these dynamics – mature love, revelation of Jesus, partnership, obedience, and expressing the divine life – as a lens to let God speak to you about the radiance of your faith and about the radiancy of the church.

7

Resolute: Glimpses into the End-Time Church in the Book of Revelation

If the Song of Songs focuses on the radiance of the church in the end times, I would like to turn to the book of Revelation to consider her resoluteness.

This prophetic vision was written down by the apostle John to encourage his churches in the 'suffering and kingdom and patient endurance that are ours in Jesus' (Rev. 1:9). The followers of Jesus are exhorted to persevere in their faith under pressure, as they see the reality of heaven and the future certainty of God's triumph. In Revelation, the church has an important function in the heavenly scenes – in the worship and prayer rising before God's throne. It also appears to have a dramatic role to play in the Tribulation drama during the reign of the Antichrist. In the glimpses of God's people in Revelation there is both a call to and a demonstration of resoluteness, determination and discerning discipleship.

When I think of resoluteness, I think of soldiers. The Buckingham Palace guards in London are recognizable worldwide with their bright-red outfits and tall busby hats. People queue outside the palace gates to watch the Changing of the Guard, a fascinating and historic ceremony, or to see them stand motionless for most of their two-hour shifts. Yet not many of the watching tourists will be aware that these men are not just playing a ceremonial role. They are elite soldiers who have done distinguished service for their country in places around the world. Even apart from their palace shift in the public gaze, they are responsible for guarding the sovereign, patrolling the royal grounds and staying vigilant.

This resoluteness and vigilance in discipleship appears time and time again throughout Revelation. The church is not a ceremonial or religious institution, but a living, dedicated group of disciples, fully committed to Jesus and his kingdom. Of course, the bridal metaphor is likewise highlighted. Towards the end of the Revelation visions, the culminating scene of Jesus' return in glory is prefaced by the announcement of the imminent wedding celebration, the marriage supper of the Lamb. Heaven has been waiting for two thousand years; the church triumphant in heaven has been exhorting the church militant on earth to stay faithful to their God, and now the bridal imagery shines through like a beam of sunlight:

> Let us rejoice and be glad
>   and give him glory!
> For the wedding of the Lamb has come,
>   and his bride has made herself ready.
> Fine linen, bright and clean,
>   was given her to wear.
>
> *Rev. 19:7–8*

It is this theme of the bride 'making herself ready' that is a vital component of the end-time church, and the book of Revelation gives us helpful insights into its meaning. This is not Jesus' atoning work to make us righteous, but his people's response in radical devotion and service to him in the sanctifying strength of the Spirit. This is true at all points in church history, but especially so in the last days.

Despite the many varied interpretations of the message of Revelation by theologians, from historists to preterists to idealists, there is a clear future-oriented fulfilment of the apocalyptic prophecy of John. As Bible scholar Robert Mounce writes: 'With the futurist we must agree that the central message of the book is eschatological, and to whatever extent the End has been anticipated in the course of history it yet remains as the one great climactic point toward which all history moves.'[1] I believe that the book of Revelation is an end-time training manual as well as a glorious depiction of heaven's triumph over evil. There is a real future drama described here which real believers will go through. Although Christians of all time have taken great comfort from the words of Revelation when enduring trials and trusting in God for future glory, the church in the generation before Jesus returns will look at this book as a relevant prophetic and discipleship guide for how to navigate the Tribulation times and overcome through it all. We are always being called to make ourselves ready for Jesus' return as our bridegroom King; it is always a response to his love. However, a deeper surrender, a greater refining, a unique preparation will somehow mark the final generation of believers that will close the church age. In the end, it is our holy and resolute nature as his people that will make us truly ready for union with Christ as his bride.

Pause for Thought

- Have I ever thought that the book of Revelation could be a training manual for the church in the end times?

There are four aspects of the bride being prepared for Jesus' return that I see in the book of Revelation: becoming prayerful, being courageous, longing and overcoming. We will look at them in turn.

Prayerful: The Mature Worship and Prayer of the Church ('Come Up Here')

Jesus calls us to be prayerful. His command to the apostle John to 'come up here' (Rev. 4:1) was initially a call to enter into the worship and prayer meeting of heaven. The end of the seven letters to the churches (chs 2 and 3) turns abruptly for John into a time of heavenly visions. Before the apocalyptic insight of cosmic judgments and end-time conflict, God gives him a vision of the throne room in heaven. The visions of Revelation chapters 4 and 5 are such awesome and precious passages of Scripture. God wanted to help his suffering church in John's day to gain a new perspective of what is happening in the heavenly places. God is on his throne, ruling in glory and power. Angels, living creatures and elders surround the throne with constant worship and adoration. Jesus, the 'lion and the lamb', is about to take the scroll of God's end-time plans and initiate heaven's countdown to his return. Christians throughout the ages have mined this passage for inspiration for their hymns and prayer liturgy. Yet there is an immediate relevance for the church in the last days.

Right now across the earth, there are tens of millions of believers joining in an unprecedented explosion – the global worship and prayer movement. These worshippers and praying people are continuing the earthly partnership with heaven's worship and prayer meeting that has been ongoing through the church age and will soon culminate in the end-time glory and shaking, the time of the great harvest and the Tribulation.

You may notice in the book of Revelation that at key moments before the releasing of the scrolls, trumpets and bowls – containing end-time judgments – we find a profound moment of worship and prayer. In chapter 5, when Jesus takes the scroll from the Father on the throne, 'the four living creatures and the twenty-four elders fell down before the Lamb. Each one had a harp and they were holding golden bowls full of incense, which are the prayers of God's people' (5:8). In chapter 8, when the seven trumpets are given to the designated angels, 'another angel, who had a golden censer, came and stood at the altar. He was given much incense to offer, with the prayers of all God's people, on the golden altar in front of the throne' (8:3). Then in chapter 15, as the vision of the angels and bowls of plagues begins, John sees 'those who had been victorious over the beast and its image and over the number of its name. They held harps given them by God and sang the song of God's servant Moses and of the Lamb' (15:2–3).

We see here the mingling of the worship and prayers of the church on earth militant alongside those of the church in heaven triumphant. There is a genuine mystery that we glimpse in Revelation in terms of how God accomplishes his end-time purposes, what we see on earth, and what the saints and angels see from heaven. Yet this throne-room revelation for the church in the end times shows us that God calls us to a higher place of privilege, revelation and discernment in prayer than we are used to. God wants us to be prayerful in the midst of end-time troubles, because our prayers will make a difference. More crucially, for this coming generation, the sense of privilege will embolden us as we realize that Father God wants his people to partner with him in how he fulfils his endgame plans on planet earth. Our prayers will carry real authority as we pray out the purposes of God. Will our mercy cries in the midst of persecution bring deliverance and relief? Certainly. Will our praying against the injustice and oppression of the Antichrist regime affect earth? Without a doubt. Will our intercession for a great harvest of people coming to faith bear fruit? Absolutely.

The sense of prophetic revelation of the heavenly throneroom will captivate us, for God wants to ground us in a deep and living place of awe and worship through troubling years. The vision of God's greatness will grow even as darkness increases. The sense of discernment will make us wiser, as a biblical worldview will coincide with the best way of interpreting the signs of the times. Put simply, we will be the worshipping and praying church living out in a most vivid way the Lord's Prayer, as we say 'Your kingdom come, your will be done on earth as it is in heaven'.

Pause for Thought

- Do I believe God uses our prayers in the releasing of his global plans and purposes?

Courageous Witness: The Bold Testimony of God's People ('They Triumphed')

Jesus calls us to be courageous. The Tribulation time is an opportunity for the church to triumph in her faith. There are three occasions in Revelation when the church is depicted as a bold and prophetic people in the face of evil.

In Revelation chapter 11, there are 'two witnesses' described by John: "'I will appoint my two witnesses, and they will prophesy for 1,260 days, clothed in sackcloth." They are "the two olive trees" and the two lampstands, and "they stand before the Lord of the earth"' (11:3–4).

Who are these mysterious figures? They are bearers of light and the ones anointed by the Spirit, as prophesied in Zechariah 4. They are last-days prophetic voices coming in the spirit and power of Elijah and Moses, as foretold in Malachi 4. Although the description in Revelation could refer to two anointed leaders in the end times, it seems more likely to refer to the whole witnessing church in that tumultuous time of Tribulation. They will have a prophetic ministry to the world. Like Moses and Elijah, they will be clothed in the 'sackcloth' of humility yet be uncompromising in their message, operating with dramatic signs and wonders. This could well indicate the completion of the Great Commission as everyone hears the gospel in a context of outpourings of the Spirit. Even when killed by the Antichrist, the witnesses are carried up to heaven and vindicated by the Lord. This could be symbolic of a near obliteration of the church but then a final revival of millions coming to faith. Certainly, in the future there will be a time when blatant evil and demonic power are openly displayed. At the same moment, the church will move into a time of tremendous boldness of prophetic witness in all nations, aligned with signs from heaven to vindicate its message of God's coming. The gospel will not be stopped from reaching the ends of the earth.

In Revelation chapter 12, an end-time battle in heavenly places between angels and the devil marks the beginning of the end. The devil is hurled down to earth and wages war against the church with rage and hostility. This is the time of the Great Tribulation mentioned by Jesus (Matt. 24:21) – a period of intense persecution of Jesus' followers. Yet this is also the greatest hour of the church. Having witnessed in the anointing and power of the Spirit in chapter 11, Christians now face the rage of Satan trying to oppose the church, and they witness in the face of death:

> They triumphed over him
>   by the blood of the Lamb
>   and by the word of their testimony;
> they did not love their lives so much
>   as to shrink from death.
>
> *Rev. 12:11*

There are two layers of meaning here. They triumph because Satan has no power to silence the message of the gospel and the saving work of the cross. Yet they also triumph because their determination to proclaim that message overcomes their fear of death. There are already more people being persecuted for their Christian faith than at any previous time in history. There will soon be a time when millions of believers pay the price of martyrdom or severe persecution, following Jesus in the way of the cross, and sharing a radical gospel before a watching world. The devil has no power over Christian believers who have died to the world and to their own selves. As the saying goes: 'He is no fool who gives what he cannot keep to gain what he cannot lose.'[2]

In Revelation chapter 14, John is given a vision of Jesus standing with 144,000 believers on Mount Zion. It is a scene of triumph and praise. Who are the 144,000? It is unfortunate that Jehovah's Witnesses, with their own strong interpretation of this, have prejudiced a serious treatment of these verses by Christians. Some commentators say this is the full number of the redeemed church of all ages. Others would say it is a literal number of chaste and radical 'super-saints', perhaps even a saved Jewish remnant. I think the 144,000 is a symbolic number in this apocalypse. It describes the end-time church in its wholehearted discipleship and witness: 'These are those who did not defile themselves with women, for they remained virgins. They follow the Lamb wherever he goes. They were purchased from among mankind and offered as first fruits to God and the Lamb. No lie was found in their mouths; they are blameless' (14:4–5). They are not literal virgins, but rather those who will have resisted the lure and defilement of the Antichrist empire. They will live as ones wholeheartedly following Jesus' teaching and example. This is a picture of the church in the heart of the dark Tribulation years. They will give themselves sacrificially as a first-fruits offering so that, through their lives and love, God will bring in the full harvest of people finding salvation in Jesus. I fully expect that the church will experience such a sanctifying work of the Spirit in coming years and that its ministry will be led, not so much by people in functional priestly and pastoral vocations, as by a great band of unknown Christian leaders sold out for Jesus and living radical lives of prayer and service that deeply challenge the world around them.

These three passages give us a powerful insight into the courageous witness of the end-time church in coming years. There will be an anointed prophetic voice coming from the worldwide church, challenging the world to give honour to God. There will be a brave martyr witness from the global body of Christ, not bending the knee to the Antichrist system. There will be a pure, wholehearted and sacrificial discipleship-making body of believers across the earth, who will stay true to Christ in the midst of all the shaking and pressure of the last days. What a way of preparing ourselves to meet our Lord as he returns!

Pause for Thought

- Where do I see the brave and courageous witness of Christians in the world right now?
- Do I believe I can be like them?

Longing: The Increase of Holy Desire for the Presence of the Bridegroom ('Come, Lord Jesus')

Jesus calls us to long for his appearing. In the closing remarks of the book of Revelation, John again hears the words of Jesus confirming the weight and truth of this end-time apostolic vision. The twice-repeated promise 'I am coming soon' draws from John a beautiful prophetic cry: 'The Spirit and the bride say, "Come!" And let the one who hears say, "Come!" Let the one who is thirsty come; and let the one who wishes take the free gift of the water of life' (22:17). Some commentators think this whole verse is about the evangelistic testimony of the empowered church in the last days. I, like others, don't think it refers just to the call to the hungry for salvation; I think the first half reflects the ache and longing in John's heart, and in the heart of God's people for Christ's return.

Remember that Jesus taught about wedding guests holding a fast for the bridegroom (Matt. 9:15). When Jesus is taken into heaven, his followers will long for his return. Jesus also taught that his people should be like wise young women, listening for the midnight cry: 'Here's the bridegroom! Come out to meet him!' (Matt. 25:6). There should be a longing and an expectancy among his people for his return from heaven in glory that causes us to pray 'Come, Lord!'

As I have mentioned earlier, the first couple of generations of Christians in the early church lived their lives vividly in the light of Jesus' imminent return. As the decades stretched into centuries, that hope dwindled; our expectant waiting was reduced to the Bible focus on the first Sunday of Advent, or to the recitation of the creeds. However, Jesus encouraged his followers to be always ready. In Matthew 24 he taught that there will be a last generation of the church still alive when he comes back and ready for him (Matt. 24:31).

But there is a difference between just readiness and *longing*. A longing speaks of our desire, the cry of the heart. Paul speaks of this yearning in Romans 8:23: 'we . . . groan inwardly as we wait eagerly our adoption to sonship, the redemption of our bodies.' Christians should have a longing, not just for heaven, but for the final part of the story, the end of our redemption story. Revelation takes this one stage further in the 'Come, Lord Jesus' cry. The readiness for the Lord, even the groaning for our redemption, will transform into a global longing in the church as she realizes that her bridegroom is about to come to meet her. I believe a bridal yearning for him will mark the church in the end times. It will be a longing stirred by the Holy Spirit in this final process of renewal in the church. There is no point in having a bride who doesn't want the presence of her husband. God's passion for his Son's return will be joined at last by the church's yearning for his coming. As Bible scholar F.F. Bruce says, commenting on the phrase 'Let the one who hears say, come!': 'every one who listens to the reading of the book (cf. 1:3) must at this point break in with his personal response: "Come!" The Aramaic form of the invocation, Maranatha, "Come, O Lord!" (1 Corinthians 16:22) was retained even in Greek-speaking churches, especially at the celebration of the Eucharist.'[3]

After two millennia of the eucharistic cry 'Maranatha', it will be the final part of the preparation of the bride in the coming years. She will have made herself ready and she will be fully mature and expectant, waiting and longing for the bridegroom. The 'Come, Lord Jesus' cry will resound around the world in the closing time of Tribulation and shaking. Our longing for Christ's return will make us resolute in our faith and convictions during a dark time of history. At that point it will be all too obvious that we are in the very end of the age, and the prayer and desire for his return will fill the hearts of his people like never before.

Pause for Thought

- Do I truly want Jesus to return in glory?
- Is there an ache in my spirit to be with him forever?

Overcoming: Jesus' Encouragements to the Seven Churches ('to the One Who Overcomes')

Jesus calls us to overcome. This unique preparation of the bride of Christ in Revelation starts in the letters to the seven churches. In the opening chapters of Revelation, before the end-time apocalyptic visions of chapters 6 to 20, John records a vision of Jesus, revealed in his heavenly glory, speaking to seven churches in ancient Asia that are under John's care. These were real groups of Christians, and the letters offer insight into the struggles of faith in the second generation of the church in a hostile Roman Empire. The fact that these communities were also on a circular trade route of that time provided an opportunity for the messages to spread to other believers further afield and to be generally disseminated throughout the early church. However, the symbolic number of seven here also suggests that these messages from Jesus speak more widely to churches of all generations in history. So we could consider these seven 'types' of churches, or seven spiritual conditions in which churches find themselves. What insights can we glean about overcoming in the end times from these letters?

The following is a breakdown of the seven letters:

1. *Ephesus (Rev. 2:1–7) – the church that has lost its first love for Jesus in the midst of good works.* The call to the members of this church is to return to their early passion and devotion to Jesus. For all of God's people, truth and love must go hand in hand. Dogmatic fervency or great tasks done in the name of the Lord in the last days must not take the place of cultivating intimacy and a living flame of personal devotion. Passion for Jesus needs guarding, especially in times of difficulty. The reward for overcoming is the tree of life – eternal life and enjoying the paradise of God.
2. *Smyrna (Rev. 2:8–11) – the church that has been persecuted for its faith.* The call is to remain faithful to Jesus through suffering. We are encouraged that our future glory outweighs our temporal suffering. The end-time church will, like the early church, be severely tested by religious persecution; we are forewarned so as to be forearmed. We overcome by never giving up our faith. The reward for overcoming is the crown of life – our full rights as heirs of the kingdom.
3. *Pergamum (Rev. 2:12–17) – the church that has compromised its beliefs.* The call is to overcome compromise and stay aligned to gospel truths. We all need to be wary of diluting gospel values and conforming to society. The temptation to

hide our faith and go with the flow of the culture around us in the end times will be great, and we need to warn each other if we are going astray. All belief systems are not the same. To overcome is to stay true to the revelation of God in Scripture and to let that direct our lives. The reward for overcoming is hidden manna – our deep relationship with Jesus in eternity; also a white stone with a new name – possibly our invitation to the wedding feast or our particular identity in God's sight.

4. *Thyatira (Rev. 2:18–29) – the church that has followed false prophets.* The call is to holiness and to deal with immorality. If Pergamum struggled with watered-down belief, Thyatira was dogged with compromising behaviour. God's people need to watch out for immorality, sin, and any false teaching that justifies our conduct but is out of line with Scripture. Deception will be intense in this coming last generation, when persuasive voices both within and outside the church will subtly twist truth and morality. In order to overcome we will have to be on our guard – to let God's love be our guide and to stay deeply rooted in fellowship and the word. The reward for overcoming is authority over the nations – a sharing in the future rule of the dawning new age.

5. *Sardis (Rev. 3:1–6) – the church that is nominal and close to dying out.* The call is to be spiritually revived. Every church walks a fine line between a living relationship with the Lord and religious duty. Formalism and nominalism in faith, if unchecked, leads to a dying community in need of the Spirit. The choice for believers in the end-time church may well be between accepting nominalism and adherence to an approved 'state church', or belonging to a dispersed and officially frowned-upon underground church that maintains its vibrancy. To overcome may involve hard

choices – resisting the pressure of being approved by society, and possibly leaving churches that are caught up in nominal religious practice. The reward for overcoming is a gift of white garments – the glorious clothing of the redeemed in heaven; and also a name that will endure – the guarantee of heavenly citizenship.
6. *Philadelphia (Rev. 3:7–13) – the church that is faithfully enduring despite being weak.* The call to the Philadelphians is to continue in their faithfulness and to trust in God's vindication for their gospel stand. Every Christian can be encouraged to know that faithful perseverance in following Jesus is ultimately blessed by God, and apparently weak but true faith will one day become a strong witness to God. The presence of the Lord will be strong among end-time communities of faith; we will have great confidence in God's sovereign care and our eternal destiny. To overcome may involve maintaining a simple but living flame of faith in Jesus in the midst of darkness and social despair around us. The reward for overcoming is becoming a pillar in God's temple – having a place of purpose in God's future reign; and receiving the name of God and his holy city inscribed upon us – signifying our secure heavenly relationship and citizenship.
7. *Laodicea (Rev. 3:14–22) – the church that has become lukewarm in its faith.* The call to these Christians is to repent for their condition and to receive afresh the presence of Jesus in their midst. Personal prosperity and outward success in any church is no substitute for spiritual fruitfulness or Jesus' living presence among us. The end-time church will be one which has been shaken out of its comfort zone and spiritual lethargy. We will have woken up to the signs of the times and the captivating call of Jesus to fellowship with him, even through the Tribulation. Our challenge will be to shake

ourselves out of spiritual dullness into white-hot faith. The reward for overcoming is to sit on Jesus' throne – the vindication of our live of faith and a sharing in Jesus' royal rule.

There are two things which set apart these letters as supremely important for every church generation. The first is the revelatory truth that the dynamic presence of the glorified Jesus is in the midst of the local Christian community. He comes with full knowledge of our faithfulness and failings; he looks to judge, refine and encourage; he holds the present and the future, and he beckons his people on in their life of faith. The second is the awareness of the opposing temptations that beset the Christian community. On one hand, there is a struggle to bear faithful witness and not to deny Christ in a hostile world that persecutes believers; or to become nominal and passive in religious duty. On the other hand, there is a temptation to be subtly enticed into error or to accommodate ways of life that do not honour Christ. Passivity and compromise are the chief pitfalls for devoted faith, according to Jesus in Revelation.

So why highlight these letters as useful for the end-time church? If they are relevant for churches throughout history, what is special in their application to Christians in the last days? I believe that the two elements just mentioned will increase in the coming years.

I believe that the revelation of the risen and glorious Jesus in our midst will increase in the church. We will become more gripped by the glory and majesty of Jesus, reigning on a heavenly throne and moving in our midst. The power of the Revelation 1 vision of Jesus in his risen majesty, which John saw, will touch believers and congregations worldwide in coming years. The more we see the Lord, the more we will love him. Deep encounters with the risen Jesus among us will deeply challenge us, and freshly motivate us to worship, follow and serve him in a radical way. Even his promises of eternal rewards will become more relevant to us: the longing to be in the paradise of God, to reign and rule with Jesus as he returns, to share in the wedding banquet, to be marked as citizens of heaven, to have a role to play in the dawning of a new age – all of these will quickly become more important to us than any worldly prestige, position, possessions or popularity.

This will be important because God knows that the temptations to compromise or become passive in our faith will also increase in coming years. The pressures in the end times that Jesus mentioned in Matthew 24 – to be enticed into false teaching, or to suffer hostile persecution – will cause the love of many believers to grow cold. The seven conditions of the Revelation churches will be conditions especially relevant to this coming generation. Issues of suffering, lukewarmness, compromise, nominalism, losing radical devotion, and being deceived, will be more prevalent in the end-time global church.

I truly think that the call to overcome is one of the most important messages we can receive from the Lord. His encouragement and exhortation to overcome anything that might test or shipwreck our faith is a word for an end-time generation, because the Lord knows what the church is soon to go through – all the glory and shaking that Christians will experience. The revelation of his risen and glorious presence will be our strength, and his call to us to stay true to him will be both immediate and urgent. Will we take to heart the messages to the seven churches as written for us today? Will we cry out to God, asking that the revelation of our glorious Jesus would permeate and fill the worldwide church? Will we stop at nothing to find the anointing and spiritual strength to carry us through Tribulation temptations and troubles if we are called to walk through them? I hope we will.

Pause for Thought

- What does the church in my city or nation most need God's help with to overcome?
- Are there any obvious areas of compromise or passivity to repent of?

Summary

The book of Revelation, rather than being viewed as a set of obscure prophetic dreams, can be seen as a training manual for the end-time church. In it we find ways in which the people of God rise up in the middle of global turmoil and Tribulation persecution. They become deeply prayerful, anointed in worship and prophetic insight, as they partner with God's coming kingdom and pray into being the final harvest and judgments. They become very courageous, finding a strength in God to withstand opposition and bring a brave and joyful witness to Jesus, devoted and dedicated to him. They are filled with longing for Jesus' return, their expectation growing as the Great Commission is completed and as biblical prophecy lines up with contemporary news. They find the grace to overcome the temptations that beset them, rising above compromise and shaking off spiritual dullness to maintain a shining witness to the light and love of Jesus that burns within them. In Revelation we see clearly a bride who is resolute, making herself ready for union with the Lord who loves her and who will soon be joined with her for eternity.

8

God Will Finish What He Has Started: The Book of Acts and the End-Time Church

The End Is Near the Beginning

I would like in this chapter to consider the relation between the early church and the church in the end times. While their contexts for faith were very different, there is much that is strikingly similar and will prove to have great value for reflection.

I love hill walking and in particular good circular hikes. I much prefer fresh views around every corner on the way to the car rather than backtracking or waiting for a bus to take me back. The Lake District in England is wonderful for the high fells and amazing vistas, and, if the visibility is good, there are few places more satisfying to walk in the UK. I undertook a great walk with my son around the 'Fairfield Horseshoe' near Ambleside a few years ago. The initial ascent was tough but, once on the tops, we traversed the edges and summits in a circular fashion, able to see over to the distant fells and lakes, down into the valley and across to the start of the walk we had just done. The clouds were high, the midges non-existent, and the walk was exhilarating. We ended up close to where we had begun – and to a good teashop to boot!

The journey of the church through history is not an aimless walk, but sometimes it has taken us further away from where we started than God may have intended. We can trace the life of the Spirit in every age, and can sense the same power of the Spirit that the first followers of Jesus experienced, but we have often ended up far from our initial charisms. I believe that the closing years of history will bring the church full circle to the dynamic that was at work in the early church. The end is near the beginning, and the book of Acts can be a relevant and lived experience for those followers of Jesus alive in the last days.

So far, we have spoken a lot about the church as a bride being prepared for Christ. The work of the third person of the Trinity, the Holy Spirit, is fundamentally important in this process. The Spirit is the great advocate who comes alongside to help us when we are weak in faith or prayer. The Spirit is the empowerer of mission who urges us on in our witness and works of justice, thrusts us out of our comfort zones and makes us stand strong in Christ. The Spirit is the wonderful reviver who plunges us into his river of life so that our discipleship is not weary or dry. The Spirit is the sanctifier who purges our lives and communities of faith. The Spirit is the great teacher who always testifies that Jesus is Lord, and glorifies the Father and the Son. The Holy Spirit is our fellowship with the Trinity, drawing us and creation deeper into union, and ultimately preparing his people to become the bride the Son longs to be united with. The early Christians relied radically on the Spirit as the divine presence in their midst; they were breathed upon and led by his numinous power. The followers of Jesus in the end times will live in a similar radical fashion, and walk a similar path as we draw on the Spirit's power and presence in the midst of glorious and dramatic days.

Spiritual DNA

Let us for a moment consider the 'DNA' of the church that is placed there by the Holy Spirit. DNA fascinates scientists. From the discovery of the structure of DNA, the genetic code, by scientists Crick and Watson in 1953, there has been a rush to unlock what its mysteries can tell us. DNA, that unique double-helix structure found in every living cell, carries all the instructions needed for an organism to build, maintain and repair itself, and to pass on that code when reproducing. Understanding how DNA molecules replicate themselves, and recognizing genes and their variations in DNA sequences, has already helped scientists achieve very useful things such as the ability to personalize medicines, solve crimes and test for a person's ancestry.

Is there a spiritual DNA, implanted by God into the church at its birth at Pentecost, which should be reproducible in every subsequent generation of God's people? Many people believe this is the case. One could point to the elemental forces on the day of Pentecost – when the wind, fire and ecstatic tongues in the upper room birthed a people who were blown by the Spirit, inwardly renewed by the fire of God, and empowered to move out into the world in praise and witness (Acts 2:1–4). One could look at the unforced fellowship of the early disciples (2:42–47), to the egalitarian and cross-cultural nature of the first congregation (2:5–11), and to the successful, unplanned seeding of new Christian communities wherever the disciples went (8:4–8; 11:19–25). The church in Acts is a people with a living Holy Spirit DNA, from which every church denomination and expression traces their lineage. One could even see the four classic marks of the church, stated as early as AD 381 in the Nicene-Constantinople Creed – 'one, holy, catholic and apostolic' – as stemming directly from the life of the early church. We are linked organically together, both historically and globally. There is a *unity* with God and each other through his dwelling with us; there is a *set-apartness* and a holy quality of spiritual life which he imparts to us; there is a *universality* and link in faith with all believers of all time; and there is a *sent-ness*, a spiritual task to obey and an inspired mission to which we are always called.

Yet many would agree that the church at different times in its history has looked very different from the early church with its dynamic life. Often institutionalized, too easily settling down, too quickly accommodating to the cultures in which it is set, the church over the centuries has dimly borne the four marks, and has certainly not always imbibed the life of the Spirit and the sense of an organic messianic community which were the hallmarks of the church in Acts. Rather, it has been the missional orders of traditional streams, the church planters, the cross-cultural missionaries, the apostolic pioneers in history who have seemed closest to the ecstatic, praising and gospel-preaching first disciples. It has been the Reformers, the missionary monks and the persecuted, renegade preachers who have appeared most like the early Christians, blown by the winds of the Spirit. It has been the revivalists, the prayerful renewal movements and the mystics who have felt something most akin to the fiery tongues that purged the early followers of Jesus.

It could well be that the wind, fire and exuberance of the Spirit will be demonstrated once more in a last-days move of God across the whole earth. Right now, the wind of God's Spirit is blowing across the church in the more hidden parts of the world – in the underground disciple-making movements in the Middle East and Asia. God's renewing power, given by his Spirit, is never finished. The wind will blow again on his people. The fire of God will soon again burn uncontainably in his church, purging, sanctifying, cleansing and setting apart. The tongues of praise and ecstatic witness will once more mark the life of God's people the whole world over as the Spirit moves to revive, renew and make us bearers of the good news to a lost and troubled generation.

Pause for Thought

- Do I think the Holy Spirit DNA in the early church is alive and well in my church?
- How could I pray for renewal and fresh life in this group of believers?

A Close Correlation between the End-Time Church and the Early Church

I have already mentioned how the prophecy of Joel highlights a bookending of moves of the Spirit at the start and end of the church age. The Lord's promise 'I will pour' in Joel 2:28–32 was fulfilled initially in the early church on the day of Pentecost but will be fully experienced by the last generation of church, both in scale – the Spirit outpouring 'on all people' – and in the cosmic shaking dimension of the prophecy. The logic now would suggest that we should expect a particular and wonderful close correlation between the church in the end times and the church in the book of Acts.

There are a number of reasons for this, which we will now explore.

Holy Spirit revival dynamic

First, there is a Holy Spirit revival dynamic at work in the book of Acts that we should clearly expect to experience in these last days. Revival theologians and commentators have often considered the experiences of revival in the church and community to be a kind of repeat of Pentecost. Martyn Lloyd-Jones is typical of these when he says: 'When you read the history of revivals, are you at once reminded of the book of Acts of the Apostles? The church always looks like the church in the New Testament when she is in the midst of revival. The New Testament was a period of revival; the great outpouring on the day of Pentecost was continued.'[1]

It took the power of the Spirit to overcome the disciples' fear of persecution and to push them out of the upper room as ecstatic witnesses to Christ. It took surges of Spirit energy to move them ever outwards from Jerusalem towards the ends of the earth. In Acts we see how the gospel spread through the Roman world in waves: waves of the Holy Spirit's presence coming upon God's people, waves of opposition that actually strengthened the resolve of the church, waves of power evangelism that brought people face to face with God, and waves of prophetic disruption that led the church in unexpected directions.

John McGinley, writing about the church of tomorrow, suggests that one of the key hallmarks of Christian communities will be a great dependence on the Holy Spirit, as in the days of Pentecost:

Once we realise God can do the same wonderful works in his Church today as he did in the Church in the book of Acts, we discover a longing for more of God rising within us. Throughout history when this longing has reached a crescendo it has caused people to cry out to God for revival – from the Moravians, to Kenyans, to the Wesleys, to a handful of people in Argentina, to Evan Roberts in Wales, to two elderly sisters in the Scottish Hebrides.[2]

If many periods of revival and fresh mission in the church have hallmarks of the book of Acts, then we should expect the last outpouring of the Spirit to share many of those hallmarks in the most powerful way. If, as I believe the Bible predicts, there is a genuine global outpouring of the Holy Spirit in the coming years, the spiritual DNA of this worldwide time of awakening will be very similar to that of the church in her early days. A great longing for more of God will increase across the church. It will cause people to put up their sails to catch the Spirit's wind in more radical ways. They will become radiant and resolute witnesses to Christ, riding on the waves of the Spirit's renewal, and navigating troubles and opposition with courage.

Preacher R.T. Kendall speaks about what he believes will be a coming together of 'Word and Spirit' (i.e. the proclaiming of the gospel in the power of the Spirit) in a coming great revival, similar to Pentecost:

> When the Word and Spirit come together at an optimum level – as in Acts 2 – the simultaneous combination will result in spontaneous combustion. It is my view that the Midnight Cry of Matthew 25:6 will result in the ultimate coming together of the Word and Spirit as seen initially in the Book of Acts. This is when authentic apostolic power in preaching the gospel will be restored to the church before the second coming of Jesus Christ.[3]

It should not surprise us that the first and the last generation of the church should share similar Holy Spirit revival dynamics. As it was God's power that birthed the church, so too it is his power that will prepare his church for the end.

Eschatological pull

Second, there is a powerful eschatological pull in the Acts story in both the experience of Jesus' ascension and the experience of the Spirit at Pentecost. This shaped the life of the early church, and will shape the last generation of the church. The same understanding – that we conduct our life and mission between the ascension and return of Jesus – will strongly motivate the church in the last days. It could be called the 'ascension–Pentecost–eschaton' vector. Or you could say it is the 'now and not yet' tension of kingdom discipleship. There was a dynamic force moving among the early believers whereby, empowered by the knowledge that Jesus was seated at God's right hand, and greatly hopeful of his impending return to renew all things, their mission was filled with urgency, power and the presence of Almighty God.

The book of Acts reveals this ascension–Pentecost–eschaton vector (i.e. trajectory) for the church's witness. Jesus prophesied the outpouring of the Spirit, he ascended into heaven, the Spirit was given, and Jesus promised to return. The era of the church's mission is conducted in the power of the Spirit, not in a vacuum, but precisely between the poles of Christ's ascension and return. The early church knew this deeply, and the end-time church will know it profoundly too.

When you look at Acts chapter 1, the ascension of Jesus (1:8–10) prepares his followers for the experience of both absence and presence – his physical absence until he returns and yet his presence in the life of the Spirit. Jesus' absence was not discouraging, because the disciples knew he had ascended to God's right hand. As they looked into the sky, angels told them that their beloved Jesus would return in the same way they saw him leave. They were not to look into the sky and wait passively for their Lord but live in an epoch of his ascended glory with his Spirit empowering them on earth for life and mission.

This passage in Acts 1 is the only place in the New Testament in which Jesus' ascension to heaven and his return are mentioned in the same phrase. As author Douglas Farrow explains: 'The ascension (not the resurrection or parousia) thus becomes the climax of Jesus' history and the eschatological event fulfilling all the prophetic hopes of Israel. And this eschatologicalizes what is left of history by setting it within the tension of his departure and still-impending return.'[4] So the presence of the Spirit as wind, fire and tongues formed an eschatological community in Acts – people living and witnessing in the tension of knowing their Lord had ascended and had promised his return. The followers of Jesus in the book of Acts realized the eschatological significance of Pentecost for their life and witness; their life was a foretaste of the coming kingdom, their witness a beckoning to the world to feast at the kingdom banquet. All this was anticipated by the disciples in the experience of Jesus' ascension and their hope of his coming back to reign.

This eschatological pull has waxed and waned in the church over the years. It has at times given rise to a church which conceived itself as the full embodiment of the kingdom of God, not looking for any transcendent breaking in of heaven, with all the problems around politics and power that the church in cultural ascendancy will generate. A church content with presence. Yet history has also seen the rise of Christian communities and generations on the cultural margins, under persecution, or with great missionary urgency, for whom the kingdom is very much future and who are desperate for its consummation. A church aware of absence.

The tensions created by this and the eschatological pull will grow strongest for the church in the last days. For the end-time church, the realization of Jesus' impending return will be the greatest motivator in mission and discipleship. The church will be filled with the presence of the Spirit, yet will simultaneously be aware of the need for the full in-breaking of the kingdom. People will sense more deeply the groaning of creation and the expectancy of the age to come – that it is about to fully burst in. Powerful experiences of the Spirit at work in their midst will be a massive impetus to their witness as they see that the renewal of all creation is at hand. There will be a close correlation between the early church and the end-time church in this ascension–Pentecost–eschaton vector.

Pause for Thought

- Do I believe we live with an eschatological tension of the 'now and not yet' of the kingdom?
- How does that make me feel?

Missionary motivation: ends of the earth and back to Jerusalem

Third, there is a missionary motivation that marks the start of the church and also the end of the life of the church age. Jesus

God Will Finish What He Has Started 161

told his followers: 'you will receive power when the Holy Spirit comes on you; and you will be my witnesses in Jerusalem, and in all Judea and Samaria, and to the ends of the earth' (Acts 1:8). The revival and missionary impetus of the Spirit compelled the early church to seed the gospel, either by persecution and dispersion, or by church-planting missions moving out from their cultural boundaries to the heart of the Roman Empire. There was in Jesus' exhortation an embryonic programme of world evangelization. The continued sporadic and expanding waves of mission have of course moved the church literally to the ends of the earth in the last two thousand years. Many Christians are sensing that the church in these last days will be compelled to finish this work (the Great Commission in Matthew's Gospel), as I have mentioned earlier, and also to enable this impetus to rebound back towards Jerusalem.

I believe what we see emerging at the moment is both a 'to the ends of the earth' push and a 'back to Jerusalem' push in the global church. The ends of the earth are in sight. On one hand, for example, the Call2All initiative has been developing over the last twenty years, birthed in a coming together of six hundred church and mission leaders from the Amsterdam 2000 World Conference of Evangelists. The defining question now shaping the modern mission movement is 'What would it take to complete the Great Commission?' The Call2All initiative is moving forward through strategic summits to measure the remaining task of sharing the gospel. The five finish lines in sight are: reaching the least, the last and the lost of unreached people-groups; everyone having access to the Bible in their own language; a church presence in every neighbourhood; proclamation of the gospel to every person; and every believer practising compassion. Such movements are stirring the global church with the possibility that we will complete Jesus' commission within a lifetime.[5]

On the other hand, the 'back to Jerusalem' push in the global church is spiritual, symbolic and literal. This is about a boomerang effect of Holy Spirit mission whereby mission rebounds. There is a spiritual 'back to Jerusalem' missionary initiative that has emerged from the Chinese church in the last one hundred years and sees this as a Great Commission closure. The vision is for the Asian church to bring the gospel to the most unreached and resistant nations in the 10/40 geographic window between China and Jerusalem.[6] A current generation of Asian Christians are pioneering cross-cultural and sacrificial evangelistic missions into these nations. Once-closed people groups are opening to the gospel, and radical mission and church planting is taking place across the Asian subcontinent.

There is a symbolic 'back to Jerusalem' focus in the prayers of the church for Jewish people to rediscover Jesus as their Messiah. Even Paul, the great early pioneer missionary, saw his work among the Gentile nations as a massive detour towards his goal of seeing his own Jewish people turn to the Lord. The modern missionary work, done in sensitive ways, is suddenly starting to see great fruit in the planting of large numbers of Messianic congregations in Israel as well as various other places. The fullness of the global outpouring of the Spirit will culminate in many Jews finding Jesus as Messiah, and the joining of Gentile and Jewish believers into the one bride of Christ.

There is a literal 'back to Jerusalem' surge as millions of Jews have made the 'Aliyah' return to their religious and national homeland over the last seventy-five years, and continue to do so, helped by the Israeli 'law of return' and assisted by some Gentile believers convinced of the importance of this prior to Jesus' return. Several Old Testament prophecies, such as Jeremiah

31:8–9 below, refer to a massive move of Jews, prompted by the Holy Spirit, to come back to their promised land:

> See, I will bring them from the land of the north
>   and gather them from the ends of the earth.
> Among them will be the blind and the lame,
>   expectant mothers and women in labour;
>   a great throng will return.
> They will come with weeping;
>   they will pray as I bring them back.

This Aliyah movement will undoubtedly reach a climax in the years before Jesus returns. God has a reason to draw many Jews back to the promised land: to have a reconstituted natural Israel, a people in a land with a promise, and waiting for their Messiah to come. Their coming to faith will be the greatest move of the Spirit in history.

Pause for Thought

- The Great Commission will one day be fulfilled. How close do I believe we are to that time?

Summary

To summarize this discussion so far, I argue that we can notice a general spiritual DNA in the early church in Acts which marks us today. More importantly, we can see a correlation between the early church in Acts and the end-time church that is starting to emerge right now. We can hope for it in the revival dynamic that will come in the last-days outpouring of the Spirit that many are prophesying about. We can see it in the sense of an end-time pull in our spirits as we live vividly aware that Jesus who went into heaven is soon coming back, and as the Holy Spirit stirs the church to live in anticipation of the renewal of all things. We can see it in the missionary motivation to fulfil the church's mission both to bring the gospel to the ends of the earth and finally to let it rebound again to Jerusalem, the centre of God's eschatological purposes on earth.

This Holy Spirit dynamic of reviving, stirring and sending in great outpourings could well bookend the church age, framing its start and its ending. God's intentions for the church are awesome to comprehend, and they provoke us to pray and prepare for the greater fulfilment of the book of Acts in the coming years – a place of empowering for mission and witness that we have not seen the like of before.

I hope in Part Three to explore some of the visible marks we should expect to be seen in the emerging end-time church, marks that stem from its spiritual DNA and its close correlation with the church in Acts.

Pause for Thought

- What does it mean to me to think that a great move of the Spirit could bookend the life of the church, framing its beginning and its end?

Part Three

The Unexplored Country of End-Time Ministry

We must go beyond textbooks, go out into the bypaths and untrodden depths of the wilderness and travel and explore and tell the world the glories of our journey.

John Hope Franklin

Introduction to Part Three: Marks of the Emerging End-Time Church

So far in this book, I have set a big stage for exploring end-time themes as they relate to the church. I have laid a foundational understanding about end-time dynamics of glory and shaking, and how God can use both to bring about a victorious church. I have taken us through some key scriptures that look at the bride of Christ becoming ready to meet him in her radiancy and resoluteness. I have noted the close correlation between the church in Acts and the church in the last days. I come now to looking more closely at the journey ahead of us and the marks of the church that could emerge in the years before Jesus returns.

In the children's fantasy book *The Voyage of the Dawn Treader*, part of C.S. Lewis's Narnia series, Prince Caspian and his companions are on a quest to find the lost lords of Narnia, who disappeared years before, and to explore far-off lands. Dangers and challenges await them at every island or on each new course they set across the seas. There comes a point where the quest has nearly been accomplished, and the seven lords are all found or accounted for.

Yet there is a tantalizing last adventure facing the friends, and they must choose either to embark upon it or return home. The crew have gone as far east as any have traversed in their world. There is an unexplored land ahead that awaits them – the world's end and Aslan's country. Prince Caspian is in a dilemma about their journey:

> It would break my heart not to go as near the World's End as the *Dawn Treader* will take us. But I am thinking of the crew. They

signed on to seek the seven lords, not to reach the rim of the Earth. If we sail east from here we sail to find the edge, the utter east. And no one knows how far it is. They're brave fellows, but I see signs that some of them are weary of the voyage and long to have our prow pointing to Narnia again.[1]

Curiosity and daring win the day, and the companions do indeed sail to the edge of the world and espy the distant land that is Aslan's country.

There is an unknown journey for God's people to traverse in the coming years. It is the unexplored country of end-time ministry. We will follow in the footsteps of the saints, to be sure, and will be carried on waves of the Spirit similar to those that carried the early church. Yet no one has been on this precise journey before. Who can tell exactly what dangers and privileges await the church in the closing years of history? For the Lord calls us to partner with him as we live out a vibrant faith in the midst of darkness and great spiritual need, a time of glory and shaking.

As those drawing ever near that time, we must ask ourselves: are we willing to go on this adventure with the Lord? Are our hearts weary and longing to go back to our 'Narnia', to life as normal, or are we able to accept the joy and challenge of end-time ministry, navigating the best and worst of times? If we choose to say 'yes' to the Lord, he will bring out the best qualities in his people as we travel through this unexplored country. The journey will lead us to become a radiant and resolute bride.

Therefore, this part of the book will help us to explore seven marks of the emerging end-time church which the Lord calls us to exhibit (see diagram).

Introduction to Part Three

Seven Marks

1. The Overshadowed Community
2. The Fervent Community
3. The Anointed Community
4. The Outpoured Community
5. The Cruciform Community
6. The Grown-Up Community
7. The Transfiguring Community

In each case, I will note how that particular mark was evident in the early church, and how I believe it will resurface powerfully in the end-time church for those who are willing to give everything to follow Jesus. In one sense, the church in every age could be said to have borne these marks, and one might notice them standing out at different points in church history. Yet in another sense, at the bookending of the church age, these seven marks will be vividly apparent in the church in the coming decades. It won't happen across the whole church, for many Christians will choose an easier path, and what I am describing is a higher call of discipleship. And it may not come all at once. These facets of end-time ministry will emerge as the brightness of the church grows. It behoves me to lay out these themes to allow people to evaluate the cost and high privilege of a true Christian walk in the coming years, whether we choose to enter into it or not. Yet, in the context of the fiery outpourings of the Spirit, and the turbulence of the world's troubles, the Bible clearly speaks of the rising and shining of many of God's people; they will mirror the vibrancy and intensity of the life of those first Christians, and on a global scale.

I deliberately use quite strong visionary language in describing how the emerging church of the end times will look. The purpose is to give a picture of possibilities and how the Lord may well prepare us as his bride. Among these I share a handful of prophetic visions I received during the first writing of the manuscript. I nearly left them out as they are my own and not tested by a particular group; but I felt that, since they are illustrative of the main points, they were still worth including.

So let us now explore some of the terrain of end-time ministry.

9

First Mark: Known for the Numinous Presence of the Lord (the Overshadowed Community)

God's Manifest Presence

The church in Acts was birthed amid glorious signs of God's power and presence and was marked by that in the early years. The Holy Spirit filled the early Christians both individually and corporately, and also rested on them with his numinous presence. The cloud of glory that accompanied the wilderness wanderings of God's people and that filled the holy places of the tabernacle and temple, but then departed in the exile, now indwelled the community of faith in a raw and awesome way. God's presence shook buildings in which they prayed (4:31), brought about an awe and fear of him as they taught and discipled new believers, and overshadowed them in ways that brought physical healing to those around (5:12–16) and healing of relationships within their own multicultural Christian community (2:44).

In my life, I have occasionally experienced those rare times when the Lord seemed to overshadow the place and people I was among. For example, in some revival meetings in America, where people were lost in wonder, love and praise, the Lord's presence was just . . . close. There was a holy atmosphere, a sense of pregnant possibilities, something almost electric in the air. Yes, 'overshadowing' is a good word for this.

What has the church done without this vital sense of the manifest presence of the Lord? Of course, the church is never totally devoid of the presence of the Spirit; every believer lives in the life of the Spirit to some degree, and every congregation's life is dependent in some way on the inspiration of the Spirit, renewing its heart in word and sacrament and stirring it to fresh mission into the world. Yet this vivid experience of the Spirit among us has not been our normal experience; it is the narrative of revival, mysticism and ecstatic religious enthusiasm.

God is inviting us in the last days to prepare ourselves as his people to be the resting place for his awesome presence. This numinous presence of the Lord in our midst will not be of our making, but will be the sovereign work of God among those of his people who are most hungry for him. The promised glory of God will rise upon us in a way that has not been seen since Pentecost days. The knowledge of his glory will cover the earth as it is seen in the church worldwide. What will it look like? I think the mysterious yet tangible presence of the Spirit will rest on the church in unusual ways. His presence may sweep across large festival worship and preaching gatherings, changing them from events to seasons of tabernacling with God. It may turn old prayed-in cathedrals into holy places that people will flock to in order to find him. It may fall like sweet refreshing rain on weary congregations and cause a renewal of faith and witness in every church stream. The bread of his presence will return to his church, and God's people will again be known as the house of bread where the spiritually hungry can receive his grace and forgiveness. This overshadowing will happen in workplaces, in internet chat rooms, in homes, in parks, in schools and on the streets – wherever God is welcomed. It will most likely happen among the upcoming generation, amid groups of young people coming together physically or virtually. I expect there will be some astounding signs of the Spirit's overshadowing – in geographically 'thin' places between heaven and earth – where angelic activity will be obvious, where spiritual encounters with the Lord will be commonplace, and where people, whether religious or irreligious, will know that the Lord is in that place and lives are being changed.

Divine Visitation

Isaiah the prophet writes of the times when the presence and activity of the Lord increases in visible ways:

> Every valley shall be raised up,
>   every mountain and hill made low;
> the rough ground shall become level,
>   the rugged places a plain.
> And the glory of the Lord will be revealed . . .
>
> Isa. 40:4–5

Times of visitation of the Spirit tend to be times of both dismantling and restoration in the church and in our hearts. If the presence of the Lord is going to increase in his church in such a manifest way, then it will greatly impact our lives. There will have to be an adjustment in the church to accommodate the increased manifest presence of the Lord. The visitations of the Lord to people in Scripture were usually accompanied by a sense of his holiness and majesty, and provoked awe in and change of life among those who received them. In the presence of the Lord our words and thoughts, our motives and actions, will need cleansing.

A couple of years ago I had a prophetic vision of Jesus coming among us. I sensed being invited to come close to the Lord as he sat in an open garden-room. There was a fire pit in the middle and we sat opposite each other. Jesus then took a coal and tossed it to me, though it didn't burn my hands. He told me to put it to my lips and, as I did so, I felt a cleansing. Then there were many others coming close to the Lord and similarly being cleansed. I felt as though there was much polluted talk, careless words, unholy thoughts, that needed dealing with before we could sit further with the Lord. I felt that not just our lips were cleansed, but also our hearts, our thoughts and our motives. As we sat longer with the Lord, it was as though our heartbeats became one with his, and our thought patterns changed to be in tune with his. As we continued to dwell with the Lord, his clothes started becoming brighter, as though he was revealing more of his glory. Our reverence for him simultaneously increased and we bowed down. At first, I assumed that the people gathered there were leaders asking to see more of Jesus' glory. But then it felt more like a gathering of all those who were hungry, holy disciples – those drawn to seek him more. The glory of Jesus was being revealed in that small chamber, but also simultaneously out in distant places, as that dynamic of intimacy and intercession continued.

The story of historic revivals in the evangelical churches is filled with accounts of people transformed by encountering Jesus in a fresh way, and the experience of being baptized in the Spirit in the groups of people affected. They would literally run into an encounter with God that they had never experienced before – a revelation of his nature that powerfully changed them. Author Bob Dunnett comments on this revival dynamic in previous generations: how it brought profound encounters and revelation of God's love and holiness, which led to subsequent explosions of church growth and mission:

> This element of revelation is something which has always been present in the most powerful baptisms in the Spirit. It has been a crucially important source of motivation for God's people in the work of the Kingdom. It is revelation of a kind that has instigated and sustained dynamic calls to service for God. Not only that, but such revelation, burning in the hearts of those who have received it, has been the foundation for the most potent preaching and teaching of the Word, particularly in times of revival.[1]

I fully expect these transforming encounters with God to increase in the church globally in the coming years. The endowment of power from on high, desperately needed by the first apostles, will simultaneously refine us and make room for more of his brilliant holiness and glory, both in us and among us.

Repentance from sin and a seeking for the empowering of the Spirit always create a joint crucible of the heart in revival times, and the coming end-time waves of revival will reform many parts of the church beyond recognition. They will need to do so if the church is to bear authentic witness to the kingdom of God at work in the nations amid the global shaking.

In the following passage, Pentecostal theologian Frank Macchia discusses the reality of both repentance and empowerment in the core of revival moves of the Spirit: 'The Kingdom of God thus transcends the Church and constantly calls it to repentance and renewal. There is a critical dialectic between the Kingdom and the Church that cannot be resolved this side of eternity and by any other power than the power of the Kingdom itself.'[2]

Thus, the presence of God and the dynamic vitality of his kingdom life in awakening will call the end-time church into a deep place of changed hearts and endowment with his power.

Divine overshadowing will truly change the lives of the people of God, as we point to the greatness of his coming kingdom.

Pause for Thought

- When and where have I most encountered the reality of God's presence?
- What would a divine visitation look like in my nation?

Presence in the Midst of Struggle

One beautiful aspect of the increase in God's numinous presence that we should expect to see will be the counterbalance of his glorious presence in the midst of struggle and difficulty. As we read in Isaiah:

> For this is what the high and exalted One says –
>   he who lives forever, whose name is holy:
> 'I live in a high and holy place,
>   but also with the one who is contrite and lowly in spirit,
> to revive the spirit of the lowly
>   and to revive the heart of the contrite.'
>
> Isa. 57:15

God's heart is especially drawn to his people in humble and difficult situations; he brings glory in the midst of brokenness. Christian agencies working alongside the persecuted church in various parts of the world have often commented how, in the midst of hostility, war, and antagonism towards faith, the joy of the Lord has been remarkably present in his church. We know from Scripture that if we are suffering for being a Christian, 'the Spirit of glory and of God' can rest on us (1 Pet. 4:14). As more global troubles affect nations and communities, I believe the powerful reality of the praise and joy of God's people will mingle with the tears and pain of their context, and his dwelling in our midst will bring outbreaks of healing and salvation, profoundly convicting unbelievers around us.

Canon Andrew White, after years of working for reconciliation in the Middle East, became the vicar of St George's Church in Baghdad, Iraq, at the height of the 2003 war and in the aftermath of conflict in that nation. He pastored a church which was both congregation, medical centre, and reconciliation and relief agency. His community saw much suffering, but also experienced amazing ways in which God's presence was very real to them. He writes about it in this way:

> Here in the heat of the fire, I have experienced God's presence to an altogether different magnitude. It seems to me that the more dire the situation we find ourselves in, the more God is willing to manifest His presence. He reveals Himself to us in such a way that His presence overwhelms and diminishes our present troubles. All of our people at St George's testify to this. In our main services every Friday and Sunday, we always have a time when I ask people to tell me what has happened to them over the past week. As they share their stories I regularly hear two things: one is how they or their loved ones have been affected by the violence, and the other is the glorious ways in which God has intervened in their lives. These stories are always deeply moving. They tell tale after tale of the manifestation of the glory of God.[3]

Why will God allow such signs of his dwelling in our midst in the end times? As well as empowering and renewing his people, as well as creating a sense of awe among communities that God is real, and as well as his presence vindicating and overshadowing his beloved people under pressure, there is, I believe, one more reason. It is because the Lord wants to bring a global foretaste of what will happen in the greatest manifestation of his presence as Jesus returns in glory. Isaiah 59 speaks of the build-up of a worldwide awareness of God's glory in an end-times scenario:

> From the west, people will fear the name of the LORD,
>   and from the rising of the sun, they will revere his glory.
> For he will come like a pent-up flood
>   that the breath of the LORD drives along.
>
> Isa. 59:19

There may well be a growing momentum of the experienced presence of the Spirit all over the world in the years preceding the second coming of Christ. Perhaps the best way of saying it is that the atmosphere will become more spiritually charged, the breath of the Lord driving the transformation of the church as his bride and opening the eyes of millions to him for salvation, and angelic activity being witnessed across the earth, ahead of Jesus' glorious coming on the clouds. The numinous presence of the Lord felt by humanity will grow in intensity in the coming decades, and it will be awesome to behold.

Pause for Thought

- If God's Spirit rests on Christians in the midst of struggle, who might I want to pray for today to know his glorious presence?

10

Second Mark: Devoted in Love for the Lord and for Each Other (the Fervent Community)

Fervency

The transforming work of the Spirit in the early Christians marked them immediately with two characteristics: they became radically devoted to the Lord, and radically devoted to each other. What Jesus had modelled to his disciples, and what they had so spectacularly failed to copy, actually became a hallmark of their lives after Pentecost – namely great love. In Acts we see devotion to the Lord – demonstrations of deep worship and prayer, and the community of faith submitting to God's word and taking on kingdom habits and a lifestyle that honoured him (2:42–43). We also see their devotion to each other – expressions of genuine fellowship, of sacrificial giving to help their Christian brothers and sisters, and of great togetherness in the community where they held fast to each other through times of growth and testing (4:32–34). In short, we see remarkable love and devotion in the early church.

'Fervency' is an old word, conveying the idea of an enthusiastic, glowing spirit. I have at times enjoyed Christian fellowship of such fervency that I felt I was part of something truly alive. I have seen this especially in missionary training camps and discipleship schools I have visited, where people have given up everything to serve the Lord and have been forged together in deep bonds of love. Hot, burning, fervent devotion can really mark the Christian life.

The Lord is inviting us in the last days to become people marked by radical devotion. Mere adherence to institutions and attendance at meetings will not be enough for many Christians. Their spiritual desire will push aside mere religious duty, transforming it into a fervency of faith, love and obedience to the Lord. It has been said that today God is restoring the great commandments into their rightful place in his body: loving God with all our heart, soul, mind and strength, and loving our neighbour as ourselves. Just as the Great Commission's task of mission will be fully attended to, so the great commandments will be embodied in a wholehearted way in the end-time church globally.

Radical Devotion

The world knows what radical extremism looks like, faced as it is with the distorted worldviews and zealous hatred that come from religious fundamentalism. However, the world will watch in amazement as the church starts to move more publicly in the opposite spirit, that of a radical devotion to God which is peaceful yet ascetic, fervent yet pure, culture-denying yet loving. It will look so different from a religious spirit as to be a threat to society's ways of marginalizing religious groups, and yet it will also be magnetically attractive to masses of people looking for authentic spirituality, for something to give their lives to.

The end-time body of believers will, I believe, embody the mysterious 144,000 in Revelation chapter 14 who 'follow the

Lamb wherever he goes' (14:4). There will be a spirit of holy abandonment to the purposes of God in the coming hour, whereby Christians will go to the gutters of their cities or to the ends of the earth to serve and obey the Lord. A passion for Jesus will be all-consuming, and reverence for the word of God – in Scripture and in modern prophecy – will be unprecedented. The battle to overcome compromise with the world's values or spiritual dullness will be a fierce one, but many will choose this higher path of full devotion to Jesus, whatever the cost. A kind of spiritual lovesickness may well overcome the church as we pour out our hearts and lives to the Lord, longing for his likeness in us and praying for his return to us.

If end-time prophetic passages of Scripture are to be trusted, believers in the last days will also be endowed with the spirit of Malachi chapter 4, where the prophet says that God 'will turn the hearts of the parents to their children, and the hearts of the children to their parents' (4:6) before the coming of the 'dreadful day of the LORD' (v. 5). This speaks of an intergenerational move of God in which deep relationships of love become the mark of congregations and across streams, and generations walk together through spiritual awakening. Even in the context of apostasy and a falling away of faith in coming years, believers will be drawn into expressions of fellowship and common discipleship which will be incredibly strong and healing. God does not want us to put up with inherited generational or denominational divides in the church any more. Walls will come down; the church in each city will be far more important than any one congregation. As the testing of faith increases, young and old will bless, worship and care for each other. Much dysfunction in broken families will be dealt with at the foot of the cross; deep healing of relationships will be commonplace; heartfelt repentance for abuse in the church by perpetrator to victim will be offered and received. New definitions of Christian fellowship will have to be invented, as the move of the Spirit restores fractured relationships across the body of Christ at many levels. Even the breaking of institutional fellowship over heresy or apostasy, which will undoubtedly occur, may well be unable to destroy a deep love for fellow believers who are walking a different path.

God the Father is preparing a family to be with him forever, and he is determined not to have a household of faith that is ready to meet Jesus yet is still squabbling, barely tolerant of other Christians, and prejudiced towards many. Jesus' prayer in the upper room will be answered before he returns: 'I have given them the glory that you gave me, that they may be one as we are one – I in them and you in me – so that they may be brought to complete unity. Then the world will know that you sent me and have loved them even as you have loved me' (John 17:22–23). The overwhelming love of God in Christ will work its way deeply into the heart of the global church family, and he will melt us and reconcile us to each other in a remarkable way. What a church to be part of and identified with, one marked by passion for Jesus and love for the saints!

To give an example of what is possible for a church modelling devotion to Jesus and to others, I would point to a church in an Argentinian prison. Olmos Prison, just south of Buenos Aires, is a maximum-security facility that for years was notorious for lawlessness, Satanism and mafia-run gangs. In 1985 a Christian pastor, Juan Zuccarelli, became a guard there and began holding evangelistic meetings, and subsequently started a church in the prison. Today, around 60% of the prisoners are born-again believers, and the reoffending rate on release is less than 5%. As retold by Rick Heeren in *Marketplace Miracles*, the next step was even more remarkable:

The governor asked Juan if he would be willing to operate a completely Christian prison. Juan agreed. The governor turned over Prison Number 25 to Juan and suggested that Juan rename it 'Christ the Only Hope Prison.' This would be a low-security prison, with a Christian warden, Christian guards and Christian inmates. The inmates would not have bars on the doors of their sleeping quarters, and they would have great freedom to move around the prisons. Their days would be filled with Bible study, worship and prayer. They would also participate in career-development training and would have access to hand tools that would never have otherwise been allowed in a maximum-security prison.[1]

In Christ the Only Hope Prison, inmate believers form prayer chains, praying and fasting for seventy-two hours at a time. They adhere to spiritual disciplines of fellowship and discipleship, donating food and clothing into a food bank for others in need, and living as a spiritual family. This church, made up of both prisoners and guards, is found in the most unlikely place.

Pause for Thought

- What would fervent love and unity look like among the churches in my town or city?

A Renewal of Holiness and Unity

God is reforming his church in these days, whether in a prison, a wealthy neighbourhood or a tribal village. There are multiple ways in which the Lord will transform us by his love in the end times, and so many levels at which it will touch and change the church. Here I mention two to illustrate what the Lord will do.

One is that God is going to release us into greater levels of purity and holiness in our pursuit of him. In 2 Timothy 2:20–21 we read: 'In a large house there are articles not only of gold and silver, but also of wood and clay; some are for special purposes and some for common use. Those who cleanse themselves from the latter will be instruments for special purposes, made holy, useful to the Master and prepared to do any good work.' So often, Christians hold back from wholehearted service to the Lord because of besetting sin and hidden wounds which we feel disqualify us for his use.

A friend of ours, Julie Brown, who has a prayer and teaching ministry in the UK, had a profound life-changing vision when attending a conference we held at the Beacon House of Prayer in Stoke-on-Trent. She saw Jesus coming to kneel at her feet, with a golden crown on his head, and then placing a heavy mantle around her shoulders. It was a mantle of purity, made of silver-coloured fabric about an inch thick, tied around her neck and reaching down to her feet. In this vision, Julie felt the absolute purity of Jesus infusing her being, like a river that washed away any defilement and scars. She wrote a book reflecting on this experience as a picture for the whole body of Christ today, and said the following:

> In times like these there is more pressure than ever before, bringing temptation and the opportunity to compromise into our lives. Daily we are bombarded with sights and sounds that defile us and through lack of power to live a holy life, the bar wavers to the extent that the Body of Christ is no longer certain how much freedom we can expect to have. We may even wonder what holiness is.
>
> The truth for this hour is that Jesus is raising that bar to its ultimate level as He releases His purity into our lives to the extent

that we are not only free but we can ascend and rule over all the defilement that the enemy sends against us!²

It is wonderful to consider the kindness of the Lord. Can you imagine how he is going to infuse the church with such a level of purity and wholeness that it will liberate his people to give themselves wholly to his kingdom purposes, without the baggage that holds many back from full devotion?

The other aspect to mention is a measure of organic unity which the Lord will bring into his church, across streams and denominations. We can see this at a local level, with city unity, prayer and mission movements now vibrant and even commonplace in the UK. We can see this at an international level, with the search for ways of embodying visible unity prominent in discussions, concords and renewed fellowship between Protestant, Catholic and Orthodox streams. We can even see this in the level of reconciliation between Jews and Gentiles, the natural and grafted-in olive branches. Messianic Jewish believers and Arab believers are finding new ways of standing together, particularly in the Middle East. I have personally witnessed gatherings of Christians, both Jewish and Arab, praying together for 'highways' of worship, mission and unity to be established (as in Isa. 19:23–25) and standing together as the one body of Christ to contend for the fullness of his purposes to be released across the Middle East in these end times.

Peter Hocken, from the Catholic charismatic renewal tradition, argues powerfully for the unity which will come through the fullness of renewal in the generation before the Lord returns:

> The completion of all things requires that the church as the body of Christ embodies the full witness of the Holy Spirit to Jesus, so that the distinctive witness of every church and tradition finds its place in the one body. The Lord is coming for his bride. Without

the work of the Holy Spirit in every tradition the bride is not prepared. She is only half clothed . . . We can say that the adornment of the bride includes the full work of the Spirit: in theological heritage, in worship, in lived communion, and above all in the lives of the martyrs and the most holy witnesses to Jesus. The Pentecostal-charismatic outpouring of the Spirit has to be important for this preparation, precisely because it is awakening living faith and hope across almost the whole Christian spectrum.[3]

What this will look like no one knows, except that the devotion to Jesus among believers who differ in some doctrinal issues will be so strong as to overcome antipathy and bring a oneness around the cross. Passion for Jesus and his kingdom, I believe, will draw Christians together who might differ on 'hot potato' issues of gender or politics. The pressure of end-time shaking and antagonism towards the church will force deep fellowship, and create a culture of a band of brothers and sisters who will stick together and fight for each other. The vibrant awareness of Jesus' near return in the years of Tribulation will bring a collective standing together, with people bound to each other in love and courage for the faith once delivered to the saints, as rampant persecution of believers increases.

Soberly, Scripture indicates that this unity and love will be a feature of the end time in spite of a great falling away from faith, and a splitting of the church into branches of nominalist Christians and those wholly devoted to God. Not all in the body will come into a place of holy purity and organic unity. Yet this radical devotion to the Lord and to other believers – honouring the work of God in each other and in every Christian tradition that truly is sold out for Jesus – will mark the emerging end-time church so clearly as his bride. God is calling us to stand together shoulder to shoulder as his people. The end-time overcoming of the church will not be an individual journey but a corporate reality. We will come through the Tribulation time together, walking side by side, in a multifaceted unity, with a great passion for Jesus and deep love for the saints. What a wonderful work of God in the church to praise him for!

Pause for Thought

- How does this lead me to pray about my fervency of faith in Jesus, and my fervent love for other believers?

11

Third Mark: Spreading the Gospel in Word and Spirit (the Anointed Community)

Impacting Evangelism

A simple reading of the book of Acts leaves one breathless with the pace of the early church's missionary expansion. Its dynamite nature of witnessing to Jesus in the power of the Spirit marks every chapter. Starting from Jerusalem, the very place of Jesus' execution, and amid ongoing hostility to his followers, the first Christians found themselves thrust out of the upper room by the Holy Spirit, anointed with power and sharing the gospel at every opportunity. Their prayer strategy seemed to be to ask for boldness to proclaim Jesus and then for the Spirit to back up the message with signs and wonders (Acts 4:29–30). And the marks of their preaching often followed this pattern: a sudden conviction of sin and revelation of the need for Jesus among their hearers (2:37–41); the power of the Spirit falling on new believers (10:44–46); and the sharing of the gospel, either preceded by or accompanied by signs of healing and demonic deliverance (8:5–7). The early church's mission was clearly a mission of both word and Spirit.

God is inviting us in the last days into a dynamic experience of Holy Spirit-anointed evangelism that impacts communities in every nation and on every continent. The church today is growing fastest around the world in places of trouble or hostility, where the gospel of Jesus is shared in new places and twinned with the expectation of miracles, healing and answered prayer that reveals the power and mercy of the Lord.

In the West we often forget that other parts of the church live in a different dynamic, because we are inheritors of a relatively powerless and failing religious tradition. Our sharing of the gospel has been wedded to a rational defence of the gospel, of mental assent to religious truth. Our church-growth strategies have been embedded in a model of Christendom where our expectation is for the surrounding culture and communities to be nominally baptized into the life of the state church, and where we assume that people instinctively know the tenets of the Christian faith which have underpinned our morality. These assumptions are no longer true. Within two generations, suddenly the rug has been pulled from under our feet in the western church. A secularized, post-Christian society has gradually and conveniently marginalized the church and our witness. Most Christians feel timid, slightly irrelevant, and generally unheard when sharing the gospel in the public sphere, and out of kilter with now-dominant cultural values.

Yet convictions and boldness are starting to return to the church in this stripped-down and newly vulnerable position. Even the barren wastelands of Europe have been tilled over by prayer in recent decades to become ripe harvest fields, and this exiled church is beginning to return to an experience of renewal and confidence in the gospel, and starting to move out in bold witness and mission.

I remember joining the mission staff of a Methodist Bible college in the Peak District of England in the late 1980s. We would lead teams of students into various towns across the country, partnering with churches in sharing the gospel in their communities. The mission staff had been recently influenced by the 'signs and wonders' conferences led by American speaker John Wimber. It was a scary yet exciting time to join the team, as we added healing services and ministering in words of knowledge to traditional forms of preaching the gospel. Particularly at young people's events we began to see the power of Jesus in deliverance and healing, and the Spirit resting on people, often leading them to salvation.

We need the anointing of the Spirit for evangelism like never before. This can never be functional, a mere discharging of our duty to share the gospel. It has to start in the place of renewal – to flow from the Spirit's empowering of our inner faith and life. Bill Johnson, pastor of Bethel Church in Redding, California, and one of the leaders of the current charismatic renewal, writes about the anointing of the Spirit for mission:

> The more profound the work of the Spirit is within us, the more profound the manifestation of the Spirit flowing through us. That in essence is the purpose behind the promise found in Ephesians 3:20: 'Now to Him who is able to do far more abundantly beyond all that we ask or think, *according to the power that works within us*' (emphasis added). Notice that what goes on around us is according to what goes on inside us. That qualifier is all too often overlooked. This power enables us to present Jesus to others in a way that meets every human need. This lifestyle thrives on the impossible. Our delight is seeing the impossibilities of life bend their knee to the name of Jesus over and over again. Those who

encounter Him on this level are much more prone to take risks so that miracles would happen.[1]

Pause for Thought

- Does my church share the gospel out of duty, or from an overflow place of renewed life in the Spirit?

Word and Spirit Together

Paul speaks about the early church's full proclamation of the gospel to the Roman world in these words: 'I will not venture to speak of anything except what Christ has accomplished through me in leading the Gentiles to obey God by what I have said and done – by the power of signs and wonders, through the power of the Spirit of God' (Rom. 15:18–19). I fully believe that the end-time church on every continent will move out through the nations with a gospel of both word and Spirit – an anointing to share Jesus in the power of the Spirit again. This truly last-days revival will be the global outpouring of the Holy Spirit mentioned in Joel 2:28–32 in which all people, *all*, will prophesy. An anointed, prophetic, multigenerational church on fire for Jesus will bring in a final harvest. This has been prophesied by many godly Christians in recent years. I mention in particular the famous prophecy given by the English healing evangelist Smith Wigglesworth in 1947. Shortly before he died, he received a vision in which he saw future moves of the Holy Spirit. The final part of the vision was a coming together of those with an emphasis on the word and those with an emphasis on the Spirit. He prophesied that:

> When the Word and the Spirit come together, there will be the biggest movement of the Holy Spirit that the nation, and indeed the world, has ever seen. It will mark the beginning of a revival that will eclipse anything that has been witnessed within these shores, even the Wesleyan and the Welsh revivals of former years. The outpouring of God's Spirit will flow over from the UK to the mainland of Europe, and from there will begin a missionary move to the ends of the earth . . . the last day revival that's going to usher in the precious fruit of the earth. It will be the greatest revival this world has ever seen! It's going to be a wave of the gifts of the Spirit. The ministry gifts will be flowing on this planet earth.[2]

This strong hope for a coming together of word and Spirit has been taken up by other parts of the church. Mission organizations are expectant that God will release a new surge of energy and motivation for the hoped-for completion of the Great Commission throughout the world. If the church in the majority world has been caricatured for being too charismatic-heavy and discipleship-light (a mile wide yet an inch thick), and the church in the western world has been pitied for being theologically sound yet powerless (dusty and dry), then an explosive combination of both word and Spirit – gospel teaching with anointing for signs and wonders – is about to bring the church together across the globe in the fulfilment of Joel 2. The current shaking that people are experiencing around the world may well be the catalyst that opens hearts up to the gospel of hope found only in Jesus. The current drought of revival in much of the church will soon give way to successive outpourings of the Spirit upon his body. We are 'on the cusp', as it were, of this last great move of God to equip the church to bring in the final harvest with signs and miracles before a watching world. How incredible is that!

Sometimes we think we are so far from this end-time anointed reality. Can God really revive his people in these days? Yes, I truly believe it. During a time of prayer recently, I was given a vision of Jesus holding a limp and weary person in his arms; she looked sick and close to death. I felt the person represented the church. Jesus was kissing her, massaging her body, and coaxing her back to full health and strength. As she revived and stood on her feet, this once-weary person became strong and ready to walk with him more eagerly. A sickly pallor was leaving her complexion as she stood in the warmth of the Son's love and the brightness of his life. Isn't that a true depiction of many weary saints? God wants to renew us in faith and power. In such a place of renewal, new mandates for mission can come to those who would hear; new clarity about destiny and vision can be instilled in our spirits. A greatly revived church can let go of protectionist and insular lifestyles, and freshly embrace the Lord and his ways. God's people can become more relevant for heaven's purposes. We forget how Jesus sees us in our weakness: he is relentless in his intent to bring us into fullness of life. He will have a church fully alive and relevant for his kingdom purposes in these last days.

A Global Anointing of Jesus the Evangelist

To use a different biblical analogy, God will bring his people through a wilderness time of testing into a fresh anointing for mission and ministry. As Jesus emerged from desert prayer and temptation in the power of the Spirit, he took hold of the Isaiah 61 messianic prophecy. Luke describes this in Luke 4:18, where Jesus assumed the mantle of the anointed evangelist to preach, heal, deliver, and declare the year of God's favour. The key to the path to his power was in his forty-day fasting and testing in the desert.

It is amazing how many calls to extended seasons of prayer and fasting for revival there have been in recent years. At some point soon, there is coming a tipping point where the Lord releases a fuller end-time measure of power to enable us to walk in Jesus' anointing for gospel preaching and ministry. It will certainly be linked to the power of deep prayer and fasting. Lou Engle, who has called young Christian people around the world to prayer, calls such a vision of the church today 'living in the anointing of Jesus the Evangelist'. He says: 'The church worldwide is entering a time of global reenactment of Jesus' extended fasting for a global Jesus harvest. The ancient tools of intercession are being uncovered and the spiritually violent are taking the kingdom by force.'[3]

Perhaps God has reserved a great anointing of his Spirit that only comes through deep prayer and trust forged in such a wilderness place. Undergirded by the fires of night-and-day prayer, and refined in the dryness of the desert where not much has bloomed and our faith has been stretched, the end-time church will emerge. She will carry the gospel physically and digitally to every unreached people-group and every town and city across the world, bringing what some believe may be a billion-soul harvest within the next generation.

John writes of a vision in Revelation 14 concerning this last great harvest in the Tribulation times: 'Then another angel came out of the temple and called in a loud voice to him who was sitting on the cloud, "Take your sickle and reap, because the time to reap has come, for the harvest of the earth is ripe." So he who was seated on the cloud swung his sickle over the earth, and the earth was harvested' (Rev. 14:15–16). The sense of gospel urgency, which has been borne mainly by the evangelists in the church and the cross-cultural missionaries sent out on behalf of the rest of us, will be shared by the whole church of Jesus, for the first time since the days of the early church. Maybe the gift of the Pentecostal movement, such a major missionary force in the last hundred years, to the body of Christ in these days will be that sense of urgency: a sharp awareness of the imminent full realization of the kingdom of God and our vital mission leading towards that day. The anointing of the Spirit for mission has an end-time goal in sight. As Pentecostal theologian Kenneth Archer argues from Stephen Land's work on Pentecostal spirituality: 'The impetus for the pouring out of the Holy Spirit is fuelled by a passion for the full realisation of the Kingdom of God. Jesus the King is soon coming! The outpouring of the Holy Spirit constitutes the Church as a missionary fellowship which is caught up into the trinitarian mission of God.'[4]

A key component in this end-time mission will be the Jewish people receiving their Messiah. The apostle Paul wrote about the mystery of God's plan for the chosen people in the book of Romans: 'I do not want you to be ignorant of this mystery, brothers and sisters, so that you may not be conceited: Israel has experienced a hardening in part until the full number of the Gentiles has come in, and in this way all Israel will be saved' (Rom. 11:25–26). The harvest in the nations and the harvest among the Jews are intrinsically linked in God's timing, according to Paul. There is already a turning to faith among some Jewish people, forming Messianic congregations across the world. As the spiritual harvest to the ends of the earth peaks in Tribulation years, many people believe that will be the moment when the Jews receive a great revelation of Jesus as their Messiah. The end-time church will be filled with God's great love and passion for the Jewish people and his desire that they should come into their spiritual inheritance, and this will help to prepare the church to stand with them in the midst of last-days troubles.

Pause for Thought

- How can I make my prayers more focused on world mission and evangelization?

Going Where He Sends Us

What will the church sharing the gospel in word and power look like in the midst of trouble and shaking? It will surely look like millions of ordinary Christians standing up for Jesus with great conviction in the power of the gospel, and going where he tells them to go, trusting he will accompany them with the power of God. This will be met by the questions and confusion that many in the world around feel as the global turmoil and shaking increase, and the Holy Spirit will use believers to lead countless people to faith in Christ in the urgency of the days.

Arthur Blessitt, the famous American cross-carrying preacher, tells a story of walking through South Africa in 1986, in the midst of the civil war before the end of apartheid. He felt led to undertake a twenty-one-day fast, seven days each in Johannesburg, Cape Town and Durban. He and his team stayed in central parks day and night, standing by the large cross and sharing and praying with people in pain because of what was happening in their country. Unusually for Arthur's ministry, they saw numerous miracles of healing in those three weeks as the power of the Spirit moved through the parks. He wrote in his journal:

> Crowds, crowds, crowds swarmed the park as the miraculous power of God was manifest. During these twenty-one days of fasting and prayer, we saw hundreds of people healed and thousands of people pray to receive Jesus as Savior. As huge crowds gathered, I shouted out for those wanting to accept Christ to gather in one group and those needing healing to gather in another group. We had teams sharing the gospel and following up with new converts, and we had other people praying for the sick. It was amazing![5]

Great pain and turmoil led to great opportunities for evangelism. There are certain critical and opportune (the literal meaning of *kairos* in New Testament Greek) moments when people are very open, creating a window of opportunity where God can touch hearts and change the human spirit. These will increase in coming years. There will be a growing confidence in churches across the world as the atmosphere of every culture shifts under the weight of intercessory prayer, and spiritually hungry, open people rush from shaking conditions into the arms of God, as the simple message of Jesus is preached with miracles accompanying.

Standing for Gospel Truth

Spreading the gospel in the anointing of God's Spirit will also include standing for gospel truth in these last days. Teaching and sharing biblical truth will be a great challenge in the swirling currents of cultural ideologies and the enticing sweet-shops of pick-and-mix spirituality surrounding us. The apostle Paul believed the last days were imminent and wrote to his son in the faith, Timothy, to encourage him in standing for truth. His call to preach the word, and to correct, rebuke and encourage others, carefully and patiently, was given because of the temptations all around to reject sound doctrine. He wrote a charge to Timothy that resounds to us today: 'They will turn their ears away from the truth and turn aside to myths. But you, keep your head in all situations, endure hardship, do the work of an evangelist, discharge all the duties of your ministry' (2 Tim. 4:4–5).

Alexander Solzhenitsyn was a famous Russian author and moralist who wrote the masterful tome *The Gulag Archipelago* about the Stalinist oppression of people in forced labour camps between 1958 and 1968. Solzhenitsyn himself was a political prisoner in the camps, and his memoirs and interviews with inmates make harrowing reading, revealing a state system of terror and brutality against dissidents of the Soviet regime. On fleeing to the West in the 1970s, Solzhenitsyn spoke extensively about Communism and the West's moral responsibility, about truth and freedoms, and about the existential struggle against evil. He was once asked about the aim of his writing, and responded thus: 'The artist cannot set himself political aims, the aims of changing a political regime; it may come as a by-product of it, but to fight against untruth and falsehood, to fight against myths, or to fight against an ideology which is hostile to mankind, to fight for our memory, for our memory of what things were like – that is the task of the artist.'[6]

To fight against untruth. In the coming years, it will be a challenge to continue proclaiming gospel truth about Jesus, the way, truth and life, amid deception and temptation. Standing for biblical morality will be unpopular in a wayward culture, and yet the brightness of our lives will be incredibly attractive.

To call people to repentance and a lifestyle that honours Christ will be like mounting a spiritual resistance movement. There is sometimes a kind of charismatic fantasy when people talk about the last-days revival – as though everyone will turn to Christ, and every country's population will receive the gospel en masse. That doesn't seem likely, judging from end-time scriptures. The anointed church that God is preparing will be at most a hugely significant minority, a Christ-honouring spiritual resistance movement.

Through many tough years to come, God's people will learn to be steadfast in holding to gospel truth. Like the early church, they will not bow the knee to any modern-day Caesar – to humanistic ideologies, to nationalism, to materialism; to culturally acceptable watered-down religion, to radical extremism, or to the new 'woke' orthodoxy. How much it is in the Father's heart for his people to bear a faithful witness to the gospel in a confused and darkening world!

It is from a culturally controversial place that we offer the hope of Jesus. Standing by the cross of Christ, the church will call millions into the kingdom. God will use us to challenge a globally wayward society with the righteousness of Jesus' ways. We will stand in solidarity with others against social injustice, and yet we will not compromise the gospel or our decision to give our all for it.

Yes, there will be opportunities to disciple nations and communities in the ways of the Lord in the early heady days of the coming great revival. There will be a profound work of God in many societies, even as the darkness of the last days increases. Yet, as the Antichrist empire begins to form, everything we have believed in and stood for will be tested. And in that day, as Isaiah 60:1 foresees, we will come forth shining like an overcoming bride when the glory of God rises on us. We will need the anointing of God in great measure in order to walk in word and Spirit, shining forth the gospel, holding on to biblical truth and winning lives to him, as life becomes intense on planet earth.

Pause for Thought

- Am I convinced enough of the truth of the Christian gospel to stand for it at all costs?

12

Fourth Mark: Expressing God's Heart for the Poor and Broken (the Outpoured Community)

Outpouring of Love

The life of the early church in Acts was marked by an emphasis on caring for the poor and the broken in society. It was said of the church in Jerusalem that 'God's grace was so powerfully at work in them all that there was no needy person among them' (Acts 4:33–34). Properties were sold to help anyone facing financial hardship, a system for the distribution of food to those in want was instituted, individual Christians were praised for their care for the poor, and churches took collections of money to send to disadvantaged churches (4:34–35; 6:1; 9:36; 11:29–30). The first generation of Christians set a high bar for showing God's extravagant love in practical ways, not only for their own people but for any in need. They lived out Jesus' teaching to serve others, and to serve Jesus through caring for the least in society – the forgotten ones.

The Lord is inviting us in the last days to be broken by his compassionate heart and bring waves of extraordinary service into our communities. The church through the years has always endeavoured to live out the gospel through loving service to the poor, either as part of its official mission or through individuals inspired by God's love. Whatever the faults or excesses of the church in a particular generation, ministering to the poor in Christ's love has always been a feature of her life. Whether through monastic orders, or cross-cultural mission endeavours, through opening schools, founding hospitals, or leading community projects and social action among the most marginalized, this is the most authentic hallmark of the Christian gospel throughout history.

I believe that in these last days, a key element of the revival move of God will be an outpouring of love to those most in need. The end-time community of the Spirit will express God's compassion in radical ways among the nations of the world. We can already see this emerging where the church is growing most rapidly within the poor communities of the majority world. God has been growing dynamic expressions of church in such diverse places as the favelas of Brazil, the rubbish dumps of Egypt, the factories full of child labourers in North India, the refugee camps of war-torn Sudan and the orphanages of Mozambique.

One of the most profound communities I have observed is the Hang Fook camp in Hong Kong, led by Jackie Pullinger. In the late 1980s I went to Hong Kong as a western tourist to work for a month in a Christian mission base. I visited the Walled City, joined the community a handful of times in acts of worship and met some residents of a halfway house. The eclectic group of believers was made up of many former drug addicts and prostitutes, people with broken lives that had been turned around by Jesus. It was greatly moving to see how this community was formed around the poorest and most forgotten of people. Jackie Pullinger, famous for her best-selling book *Chasing the Dragon*,[1] has been very honest about the successes and setbacks, the joys and sorrows, of ministering among the poor. As she reflected on her life in Hong Kong, she wrote:

> If you've never been broken, sorrowful and weak, you'll only have good advice to give. But, if you've not been comforted when you were wretched; if you've known insults attacking you and known what it is to be rejected by those you love; if you've known what it is like when you needed their help and they did not give it; if you've known what it is to be bereft and to have nothing and no-one but Christ Jesus for comfort – then how rich you are! Then you have something to offer those who are poor like you were. Nobody else can do that. That's why only when you've tasted those depths, will you be able to minister to those in the depths. Count it as a privilege, because it is . . . Ministry must be helping what is needed at the moment.[2]

No wonder Jesus said at the start of the Sermon on the Mount: 'Blessed are the poor in spirit, for theirs is the kingdom of heaven' (Matt. 5:3).

Compassion That Reveals the Heart of God

In this coming end-time revival, the compassion of God shown through his people will not be different from in the past, but I believe the effects will be magnified. God will anoint churches and believers to minister to social needs or respond to crises in ways that are beyond the ability of a local community or city to provide. In the midst of shaking, there will often be Christian demonstrations of mercy, for God 'relents from sending calamity' (Joel 2:13–14). Churches will find themselves to be distributors of heavenly blessing and resource to needy communities.

This too is part of a revival anointing. Some Old Testament prophetic pictures of Holy Spirit outpourings have an element of bountiful supply and blessing: his people feeding on the wealth of nations (Isa. 61:6), and threshing floors filled with grain (Joel 2:24). These things speak of the abundance of God's gracious resourcing under the anointing of the Spirit. In and of themselves, they will make the church attractive, even as it may hold a conservative moral line that is out of tune with the surrounding culture.

Humble love will necessarily accompany the church's mission of the gospel in word and Spirit. God is putting his church on display in these last days, and it will be seen shining, not just through preaching and miracles, but also through his grace in our radical humility. When the church is on the edges and ministering in the margins of society, then she is most authentically speaking to the world. This is what Jesus means when he says: 'By this everyone will know that you are my disciples, if you love one another' (John 13:35).

Jesus' presence is often found among the poor, the 'least of these' (Matt. 25:40); and the lower we get in humble service, the more of him both we and the world will see. Guy Chevreau, author and teacher, writes about his experience of being deeply challenged while visiting growing churches in Africa as a western pastor. Their context of poverty and dependence on the Spirit seemed to him to mark communities of faith with a deep humility, which led to God's outpoured blessings. In reflecting on this and the words in Scripture: 'Humble yourselves, therefore, under God's mighty hand, that he may lift you up in due time' (1 Pet. 5:6), Chevreau challenges the church in the West to learn from them the secret of humility and of bowing our knees before God:

As soon as we desire to yield, we can receive the gift of gravity and 'down we go'. I understand that this is good news, especially when I'm exhausted. I know it's good news for my friends in Africa, because so many of them know that they literally have no resources to contribute. Because they are so poor, so hungry, so weak and sick, because they are uneducated, and untrained, they have no 'strength' or 'might.' But they can humble themselves and they will wait on the Spirit. Then, in His strength and in His might, they rise with a power they know is not their own.[3]

Chevreau demonstrates that there is a release of the Spirit's grace that comes to those who yield everything to God in humility. Why then might God bring such an outpouring of grace in broken places through the end-time church? The theological reason is to reveal the heart of the Father to a very needy world, the One described by Paul as 'the Father of compassion and the God of all comfort' (2 Cor. 1:3). People may not be won to the gospel by grand arguments, but they will be softened by great love. If, in John's Gospel, the glory of God displayed in the face of Jesus was most clearly seen in his dwelling with people in their broken conditions – as the Word made flesh – and ultimately through his death, being lifted up on a cross (John 12:28–32), then God will be revealed to people around the world in their low places. I think God's delight in the last days will be to let his numinous glorious presence rest more in the places of poverty and weakness than in the places of wealth and power. God wants to let his Father's heart be seen in the most broken communities of the world.

Heidi and Roland Baker lead a network of churches and orphanages in Mozambique. They have lived through both disasters and revival and have become a model for others in pursuing sacrificial ministry in hard and dark places. In their orphanages, the Bakers have seen the Lord bring the most beautiful emotional healing to street children suffering from the wounds of the world, as they have received new life in Jesus. Heidi explains: 'After fourteen years of ministering to children in the streets and villages of Mozambique, I am beginning to understand more about the spirit of adoption. God is looking for spiritual fathers and mothers who know who they are in Him, who will go into the darkness, look for lost children (spiritual orphans) of all ages, and bring them home to the Father's house.'[4] I don't know what this will look like in different parts of the world and in different social contexts. Yet I know that, as troubles increase across the globe, as people's securities in wealth and comfort are stripped away, God will position his people within every community to humbly minister his heart and his love; the Father's house will be the only safe place of refuge for us to find. Millions of people who only knew God as a concept will have their hearts softened by his mercy and compassion, displayed through the church. This will be an intricate part of sharing the gospel in the end times.

Pause for Thought

- What are the Christian ministries that most reveal the Father's heart of love in my country?
- Can I support them in any way?

Disarming Principalities

There is another reason for God releasing extraordinary compassion through his church. It is this: serving others with love disarms the principalities and powers. Jesus taught his disciples that loving God and doing his will counteracts the devil's work against us: 'I will not say much more to you, for the prince of this world is coming. He has no hold over me, but he comes so that the world may learn that I love the Father and do exactly what my Father has commanded me' (John 14:30–31).

In the Tribulation there will be massive persecution of believers. We understand from Scripture the upside-down dynamics of the kingdom: we are called to forgive when hated, to turn the other cheek, to love our enemies. In the end times, as God's people are going to be ostracized and persecuted by the institutional powers of the world, what will we reveal of God's nature? God's desire is that we will reveal a love that transforms and ultimately overcomes the devil and evil. Our outpoured love will have to embrace our enemies and those who hate us for Christ's sake. This is what Paul's exhortation to the Romans means: 'Do not be overcome by evil, but overcome evil with good' (Rom. 12:21).

Theologian Walter Wink, in a powerful book about dealing with social injustice, war and violence, reminds us of the way and teaching of Jesus, which is to disarm principalities and powers through suffering love. Wink talks about how loving our enemy is another way of living in expectation of miracles:

> Loving our enemies may seem impossible, yet it can be done. At no point is the inrush of divine grace so immediately and concretely perceptible as in those moments when we let go of our hatred and relax into God's love. No miracle is so awesome, so necessary, and so frequent. Just when forgiveness seems impossible, the power of God is able to manifest itself most amazingly.[5]

It is a miracle that takes place in us, and yet it can also disarm and convict those who are persecuting us.

South African leader Nelson Mandela had lived for twenty-seven years in severe conditions as a political prisoner and symbol of the apartheid struggle in his nation. Within four years of his release he oversaw democratic elections and served as the first president of a united South Africa from 1994 to 1999. A profound image from those days was how Mandela used sport to help heal the nation. When the Rugby World Cup was hosted in Johannesburg in 1995, he attended the finals and decided to wear the jersey and cap of the predominantly white South African national team, the Springboks, to show that rugby could be a unifier and not a divider of the races. As he walked onto the pitch to greet the captain, the mostly white audience in the Ellis Park stadium started chanting Mandela's name. An old friend who had shared in the apartheid struggles, Tokyo Sexwale, spoke of that iconic scene: 'That was the moment when I understood more clearly than ever before that the liberation struggle was not so much about liberating blacks from bondage, it was about liberating white people from fear.'[6]

I am speaking of transforming not demonic powers but rather the people and institutions influenced by them. There are none more lost or broken than those trapped in a cycle of hatred or violence. The end-time church will brightly shine through Christians' radical compassionate love towards those who hate them, loving them in their broken state, and allowing God to convict them in that place, with the hope of opening their eyes to his love. Perfect love will drive out our fear of others, even if they oppose us and torment us. If the low place of serving the poor is a crucible of divine revelation, then how much more is the contraflow place of reconciliation and forgiving enemies?

In these coming years, let us expect an extraordinary measure of God's love and compassion to be released in our midst as his church, as he leads us to minister among the poor and broken. Through the prism of God's reign he will reveal his Father's heart and his potential to transform lives in the most difficult of places.

Pause for Thought

- What has God taught me about the power of forgiveness?
- Is there anyone I would like to pray for today?

13

Fifth Mark: Refined by Persecution and Falling Away (the Cruciform Community)

Cross-Shaped

The early Christians did not have life easy; Jesus did not leave them in an idyllic environment to grow and flourish. Rather, the members of the fledgling church had to learn to live and evangelize in a hostile situation. Their religious and political opponents were intent on snuffing out the life of this Jesus sect, but nothing could stop the work of God among them (Acts 4:18–20). Local persecution merely served to blow the seeds of the gospel out into the regions outside Israel (8:1–7). Church planting in the context of riots and antagonism actually forced rapid discipleship in young communities of believers (1 Thess. 1:6–8). In fact, for the first few generations of the church, state-sponsored discrimination and opposition to the Christian faith was their normal environment. Churches had to prepare believers to face imprisonment and even martyrdom; they had to deal with pastoral issues such as apostasy and situations where people who had denied Christ under pressure then wanted to return to the church. From this it is clear to see that trouble and persecution was the context for early Christian living. When Jesus said that anyone who wanted to follow him must take up their cross, he was being very serious. The life of the church is shaped in a cross, and I don't mean just the design of historic church buildings. We are marked by a willingness to count the cost of following Jesus; we are supposed to be cruciform in shape.

The Lord is inviting us in the last days to accept the privilege of taking up our cross and not giving up our faith despite fiery opposition. If there is one mark of the end-time church that Jesus prophesied about when teaching his disciples, it was that his followers would be severely tested and persecuted in the last days. He told them that, as the end-time birth pains began to increase, the church would be hated by all nations. Moreover, many nominal believers would turn away from faith, and Christians would betray other Christians, leading to persecution and martyrdom. In addition, confusion about truth would be rife, and people would be deceived by voices leading them astray from their faith. On top of all this, overt wickedness, either through the Antichrist regime or through a toxic atmosphere in nations opposed to true Christianity, would cause many people to back down from radical discipleship and passionate love for Jesus (see Matt. 24:9–14). These are sobering words indeed. As I have already noted, hatred, betrayal, deception and wickedness will test the life of the church and the faith of all believers.

Jesus clearly expected suffering for faith to be part of our discipleship. As he said: 'Whoever wants to be my disciple must deny themselves and take up their cross daily and follow me. For whoever wants to save their life will lose it, but whoever loses their life for me will save it' (Luke 9:23–24).

I have not been persecuted for my faith, although I know and have met Christians from other parts of the world who have paid a great price for following Jesus. The closest I have been to a hostile environment is when I smuggled Bibles into China for a week while living in Hong Kong years ago. I learned to pack bags with false bottoms, to make no eye contact with my colleagues as we travelled separately on public transport, and to go calmly through border checks and scanning machines, praying all the way, until we finally deposited our precious cargo in anonymous lockers for people in the underground church to pick up. I felt something tangible – a deep fellowship with secret and persecuted believers who are constantly watched, scrutinized and oppressed for their faith. And yet, in the 2020s in the West, I sense the same growing hostile environment around us, though in a more subtle way. Christians are being watched, scrutinized and quietly oppressed for any outspoken witness which doesn't fit with the cultural line.

Pause for Thought

- How would I describe the general attitude to Christian faith in my country?

The Brightness of the Church Contested

What sense can we make of persecution in the context of a great last-days revival? There are voices in the church today which speak clearly about an exciting coming era when the church will enjoy massive growth and influence in society. There are other voices which warn about coming deception and trouble for the church, suggesting that a more likely future scenario will be the existence of a Christian remnant or resistance movement. In a way, both predictions are probably true, and it will be a mixed picture. At some point soon, the increasing revelation of God's glory may cause a few years of tremendous renewal in the church and a great harvest across the nations. Yes, there will be opposition in the near future, but the Tribulation time may still be several years away. In some nations or regions, spiritual transformation will radically impact society and Christian influence will be prominent; in other places the dynamic life of the church will be more of an underground movement, subversive and highly attractive despite official opposition. Indeed, there is coming a time when Christians will be hated and loved in equal measure: hated by those who see them as a disturbance and threat to their way of life, loved by those who see them as reflecting the overwhelming love of God in the midst of need and trouble. One thing is clear: God wants to forge a resilient faith in the end-time church that will not be 'middle of the road' or lukewarm.

The writer to the Hebrews reminds his friends of the time 'when you endured in a great conflict full of suffering' (Heb. 10:32). This is a picture of what the end-time church will walk through. The devil will not allow the brightness of the church's shining to go uncontested. As the light of glory and faith increases, so will darkness increase – the overt darkness of radical religious extremism, and the subtle darkness of extreme liberalism towards traditional morality and a hope-denying erosion of truth. We may have thought we had seen and fought against the most strident ideologies in the form of Nazism and Communism; yet the spirit of radical Islam may well prove to be one of the church's biggest threats, as well as a fertile harvest field. We may have considered Neo-Darwinism and the theory of evolution to be a temporary philosophy, despite its infiltration into all sciences. Yet its forcefield, accompanied by other modern, secular forces, will continue to contradict all that Christianity stands for, even as the hopelessness intrinsic to its worldview causes an existential crisis for many. At some future point, the public tide of sympathy or interest in Christian faith will turn, most likely as a 'one world' system begins to emerge and demands people's allegiance. This will be the time when the church will be most tested, and yet will have the opportunity to shine most brightly. It is then that we may come closest to the vibrancy of the early church in our uncompromising witness to Jesus. And yet the testing will be very difficult.

The Refining of Our Faith

I think we kid ourselves if we think the end-time troubles will be anything less than chaotic and difficult. There will be splits in Christian communities, some tears, and rending across the church as the eddies of revival rivers surge, and the pressure of cultural conformity grows. Some will miss the boat, so to speak; parts of the church will move into nominalism and cultural accommodation while others press into more radical expressions of Christianity. The end-time church is being called onto the tight, bright path of discipleship which we see in the spirituality of Jesus' Sermon on the Mount, and that is a path that not all will choose. The blessing will be found in the middle of difficulty; the salt and the light will be costly to spread. There will be a sense of confusion as to how to stay true to Christ as the perceived threat of genuine lived-out Christianity increases. The cultural pressure from within the church, and within societies, to water down the gospel, and to be quiet about our beliefs and not be 'offensive' concerning them, will be intense. In those times, Jesus will encourage us, as he did the church in Smyrna: 'Be faithful, even to the point of death, and I will give you life as your victor's crown' (Rev. 2:10).

Matt Chandler in his book *Take Heart*, about finding the courage to be a Christian in today's age of unbelief, calls for a faith-filled perspective to the church's mission:

> Yes, these are hard days. And yes, they may get worse. Of course, I'm not saying that I want actual persecution and fierce suffering. I'm just saying that if we live through those days, they will not be unique for the church and they will not mean the defeat of the church. In fact, as we've said, in our age we're back in the place where the church thrives the most – on the margins, being seen as unique and weird.[1]

God always uses persecution that comes against the church to refine our faith. We should expect a great refining to occur in our lives through persecution and tribulations, which will strengthen our love and resolve to follow Christ whatever the cost. We don't know in the West what faith underground looks like. We haven't experienced what some of our brothers and sisters live with in countries where state-sanctioned discrimination against faith is encouraged, and even freedoms to move, trade and have a livelihood are withdrawn from those faithful to a Christian creed. We need to prepare ourselves now and pray that we will not buckle under pressure against our faith personally. I was in the prayer room in our house of prayer a few months ago, praying and listening to the Lord. In my mind I saw a vivid picture of Jesus holding a blood-red rose that was dying. Rather than throw it away, he took the rose and put it into the Calvary wound in his side. As he did so, the rose blossomed back to life again. It was such a strange picture that I pondered on it for a long time. I felt the Lord was saying that this is the church in my nation, the UK. In order to thrive we need to be freshly grafted into his wounded side. Life will blossom in amazing ways when we truly embrace the suffering of Christ, the life of the global persecuted church, and the blood of the martyrs down the ages.

The move from being casual believers to becoming radical disciples is already a move that others in the body of Christ have made. The term 'discipleship-making movements' (or DMMs) describes a major way in which the gospel is currently spreading in the hardest parts of the world. Christians in these regions are being tutored by the Spirit in how to come alongside unbelievers and bring them on a journey of faith exploration. The focus is on discipling groups of people who are learning to follow Jesus and obey his commands together. DMMs are indigenous and multiplying movements, fostering obedient disciples who then disciple others. The fastest-growing church in the world at the moment is in the Islamic Republic of Iran, with more people becoming Christian disciples in the last two decades than in the last 1,300 years. They are part of a powerfully subversive movement that is spreading to the neighbouring countries.

I sat at a meal table four years ago with one of the leaders of the underground church in Iran, as this remarkable man shared with me the cost of Christian faith and spoke about evangelism in his country. He told me that the mosques are nearly empty, and people are searching for spiritual truth. He described also how the persecution of the church becomes the very fuel for the spreading of the gospel. Christians rely completely on the Holy Spirit to lead them to people seeking faith, to show them where to meet, and to hide their movements from the secret police. This leader shared how many hundreds of his friends have been imprisoned or had to flee the country. Christians leaving their homes in the morning don't know if they will return or be arrested for their beliefs. Their faith is on the line every day, and yet he told me that the joy of being part of this move of God, of seeing miracles and faith spreading contagiously, is worth the cost.

We may all find ourselves in similar positions in the future. God will use such spiritually contested places to sharpen our faith and touch many lives. God will also allow shaking to test us and to align us with himself. The troubles that will increase in the coming years will test the genuineness of our faith and the depths of our roots in God's love. He is calling us now to strengthen our walk with him, to feed more deeply on his word, and to deal with any obstructions or compromises that would hinder our faith.

Pause for Thought

- When have you experienced conflict for being serious about your Christian beliefs?
- Has that trouble refined your faith?

Staying Close to Avoid Offence

One of the greatest temptations in the end times will be the potential for being offended by the Lord. Why? Because God's allowing of shaking and times of crisis around the world will trouble many believers. Christians have become so enamoured with a gospel of grace which has erased any sense of God's holiness or of bringing judgment in this world that many will feel offended at his supposed inaction against evil. There will be very real and public questions: Where is God in all the troubles? How could a God of love allow such shaking? In a world in which popular philosophy has divorced the issue of evil from the issue of sin, there are few reference points for revealing God's purposes in troubles and crises. Only those in the church who have learned to draw near to him, to understand his word in Scripture, and to come up higher to partner with him in prayer, will understand his ways and purposes.

Malachi 3 speaks of the day of God's coming, fulfilled in both Jesus' first and second comings. The context of that time, according to Malachi, is one of refining his people: 'But who can endure the day of his coming? Who can stand when he appears? For he will be like a refiner's fire or a launderer's soap. He will sit as a refiner and purifier of silver; he will purify the Levites and refine them like gold and silver' (Mal. 3:2–3). The coming revival will bring a refining and testing of our hearts. Will we yield our lives to God? Will we trust him to purify us in the midst of persecution and testing? Will we give glory to him in the midst of turmoil in the nations?

One encouraging picture in Revelation 15 is of the saints who have overcome in the tribulation time, as they worship God and sing:

> Great and marvellous are your deeds,
>   Lord God Almighty.
> Just and true are your ways,
>   King of the nations.
> Who will not fear you, Lord,
>   and bring glory to your name?
> For you alone are holy.
>
> *Rev. 15:3–4*

Offence may be couched in intellectual arguments, but taking offence at God actually reveals our hearts. There will be a dividing line between those Christians who have stayed close enough to God to grow in trust and find his wisdom in the troubles and shaking, and those who have become offended by God in the crises and judgments and turned away from their faith. The saints in the end-time church will be those who are worshipping and praising God for his love and sovereign purposes when all around are despairing and losing hope.

No wonder the apostle Paul ends his magnificent letter to the Ephesians with a call to be strong in the Lord and the power of his might. This letter, which most clearly reveals the nature of the worldwide church and the reality of who we are in God's sight, culminates in Paul's teaching about the importance of standing with the armour of God in place if we are to withstand the evil day (Eph. 6:1–18). 'The evil day' (v. 13 KJV) is an eschatological phrase here, translated 'the day of evil' in the NIV, meaning ultimately the time of Tribulation. The armour of God is not intellectual but spiritual – the breastplate of righteousness, the belt of truth, the helmet of salvation, the shoes of gospel peace, the shield of faith and the sword of the Spirit. Living with these attributes and taking up these weapons keeps us in a place of strength in the Lord. It protects our hearts from being worn down or defeated by the fiery darts and vicious attacks of the enemy in the heat of battle. Yes, we will be refined, by testing, by shaking, to draw out the gold of our faith in Jesus. Ultimately, the end-time church will be cruciform in shape and character, by the grace of God.

Pause for Thought

- Is my heart growing in trust in God, even when there is shaking and turmoil in the world around me?

14

Sixth Mark: Mature in Development, Growth, Influence and Prayer (the Grown-Up Community)

The Fullness of Christ

To be mature means to reach one's full level of development. The early church started out as a young church, of course; the first apostles had a lot to learn. They had to learn to deal with growth of numbers (Acts 4:4), community problems (6:1–4), doctrinal issues (15:1–6), training new leaders (14:21–23) and adapting the Christian faith to new cultures (17:16–23), all in the context of preaching the gospel and extending the kingdom wherever they went. So in what ways was the early church of Acts a mature church? Well, the first Christians were mature enough to take full responsibility for Jesus' commission, and give their lives fully to spread the gospel throughout their known world. They were mature enough to discern God's purposes for them and know the right directions to take. They were mature enough to be able to reproduce, to make other disciples, to plant churches, to nurture congregations. They were mature enough to look like their Saviour and Master, Jesus.

In fact the apostle Paul uses a remarkable expression: he says that the church is called to be 'the fullness of Christ'; that Jesus is the head and we are his body and we are growing to become like him. As Paul writes in Ephesians chapter 4:

> So Christ himself gave the apostles, the prophets, the evangelists, the pastors and teachers, to equip his people for works of service, so that the body of Christ may be built up until we all reach unity in the faith and in the knowledge of the Son of God and become mature, attaining to the whole measure of the fullness of Christ.
> Then we will no longer be infants, tossed back and forth by the waves, and blown here and there by every wind of teaching and by the cunning and craftiness of people in their deceitful scheming. Instead, speaking the truth in love, we will grow to become in every respect the mature body of him who is the head, that is, Christ.
>
> *Eph. 4:11–15*

Notice that it didn't take long, just a generation, for the early church to become a mature body. Despite faults and issues in individual communities of faith, the exalted Lord Jesus poured out the necessary charisms and gifts for the church to organically grow out and grow up. These Ephesians 4 qualities – unity of faith, depth of knowing the Lord, Christlikeness, strength of belief, great love and clear growth – certainly marked the early church.

In my experience over recent years of planting a house of prayer, as a fresh expression of church, I realized that it doesn't take long for a young community to become grown up – to take responsibility for growth, for discernment concerning God's direction, to reproduce and nurture others, and to look like Jesus. The Pentecost DNA which I mentioned earlier – the ability to be blown by the Spirit, inwardly renewed by the fire of God, and moved to carry the seed of the gospel out into the world in praise and witness – is reproducible in any culture and any age. Likewise, the Spirit's indwelling and transforming power among us is sufficient to create Christlikeness in any church community.

God is inviting us in the last days to step up and become fully mature in our faith. I believe that one of the most exciting hallmarks to look for in the emerging end-time church is astounding maturity, like that of a bride matched to her husband, or a body expressing its fullness. Never since the days of the early generations of the church have the majority of Christians been reflective of the fullness of Jesus. Fragmentation, division and doctrinal differences have kept us apart from each other. The end-time church – testing and falling away notwithstanding – will consist of a global, dispersed body of believers who will look more like Jesus than ever before in history. We will be fully mature in development, growth, influence and prayer.

We will look briefly at these four aspects of Christian maturity.

Mature in Development

Think of an Olympic athlete; there is a maturity of physical development and skill in such a person, although relatively young: someone who is operating at peak fitness and fullness of potential. The end-time church will be mature in development as the body of Christ. Maybe not perfect, but certainly operating at peak fitness and at full potential as an image of Jesus. Paul's desire for his churches was that they should 'stand firm in the one Spirit, striving together as one for the faith of the gospel' (Phil. 1:27).

Different parts of the church in the Tribulation years will not be wrongly competitive with each other, but will speak with one voice. There will be such a clarity when the gospel is declared around the world, and such a deep resonance with heaven, that it will touch people's hearts and open them to the love of God. The church that is emerging will be a repentant church: one that has dealt with her shadow side, brought her sins and failings into the light, left behind shame and inadequacy, come through division, and is now emerging as a bride who can honour the various traditions of the church in which the Spirit has so wonderfully brought renewal. She will be cleansed, whole and pure.

The church rising up will no longer be thrown off course by fickle moods of culture or winds of popular teaching, but will have gone through a refinement process to overcome the fear of popular opinion and the temptation to compromise with the world. She will be very clear about her destiny and what she has to do in the time before the Lord's return. She will be united in faith, walking in the knowledge of God, and looking like Jesus. The church will be worthy of his calling, fruitful and beautiful as she reflects his glory.

Only the work of the Spirit can create such a mature church, one which is ready for Christ's return, and united within herself. Peter Hocken, a Catholic author commenting on renewal, writes about such a future:

> The outpourings of the Spirit are to prepare for the final great work of the Spirit in the resurrection of the dead and the establishment of the new heavens and the new earth. This preparation involves a power for the proclamation of the gospel to all tribes and nations before the end comes, the turning of Israel to Jesus as their Messiah and reconciliation of the divided Christian churches. Only then will the Bride be ready for the returning Bridegroom.[1]

Perhaps the imagery of 'the beloved' in the Song of Songs is also helpful here, as I unpacked in Chapter 6. The journey towards maturity for the beloved young woman in that story is a long one, yet she ends up coming out of the wilderness leaning on the lover. That rich image embodies a journey of refining of character and unfolding of destiny, and a resultant depth of love and devotion to the Lord. Likewise, the global church will be truly transformed into God's people who lean on God's strength and walk in God's love, a church forged through the end-time drama into the true likeness of Christ.

Pause for Thought

- Do I truly believe that the church can be one in Spirit before the Lord returns?

Mature in Growth

Think of an English oak tree; it takes many years to grow from acorn, to seedling, to sapling, to tree. It may be thirty years before some oaks produce acorns, fifty years before they reach their full height and spread, and hundreds of years before old age; and throughout their lifespan they support a wider biodiversity of insects, birds and mammals than any other British tree. A mature oak tree is a marvel of nature, a wonder to behold. The church in coming years will be fully mature in growth. There will be a dynamic expression of Christian faith within every tribe, culture and people group, even if it is not apparent in every congregation. Revelation chapter 7 gives us a vision of the fullness of the church after she has walked through

Tribulation times: 'there before me was a great multitude that no one could count, from every nation, tribe, people and language, standing before the throne and before the Lamb' (Rev. 7:9). As the Great Commission is completed, we may well see the billion-soul harvest that has been prophesied. Fast growth and radical discipleship will occur in the coming generation, and more and more of the people of God on earth will be living with a kingdom vision and a fervency of faith in the midst of glory and shaking.

Christians will still feel pain, of course, over portions of the church that have become apostate, and the divisions caused by those who couldn't embrace the renewal or bought into a watered-down, culturally accommodated faith. Yet there will be so much life in the body of Christ, and so many new expressions of church in this coming generation, that God will be praised. Many believe that waves of young believers will lead the way in this multiplication and growth. Some megachurches may still thrive, but we can expect much church planting and millions of small-group Christian communities creating a last-days reformation of church life (or, as some call it, a new church 'architecture'). As the full number of Gentiles comes in, we will become more intertwined, in heart and soul, with the Jewish people turning to their Messiah. Where past generations were ignorant of God's plans for a revival among the Jews, this generation will be given revelation from his word, and will pray and partner with other believers for the salvation of his chosen people. We are already being enriched by the historic streams and new expressions of the Christian faith flowing together; we will be completed by the wonderful dynamic of cultivated and wild olive branches finally together and united in Christ (see Rom. 11:17–26). We are visibly moving towards that Revelation vision of people from every tribe, language, people and nation represented before the throne of God, the church militant on earth mirroring the church triumphant in heaven.

Mature in Influence

Think of the influence of Christianity in the world. We can easily forget, in our post-Christian society, how profoundly Christianity has influenced the West. Christian values based on the Ten Commandments did nothing less than undergird the basic moral foundation of western civilization for 1,500 years, for example concerning forgiveness towards enemies and the sanctity of human life. In moving away from these foundations, there is currently a great crisis of meaning in western civilization, affecting its total worldview. And as western lifestyle ideals have penetrated every other culture, many of which are similarly in ideological crisis, this profound 'meaning vacuum' creates great disquiet and searching among intellectuals and people on the street alike.

As well as sharing gospel truth, I believe that in these last days, God will gift the church with influence of a different kind from that in the past. Christendom is over. But God's people will still have great influence, particularly through their insight into and prophetic understanding of the crises we will find ourselves in. In the Bible, God used Joseph to steer Egypt through a time of severe famine. He also used Daniel to speak wisdom and righteousness to the ruling leaders of his day. In fact, Daniel's experience in the court of Nebuchadnezzar teaches that God is a revealer of mysteries:

> He gives wisdom to the wise
> and knowledge to the discerning.

> He reveals deep and hidden things;
>   he knows what lies in darkness,
>   and light dwells with him.
>
> *Dan. 2:21–22*

Even now, Christians are being anointed by the Lord, particularly in the spheres of politics, business, science and the arts, to use their personal influence to help address some intractable political problems, launch brilliant flagship business initiatives for the social good, create breakthroughs in science and medical discoveries, and shine rays of righteousness into the arts. The brightness of the church's witness in the generation before the Tribulation comes could be extraordinary. There will be many Christians who, while they may be unpopular socially, can nevertheless bring kingdom wisdom and influence into the mysteries of shaking experienced in communities, cities and nations. As societal life is shaken in the last days, God will use his people to give glimpses of glory and show what his unshakeable kingdom looks like in many areas of life. I believe the church in this generation will exhibit the fullness of the gifts, fruit and mind of Christ; we will represent him well, in dimensions of his power, his character and his wisdom, and that will be a blessing in the world.

Pause for Thought

- Concerning what area of national life do I most pray that God will raise Christians into a place of influence?

Mature in Prayer and the Knowledge of God

Think of those we have looked up to as spiritual gurus or teachers. In the past we may have expected Christian councils to give doctrinal understanding, or great Bible teachers to expound meaning for us; and we sought spiritual guidance from holy saints living before our time, or wiser Christians older than us, who seemed to live in a rarified atmosphere of great intimacy with God. In this last generation of the church, the Lord wants his whole people to be mature in our lives of prayer and to know him and his ways. God is calling us all higher, together. I fully expect that the current exploding worship and prayer movement around the world will infiltrate the whole church and we will increasingly function as a living global house of prayer. The benefit for the global church will be a rise in praise and deep communion with the Lord; the benefit for the world will be an intercessory people across the earth partnering with God like never before. The emerging end-time church will mature as an *ekklesia* (a Greek word for church) – a body of people who may lead kingdom breakthroughs into the life of towns and cities, and have great insight into God's ways and redemptive purposes for our world. As the early church was a praying church, so we will become a truly worldwide praying body of believers and a communion of radical worshippers. As the apostle Peter exhorted: 'The end of all things is near. Therefore be alert and of sober mind so that you may pray' (1 Pet. 4:7).

During the Covid-19 virus crisis, I was much in prayer concerning the signs of the times and the writing of this book. During one particular prayer time, I had a powerful vision of the church being called up higher by the Spirit. I could picture God's heavenly throne and significant numbers of his people being called up to stand before him; he was convening what seemed to be different prayer councils for nations. I sensed God's power connecting heaven's throne with the earthly places where his people were living. His grace and power were being released through these councils; it looked like waves of light and sound that rippled and reverberated across the land, shifting atmospheres and spiritual conditions. I saw what seemed to be scrolls being given to different groups – prayers to pray that signified spiritual authority to counteract and countermand, to disrupt and overrule some of the orders and plans and works of the enemy. It was a dynamic prophetic scene.

As I reflected on this vision, I realized it spoke about the unseen power of prayer in our world. Although the devil is making his plans to wreak havoc on the earth, and although the spirit of the age is permeating our societies worldwide, the church will rise up in humility and strength to withstand his power wherever she stays true to the name of Jesus. The enemy is making plans, but he is unaware of the masterly heavenly strategies the Lord is putting in place. God will use the end times to lift up his people and call them to stand in faithful prayer; then to move out in faith, locally and globally, to reveal his glory and his unshakeable kingdom.

So we have a choice in times of trouble: to lift our voices together in praise. We can press through confusion to seek God's face together; we can come into a mature and strong place of partnering with him in prayer. We can be a people, as Jesus said, who understand the keys of the kingdom he has entrusted us with, and against whom the gates of hell will not prevail.

A mature church – what a possibility! God longs to bring his people into maturity, into the full reflection of the likeness of Jesus. Through the coming revival and trouble, the Holy Spirit will mature us and strengthen us, enabling the unity of faith, the depth of knowing the Lord, the Christlikeness and clear growth, the strength of belief and the faithful prayer that he is looking for in a people getting prepared for his Son's return in glory.

Pause for Thought

- What vision might God want to give me for the growth of the church in my city or nation?

15

Seventh Mark: Creating First Fruits of the Coming Eschaton (the Transfiguring Community)

The Gleam of a Beauty from Beyond

In the story of the Lord of the Rings, after far-flung adventures and taking part in the great battles of Middle Earth, where the evil powers are overthrown and the dark ring is destroyed, the little hero people called the Hobbits return to their own land. One of them, Samwise, has with him a small wooden box containing soil and a nut from the enchanted land of the Elves, a realm of great beauty and little decay. He scatters grains of the precious soil all over the Shire, which itself had been scarred by the evil at work – and waits for transformation. Tolkien writes of the following spring: 'Altogether 1420 in the Shire was a marvellous year. Not only was there wonderful sunshine and delicious rain, in due times and perfect measure, but there seemed something more: an air of richness and growth and a gleam of a beauty beyond that of mortal summers that flicker and pass upon the Middle-earth.'[1] You could say that the Shire in that story had become the *first fruits* of a different realm. In a similar way, the early church was a first-fruits community of the kingdom of God. Jesus inaugurated the life of the kingdom in his ministry, and the first generations of church learned how to embody the life of his reign and also how to extend its values and life into the world around them. In biblical terms, the early church was a foretaste of the renewal of all creation promised in the Old Testament prophets (e.g. Isa. 35:1–10). Even the breath of the Spirit at Pentecost reminded God's people of the original creation story of Genesis. This first-fruits community of the heavenly world enjoyed the kind of fellowship with God which had been broken since Adam, and restored relationships between rich and poor, slave and free, men and women, Jew and Gentile (e.g. Acts 10:28; Gal. 3:26–29). It also ministered signs of that kingdom to the world around, in healing of body and mind (Acts 5:12), and in a Christian ethic which affected work, family and every area of life (Eph. 4:20–24). Moreover, the life of this Christian community overflowed its own banks as a relatively small religious sect and brought God's liberating rule into the heart of the life of cities across the Roman Empire. Corinth and Ephesus in the book of Acts (chs 18 and 19) are examples in Paul's ministry where the civil, religious and commercial centres of city life were hugely impacted or challenged by kingdom values. In the following generations, this otherworldly kingdom-dynamic rippled like a transforming current of life throughout the entire Roman world.

The Lord is inviting us in the last days to both embody and create beautiful first fruits of the coming eschaton, the eternal realm of God's kingdom. I have written already about the kind of things that will deeply mark true communities of faith – enjoying the holy presence of God, deep devotion to the Lord and each other, a love which heals and unites, great faith in the gospel, and hope that influences and inspires an alternative kingdom way of life. Like the effects of the Elven soil in Samwise's box, the church can inspire others with gleams of beauty 'beyond that of mortal summers'. In Scripture, the anointing of the Spirit for mission is never for selfish use, but to bring a kingdom witness to the earth. As the prophet Isaiah writes:

> For as the soil makes the young plant come up
>   and a garden causes seeds to grow,
> so the Sovereign Lord will make righteousness
>   and praise spring up before all nations.
>
> Isa. 61:11

The Christian community embodies the kingdom, and also extends it outwards into every area of society. There is no space here to tell of all the ways over the centuries in which the social justice and compassion of the church has led to the betterment of communities and culture. I believe that in the coming years before Jesus returns, God's people will be inspired to find new ways of bringing God's transforming touch into workplaces, cities, and the spheres of societal life.

Social Transformation

Social transformation has been a growing theme of evangelical and Pentecostal teaching in recent years. This is an antidote or correction to the premillennial Rapture teaching of the church in the last one hundred and fifty years, which denied the prospect of any real renewal of creation in our time, but told Christians to either wait passively for, or at best witness bravely in hope of, the end of the world. In its stead, new voices have been championing again the teaching of Jesus, where he called his disciples to be the preserving and flavouring salt of the earth, and a visible and shining light in the world here and now; and where he commissioned them to disciple all nations. Modern transformation teaching stands in the long line of theological wrestling over how the kingdom impacts the earth, from Augustine's *City of God*, to Calvin's Reformation experiment in Geneva. Medieval missionary monks who converted kings and then baptized their people; working-class Nonconformist preachers during the Industrial Revolution who helped redeem and empower local communities; social reformers from the Victorian era lifting people out of poverty – all would understand a measure of how God leads people to change society through the redemptive and uplifting nature of the gospel.

So, what is the difference in the work of the church in society in the last days? It is the fact that the transforming impact of the church will occur amid the great last-days revival, and the context will be the revealing of more of God's glory amid great shaking. The Spirit's empowering of the church in the coming years will happen in order to enable countless millions of ordinary Christians to carry the presence of God into workplaces, schools, hospitals, government buildings, radio stations, and all the other 'secular' places that might seem far from the church's normal remit. Instead of living with a siege mentality in the workplace or neighbourhood, Christians will increasingly think of doing as Jesus did: invading the darkness with gospel light and kingdom hope. The end-time context for Christian mission will be a world breaking open to kingdom change and, in this clash of light and darkness, people being open to heavenly solutions. The Lord will give strategies to the church in a particular local place for how to bring his love and kingdom transformation to its marketplaces and communities, before the darkest days of the Tribulation time finally overtake the world.

The famous prophetic oracle of Isaiah 61 shows a kingdom vision of jubilee, liberty and restoration, where Israel finally comes into her destiny as a kingdom of priests favoured among the nations. Jesus' ministry itself inaugurated a time of grace – good news for the poor, binding up the broken-hearted, freeing prisoners, restoring sight, and bringing God's favour so that people could experience the kingdom. This vision of renewal doesn't stop with the church or religious structures, but has been the inspiring biblical foundation for many social action initiatives through the history of the church. I believe the end-time church will again pick up this mandate, as the anointed people of God, to move out into devastated places as waves of revival cascade across nations. We will see many lives turned around through the gospel – people saved, healed, delivered and becoming oaks of righteousness. We will engage with the call to rebuild ruined cities and restore broken communities, and God's people will come into a place of great influence and blessing as we tend God's kingdom garden of righteousness and praise on the earth.

Christian leaders in the West are currently refocusing on what Jesus' intention for the church is in society. The term *ekklesia* in Greek, meaning 'the called-out ones', or the legislative assembly, has at its heart the sense of bringing kingdom change. Indeed, Jesus' words to Peter were that he would build his *ekklesia*, and the gates of hell would not prevail against it (Matt. 16:18). As author and marketplace Christian leader Steve Botham encourages us: 'I believe these are times of divine shift. God wants us to stand in the knowledge of the Ekklesia. He did not call pew fodder; He called kingdom builders. He did not call us to be ordinary; He equips us to be extraordinary.'[2] For example, Ed Silvoso leads the International Transformation Network, encouraging alliances of pulpit and marketplace ministers to grow prototypes for nation transformation. Challenging some understandings of the gospel, Silvoso says that the Great Commission is about discipling nations, not just people. He specifies that the mission of the church is to take the kingdom of God into places where the kingdom of darkness is entrenched, trusting that Jesus will then build his church.

In his book *Transformation*, Silvoso teaches about demonic strongholds in economic systems today, which he calls a prevailing 'Babylon culture'. He encourages Christians to initiate anointed marketplace ministries to combat social ills, saying that 'we are fast approaching the tipping point in terms of generating and/or accessing substantial resources for the kingdom of God'.[3] He also explains the evangelistic motive in this, whereby the lived-out values of the gospel become the answer to people's discontent about the entrenched systems of global poverty: 'We Christians should perceive in this groundswell an extraordinary opportunity to use the elimination of all forms of poverty as a masterful act of kindness to open the eyes of billions of people to the reality of Jesus Christ and His gospel of good news to the poor.'[4]

I think Silvoso is right in challenging the church to consider every sphere of culture as ripe for kingdom transformation and in widening out the commission to discipling nations in the ways of Jesus. I also think he conveniently ignores some of the end-time signs of trouble and shaking in order to drive home his call to the church to rise in faith to see much greater social transformation than we imagine is possible.

We can have a transformational mindset because God anoints us to bring his kingdom change in society, the light of the church shining despite darkness rising. Even in post-Christian Britain, God is using the church to bring gentle but profound change in areas of social need in cities and towns. In my own adopted city, I could name several Christian ministries which have arisen in the last twenty years and are making a huge difference in the name of Christ. They are creating places of welcome for asylum seekers, empowering young people who are struggling with their self-worth, working with homeless people and ex-offenders towards long-term solutions and integration into society, befriending and supporting vulnerable and lonely old people – the list goes on with many more examples of the church's transformational effects in terms of practical kingdom action, combating poverty and strengthening community. I believe these effects will be amplified in the coming revival.

Pause for Thought

- What examples inspire me when I hear of Christian groups bringing transformation into the marketplace and areas of public life?

Transfiguration

As well as a revival context for social action, the other difference for the end-time church is that we will be ministering and working within an increase of the revelation of God's glory across the earth. You could ask whether the best word for what is coming is actually 'transformation'; should it be 'transfiguration'? An acquaintance of mine, Malcolm Duncan, a well-known Bible teacher in the UK, has suggested to me that whereas 'transformation' has become a buzzword in many business sectors, 'transfiguration' is a uniquely Christian word. To transform means to change the shape of, whereas to transfigure means to make something better, more positive, beautiful or spiritual. Where things have been disfigured through sin, in this last-days generation God wants to transfigure them through his glory and love.

What happens in the story of Jesus' transfiguration described in Luke 9:28–36? It was certainly an affirmation for Jesus of his divinity and his true glory. It was clearly a confirmation of his destiny to journey towards the cross and vindication beyond it. Yet it was also a sign, for the disciples and all who would read this story, of transcendent glory in the midst of ordinariness, an unveiling of God's light and purposes on an otherwise dark mountain: 'As he was praying, the appearance of his face changed, and his clothes became as bright as a flash of lightning . . . Peter and his companions were very sleepy, but when they became fully awake, they saw his glory and the two men standing with him' (Luke 9:28,32).

Jesus' transfiguration offers people a foretaste of what God promises us in the fullness of his kingdom. And that is a work in which we are all invited to participate. Archbishop Desmond Tutu, the great Christian voice for social activism in South Africa, called for such a vision of transfiguration: 'God places us in the world as his fellow workers – agents of transfiguration. We work with God so that injustice is transfigured into justice, so there will be more compassion and caring, that there will be more laughter and joy, that there will be more togetherness in God's world.'[5]

My grandfather used to make clay pots in his retirement. As a china merchant in his working life, he brought his faith into his work ethic. As a retired man, he spent his time preaching in chapels, and also painting and making pots. There was nothing special about his vases, jugs and planters; they were quite earthy in design and plain in decoration. Yet a few years before he died, my grandfather started adding touches of gold gilt to the clay pots he was making. He loved to adorn the edges of the flowers or patterns that decorated his pots. It was, as we like to call it, his 'gold phase'.

To use this analogy, as the awareness of God's presence increases globally, how wonderful would it be if spheres of life, institutions and people groups, different areas of society, became touched by the gold of God's presence? That is what many believe is going to happen in the heightened spiritual atmosphere of the end times. It will be as though it were God's 'gold phase'! This is another way of describing how the church becomes mature in influence, as discussed in Chapter 14. In spite of shaking and troubled times, the Lord will still lead us to bring his transfiguring touch of wisdom into the financial and political arenas, into frontline advances in solving environmental problems, into peacemaking solutions in areas of conflict, into signs of hope and love in struggling communities, into creating bulwarks of shining faith and sense-making in places and institutions where a vision of truth and beauty is blurred.

Pause for Thought

- Can I already see places touched by the glory of God around the world?
- Is there a country or people group I would like to pray for to experience that?

Renewal of Earth and Restored Creation

There is one further thing to say concerning the church being the first fruits of the new eschaton. I believe that the church will come into a fresh understanding of God's plans to renew heaven and earth, one that will motivate us in our mission in the end times. Instead of the otherworldly hope of going to heaven, which the church has perpetuated for centuries, we will focus on the return of Christ to bring the longed-for renewal of earth as he comes to reign. There are many voices challenging Christians to rethink our vision of the eschaton from a biblical point of view. Our eternal destiny is not just an immaterial reality, but an embodied one. Jesus will return to rule over earth and renew the worldwide devastation caused by sin and the Tribulation. As I have mentioned, the Millennium has fascinated Christians down the centuries, precisely because it offers a hope of the life of the kingdom fully expressed on earth. The original invitation in Genesis chapter 1, for humans to partner with God in ruling over creation, will be fully realized when Jesus comes in glory. Christians in their resurrected state will have work to do: to look after creation, to disciple people in the ways of the Lord, and to be part of the healing of the nations which Jesus will bring about fully at his return.

If the millennial rule of Christ is not enough to wrap our hearts around, let us consider how the vision of Revelation leads finally to the most majestic and gracious of all divine acts: the joining of heaven and earth, as God makes his dwelling with people. If a 'literal Millennium' reading of Scripture is right, then the rule of Christ on earth is a preparation for the new heaven and earth to be revealed. As the Son fills the earth with the glory of God, the Father is preparing to reveal a union of the whole cosmos with divine love. The last judgment is the great moment when each human being finds out whether their future is in this renewed cosmos or not. As death and hell are destroyed, God's dwelling with his redeemed creation is full and final. This is the place where there are no more tears (Rev. 21:4). The new Jerusalem is the perfect city, the centre but not the entirety of the renewed cosmos, made possible because of union between the Godhead and all creation, the God who makes all things new.

In Matthew's Gospel, Jesus speaks of the promised future blessings that his followers will receive in the midst of the great renewal of the whole cosmos:

> Truly I tell you, at the renewal of all things, when the Son of Man sits on his glorious throne, you who have followed me will also sit on twelve thrones, judging the twelve tribes of Israel. And everyone who has left houses or brothers or sisters or father or mother or wife or children or fields for my sake will receive a hundred times as much and will inherit eternal life.
>
> *Matt. 19:28–29*

We sacrifice much in this life, living for eternal reward. Yet these hundredfold blessings are not ethereal but a rich recompense for that sacrifice: the fulfilment of our best desires and our greatest dreams in a renewed world.

Richard Middleton is one of many theologians helping to reassess the biblical narrative of the locus of our eschatological hope – namely a renewed earthly creation rather than an immaterial heaven. Middleton reminds us of God's original missional mandate to humanity, namely to be a faithful covenant people to bless the earth, which only became possible as Jesus dealt with sin and evil and offered a restoration of human beings in relation to God, each other and the earth. The mission of God's people since Jesus is both a gospel-bearing witness to the nations and a modelling of what restored humanity could look like. He writes the following:

> The point is that once the subplot of the sending of Israel has been successful and the nations have received the blessings of salvation, the redeemed human race will once again utilize their God-given power and agency to rule the earth as God intended – a renewal of the human cultural task, but this time without sin. The initial narrative sequence of the biblical story will finally be fulfilled. Far from being the end or cessation of history, this is history's true beginning, free from the constraints of human violation vis-à-vis God or other humans or the earth itself. The climax of the biblical story, which many have called the 'eternal state,' is fundamentally this-worldly. When God brings his original purposes to fruition, we find not escape from creation, but rather new (or renewed) creation.[6]

Middleton, however, like others, is keen to concentrate our minds on the 'already' and not just the 'not yet' of God's salvation plan. He encourages a biblical view of 'the beginning of the end in the midst of the story',[7] in which God's people bring blessing to the nations, and live as examples of restored humanity today, while awaiting the fullness of God's restoration.

I agree with Middleton's argument and want to apply it to our thinking about transfiguration and first fruits. Why get involved in justice or environmental issues in the last days if the Tribulation is around the corner, and if waves of devastation are coming upon the earth? I encourage people to see their work as that of creating first fruits of transfigured communities ahead of Jesus' millennial rule and the new heaven and earth. Jesus' parable of the talents in Matthew chapter 25 calls his people to faithfulness in stewarding God's gifts in the light of his coming to reward or judge. Tackling climate change, working to alleviate poverty, being peacemakers in the midst of conflict, staying involved in the political system to bring about change – all these noble Christian tasks and so many more are worth continuing even amid global shaking and turmoil. Not everything will be lost, not every community devastated, in the Tribulation. We are all responsible for bringing a first-fruits offering to the Lord of what we did with our gifts and opportunities. The church will have a profound impact in creating first fruits of what the kingdom looks like in our generation, which we will have the privilege of presenting to Jesus as he comes in glory.

During a time of prayer recently I had a glimpse of what the church could look like today from heaven's point of view. I sensed from God that, if the church were to rise up together, she would look like moving fabric, shimmering across the whole earth with his glory. I saw, not a cloth covering the planet, but a mesh-like living material, both reflecting his light and transmitting his light and energy. The church in this vision was God's radiant garment of glory on earth. Such, I believe, will be the impact of the end-time church in coming years – a people shimmering with his glory across the earth, creating first fruits of another world as a transfiguring sign of the coming age. When many around us will be struggling with despair, believers in Christ can bring living hope, signs of kingdom change, even measures of his glory to light a darkening world, because of our hope in the transcendent kingdom of God who will make all things new. Glory to God!

Pause for Thought

- Is my future hope fixed around an ethereal life in heaven or a more eternally fulfilled life on a renewed earth filled with the Father's glory?

Summing Up of Part Three

Looking back over this part of the book, if I am right about a close correlation between the life of the end-time church and that of the early church, we can see that the rising up of the end-time church will be multifaceted and very dynamic. These marks of the church – being overshadowed, fervent, anointed, outpoured, cruciform, grown-up and transfiguring – are, I believe, those that marked the early church as God birthed it and gave it its spiritual DNA.

We do have to ask: how on earth do we get from the church as we know it to this end-time global movement of believers? Many churches in the West are bogged down in maintenance rather than mission. Bitter infighting is breaking out over differences of opinion on the Bible and cultural morality. Power plays are rife in church leadership, and secret sins of abuse are in the media glare. Minority Christian groups in other parts of the world fight for survival under severe persecution. How can God take such a mixed, threatened and disunited worldwide group of believers and create a radiant bride? Some would resort to talking about the visible and invisible church, first touted by Augustine of Hippo in the early development of a theology of the church. In this understanding, there is always a mixture of saints and sinners, truth and error, in the church, and only God knows the elect who will be part of the heavenly kingdom. Yet the Bible seems to speak of a great work in the church that happens in the closing years of human history in which the global visible church will shine like a jewel on the dark backdrop of end-time events. This great work of God among his people is what I have tried to give language to in this book.

It might look as though I am painting a rose-tinted picture of the church in the final generation. Am I suggesting that the church will be perfect in the last days? Far from it. The biblical picture suggests there will still be flaws in the church, and different levels of responding to the glory and the shaking. There will be the tragedy of saints falling away from faith. Even in revival, there will be a varied pace and level at which churches move in step with the waves of outpouring that the Spirit brings. Yet I do think that there will also be an unusual spiritual momentum which God brings about in the end times. Periods of church renewal and revival usually peter out; they have at most a generational lifespan before becoming routinized and institutionalized in the following generation. What many are praying for is a multigenerational move of God, such as we see prophesied in Joel 2, where young and old run together in the outpourings of the Spirit. I personally believe that the twin dynamics – of God's glory being revealed in waves of revival and a fascination with Jesus growing, on one hand – and massive shaking occurring through global uncertainty and troubles, on the other – will together form the church into something very special, a precious jewel, an anointed great family of God. The pressure of the shaking will be a sustained ordeal, which will keep us sober and alert as we navigate difficult times on planet earth. The increasing brightness of God's glory being revealed will also be a sustained experience, which will keep us running in our destiny and fully alive to his purposes. This is the privileged journey into the unexplored land of end-time ministry.

There is an often-used quote I have heard said in Christian circles: 'It is not the church of God that has a mission; rather, it is the God of mission who has a church.' I love that quote.

It suggests – to use a rugby analogy – that we are not the one scoring the winning try, but rather that we are the ball, carried by God over the touchline to the cheers of the crowd. The great *missio Dei*, the mission of our God in our world, has an endpoint in sight. That endpoint is the moment when the kingdom of the world has become 'the kingdom of our Lord and of his Messiah' (Rev. 11:15). The kingdom of God is coming in its fullness, and the church age will end on a climax in the midst of Tribulation. This coming last generation of his people are a crucial part of God's mission; we will be held by God as he equips us to play our part well. The heavenly hosts are waiting to cheer us on at the close of the end of the age.

Paul offered up a heartfelt prayer for his friends in Thessalonica: 'that our God may make you worthy of his calling, and that by his power he may bring to fruition your every desire for goodness and your every deed prompted by faith' (2 Thess. 1:11). The Lord is committed to the final preparation of the bride for his Son. And if that is so, then there will be a last-days church that emerges, a church that is unusually marked by God: known for his numinous presence among us, devoted to the Lord and to each other, spreading the gospel in word and power, extravagant in love for the poor and broken, refined by persecution and falling away, mature in growth, influence and prayer, and creating first fruits of the eschaton.

What then is our practical response to the vision of the end-time church which I have laid out? We will turn to this now in the final part of the book.

Part Four

How Shall We Prepare?

'I wish it need not have happened in my time,' said Frodo. 'So do I,' said Gandalf, 'and so do all who live to see such times. But that is not for them to decide. All we have to decide is what to do with the time that is given us.'

J.R.R. Tolkien

Introduction to Part Four

In this final part of the book, we will consider our response to the end-time context I have set out, and what that calls for in our individual walk with Jesus and our life and mission as a church here and now. How does this ragtag mix of sinners and saints, found in a multitude of denominations, still so divided, move into a collective determination to explore the terrain of end-time ministry? How do we get from here to there? I can only speak from a western European perspective, but I hope it has wider relevance to you wherever you are in the global body of Christ.

Confidence That God Will Give Us All That We Need

This journey starts with confidence in the God who is leading us. One of the current popular phrases in the business world is being 'set up to fail' or being 'set up to succeed'. This relates to a work scenario where you are given a project by your boss. On one hand, a poor boss might set you up to fail by not giving you the right resources for the task, setting conflicting goals or making you face impossible odds for success. They have set you up to fail, which is not a good feeling. A good boss, on the other hand, has thought through the project and goals to enable a strong performance, has invested time in skills development so you can do a good job, and has cleared a path for the best chance of a great outcome. They have set you up for success, and you rise to the challenges because of what both they and you believe is possible.

In a similar way, Jesus clearly set the early church up for success. He knew what it needed for life and growth and perseverance. Jesus had prepared his disciples well for all that he knew they would face in the days of the early church. Despite their personal weakness and failure when he died, Jesus had invested all the training and revelation they needed to be his followers. They had the secrets of the kingdom, they had been released into mission, they had been tutored in prayer, they were eyewitnesses of his resurrection. When finally filled with the promised Holy Spirit, the apostles and other members of the early church had everything they required to prosper in the times of glory and revival they lived through. They also had the empowerment and strength to endure persecution and pressure, and overcome it. Jesus knew exactly what he was doing.

I believe that Jesus is preparing his end-time church in a similar way now. He is setting us up for success in these climactic years of shining glory and rising darkness. If we heed his call to arise, if we stay true and close to him in these early days before life gets really intense in the world, we will mature into a church showing all the marks that I have outlined in Part Three of this book. Will we have confidence in Jesus to train us to overcome challenges now to our faith, and to learn to walk in more of his anointing now, in this season? Will we have confidence, not just in the overarching sovereignty of God in the end-time narrative, but also in his specific way of preparing and equipping the saints in these coming end-time days? Paul had such great confidence in the Lord's establishing work in the fledgling churches he founded that he could say: 'He who began a good work in you will carry it on to completion until the day of Christ Jesus' (Phil. 1:6).

Do we believe that is true for the global church in the last days? He knows exactly what we need to be ready – ready to shine in the rising of God's glory, ready to navigate life in the global shaking, and ready eventually to welcome Jesus' return. His eyes are fixed on us, his hand is resting on us, his heart is for us; as he told his disciples, he likewise tells us: 'You did not choose me, but I chose you' (John 15:16). Jesus will help us get on a fast track of learning and equipping in the coming years.

Pause for Thought

- Do I trust Jesus' leadership to equip me and the church for the end times?

16

Preparing as the Whole Church

Radical Training

The journey into this end-time terrain of ministry requires a radical willingness in the global body of Christ to be trained by the Lord, and to go on a big learning curve in discipleship and thinking. Consider the level of preparation people undertake for an expedition. If you were about to go on a month-long adventure journey, and the expedition leader had just given your team your itinerary, your equipment sheet, and a map to follow, covering the unfamiliar terrain, I am sure you would take far more care and more time than if simply planning a weekend walk in your nearby park. You would buy the necessary gear, meet up with the others to plan, do training walks, familiarize yourselves with the map, become expert at orienteering, prepare for all weather conditions, work as a team, and approach the expedition ready for the challenge and excitement that it would bring.

Well, we have never walked this way before. No generation of Christians has ever faced the precise challenges and opportunities we will face in the next few decades as the glory and shaking increase. We will need to be attuned to the Lord and his word, and prepare ourselves mentally, physically and spiritually to navigate this coming end-time season on earth. In particular,

I suggest that we will have to adjust to a time of more intense discipleship, and we will have to think more clearly about biblical eschatology.

More intense discipleship

The dynamics of living for Jesus will undoubtedly be more intense the closer we get to his return. The church will see more 'God things' happening – waves of revival, outreach in the power of the Spirit, more salvation and healings, new church expressions, more kingdom transformation in the midst of the marketplace and ordinary communities. There will be more troubling things happening too – the increase of shaking, a rise in various natural and man-made crises, more societal instability, and a greater cost of following Jesus. The qualities of Christian discipleship don't change; the gospels and New Testament letters lay them down clearly. We don't get a different Bible in the end times. So our development of character, the use of our gifts, our loving relationships, our daily witness, our faithfulness in our work and destiny, our use of money and time, our growth in prayer, our steadfast commitment to God's people in fellowship – all these are as important as they always have been. But the point I am making is that everything will be at a more intense level.

The purpose of the gospel of grace, in Paul's understanding, is to help us live well in the intensity of turbulent times and to be always ready for Christ's return. God's grace 'teaches us to say "No" to ungodliness and worldly passions, and to live self-controlled, upright and godly lives in this present age, while we wait for the blessed hope – the appearing of the glory of our great God and Saviour, Jesus Christ' (Titus 2:12–13).

We need to have a different mindset if we are preparing for Jesus' appearing. To change the analogy from hiking to driving, think for a moment about how you drive a car. If you are on the roads of your neighbourhood or city, you know fairly confidently how to operate your standard family car under normal conditions. Now consider being given a 'driving experience' day on a Formula One race track. You now find yourself behind the wheel of a Ferrari supercar or a single-seater Formula One racing car, doing laps on one of the fastest tracks in the world. Your steering, pedalling, gear-changing and ability to drive are not essentially different, but everything is on a more intense level. You are accelerating from 0 to 100 mph in under five seconds; you are driving at 150 mph along fast straights, and navigating thrilling corners and experiencing the G-forces that racing drivers know well. Driving for just a few laps in those conditions would leave you feeling physically tired and mentally exhausted.

In the intensity of the coming years, as believers we will need to seek more anointing of the Holy Spirit as we live and minister in a troubled world. We will need to ask God for more strength in our faith when the cost of following Jesus goes up. We will need to be reading God's word more deeply – to become discerning and flexible when revivals break out and churches are alive in God, when there are controversial manifestations of the Spirit and a higher level of power, and when there are more young Christians needing discipleship. We will need to learn to trust the Lord in a deeper way when local and global society starts getting shaken in ways that turn normal life upside down. It will all be more intense. Years ago, my wife prophesied over our unborn son that he would be strong in revival and joyful in persecution. This upcoming generation will indeed be led by the Spirit to be strong and joyful, radiant and resolute. In short, we will all need to buckle up for the ride of our Christian lives!

Pause for Thought

- How could I prepare to get ready for a more intense time of discipleship in future years?

Thinking more clearly about biblical eschatology

I believe eschatology and the study of the end times will soon cease to be a fringe interest in the body of Christ, and become a serious topic for contemporary understanding. We have to wonder how eschatology ever got taken off the table talk of the western church. My seminary training never included any serious teaching about eschatology and the events leading to the Lord's return in glory. It was not addressed in biblical studies or in practical, pastoral teaching. It came through in some systematic theology lectures, mainly in the context of mission and ethics, but not in any way bringing an awareness that we could be training a last-days generation of scholars, evangelists and pastors. I imagine that is typical of mainline theological institutions. Is it any wonder then that church leaders don't bring this into their preaching or equipping of the flocks under their care?

The Holy Spirit will challenge us to redress this imbalance, and I am confident that we will see much greater emphasis on grappling with end-time studies across the whole church.

Our changing context and prophetic voices will demand it. In theological circles, the last fifty years have seen what is sometimes called the 'reopening of the eschatological office' – great renewed interest in understanding mission, the church, the whole faith, in the light of the end. Also, the fine work being done by some theologians recently, around biblical visions of the future kingdom consummated and the new heaven and earth, is challenging our sense of moral responsibility for the environment and social change now. On the other end of the spectrum, popular interest has surged in the last fifty years in examining biblical end-time prophecy, and sometimes those on the eccentric fringe of evangelicalism have made it their hobby horse, aligned with particular fascinations with doomsday narratives or conspiracy theories. It is, however, the large group in the middle that I am interested in helping to re-engage with the end times – the majority of church leaders and church members. For eschatology frames not just academic papers or ethical responsibility, nor just a hobbyist interest in biblical prophecy and end-time timelines, but the whole of our Christian existence and the trajectory of mission. Eschatology is all about God's future, our vibrant hope, the kingdom of God that is accelerating from the future to meet us. Clear end-time teaching provides the goal and motivation to live well. In short, we need to recapture an eschatological framework in reading Scripture.

This sharp focus is embedded in the apostles' exhortations in the New Testament. John writes: 'But we know that when Christ appears, we shall be like him, for we shall see him as he is. All who have this hope in him purify themselves, just as he is pure' (1 John 3:2–3). Peter also argues that clear thinking and purposeful living stem from a heightened expectation of the Day of the Lord: 'You ought to live holy and godly lives as you look forward to the day of God and speed its coming' (2 Pet. 3:11–12).

So if Jesus is bringing eschatology back into the table talk of the church, and if he is preparing us for more intense discipleship, we must respond to his promptings and his call to prepare to be an end-time generation. Whether it is us or our grandchildren who live through Tribulation pressure and the coming again of Jesus, the call to the church to prepare starts now. We need to start adjusting our lives *now* for what God is doing in our days. The devil may have a plan to ravage lives and to bring darkness and tribulation to the earth, but God has a greater plan to prepare the world for the fullness of his kingdom and to draw many millions into his arms of love.

As a church, our embracing of radical discipleship, and our serious attention to biblical prophecy about the future, will help us look forward to the Lord's promised coming with open arms. We take a position of faith and trust in God, whatever the outward circumstances, and we do not back down. We welcome the move of the Spirit as it comes, and learn to ride the waves of revival and to recognize the revealing of his glory in greater measure. We learn to discern what God may be doing, even in the times of shaking. We ask him to show us what he is doing, and use it as a time to be strengthened and to share the gospel. We welcome his training and equipping, helping us to grow in biblical insight so that our spirits soar in greater revelation of Jesus our beautiful King. To have an open heart, to welcome all that God is doing in our days, to be confident that his Spirit is with us, that he is always good, and to trust that he will bring us through difficulty and trial and 'present [us] before his glorious presence without fault and with great joy' (Jude 24) – that is our great privilege as his people in the end times.

Pause for Thought

- How much do people in my church or small group chat about the signs of the times and biblical prophecy?

Aligning Ourselves with God

At the beginning of the book of Revelation is a stated blessing: 'Blessed is the one who reads aloud the words of this prophecy, and blessed are those who hear it and take to heart what is written in it, because the time is near' (Rev. 1:3). The visions of Revelation contain the clearest timeline and scenario of end-time trouble, judgment and overcoming discipleship, culminating in Jesus' second coming and the start of the age to come. The time of these prophecies being fulfilled has always been near – in the sense that the church is potentially always just one generation away from Jesus' return. Yet the meaning of 'near' here means the next thing on God's timeline. Jesus is telling John that, now that the church age of mission in the power of the Spirit has been inaugurated, the next great time period on the divine calendar is this end-time countdown to his return in glory. The more alignment we see between world events and these biblical prophecies, the more we know we are right at the edge of the full in-breaking of heaven to earth. For the generation that is alert to and walks in this prophesied time, Jesus promises a special blessing. We are blessed if we read this prophetic vision with sober insight, and blessed if we hear it and take it to heart, responding to it faithfully.

This big learning curve of navigating the terrain of end-time ministry requires a deep alignment with God. We are not ready for the coming turbulent years, and only by great reliance on the Holy Spirit can we become in tune with how God is working in the world and how to partner well with him. We need to be closely aligned with God at the levels of a wholehearted embracing of the journey, a greater clarity of vision, and a stronger faith stance. We will look at these in turn.

Wholehearted embracing of the journey

My wife and I have tried to have a simple approach to following God's call on our lives, namely saying 'yes' to his leading. Even as we started courting, we agreed that we would go wherever God would lead us. From exploring missionary work, going on pilgrimages to revival hotspots, relocating to unfamiliar cities, moving into pastoral church ministry, to setting up a house of prayer, our attempt has been to constantly say 'yes' to God, even if we didn't know where his call would lead. Sometimes his leading has been clear and wonderful, at other times confusing and even painful, yet our trust in his unerring sovereign guidance has proved him faithful. All discipleship starts with a simple 'yes' to following Jesus.

One of the key questions arising from this book is this: is Jesus really calling us as a whole church to be transformed in a generation or two into a beautiful, prepared bride ready for his return? Is he really asking us to become radiant and resolute people who will help usher in the second coming as we cry out 'Come, Lord Jesus'? If so, then this invites our necessary response.

The divine invitation to navigate the unexplored terrain of end-time ministry is a sober privilege. We could be the ones who become the transitional generation, foretold in Scripture, which sees the mighty works of God displayed at the end of the age. As the early church fulfilled its calling to be his witness in the powerful dynamic of the Acts of the Apostles, God is asking the church in the coming years to step into its calling to be his witness in the face of an Antichrist rule and global outpourings of the Spirit. We cannot lightly take up the invitation to be an overshadowed, fervent, anointed, outpoured, cruciform, mature and transfiguring people of God. Yet it starts with a 'yes'. A 'yes' from an individual, from a congregation, from a city church, from a ministry, from bodies of Christian leaders.

As the Gospel of Luke reminds us, Mary the mother of Jesus is the model disciple in her response to God's call. The angel's invitation is for her to bear the longed-for Messiah, and to allow the power of the Spirit to overshadow her, enabling the incarnation of the divine Son of God. Her heart may have been troubled but, despite this, her questions did not begin with 'but'; they asked 'how'. Mary did not know the glory and the pain this invitation would entail for her life. All that mattered was her willing 'yes', her submission and openness: 'let it be to me according to your word' (Luke 1:38 ESV).

I am just one of many writers and preachers who are stirring the church to think about the end times, not as an academic subject, but as a wake-up call to follow Jesus in remarkable times. We as his people are not pawns but actors in the end-time drama. We have real choices to make, and responses to Jesus' leading that have bigger consequences than we may realize. Realizing that God intends us to overcome in times of tribulation, realizing that he is using the troubles of the end of the age to refine us and make us radiant, realizing that he is preparing us to receive and possess the kingdom in its fullness – all of this brings a sober and holy assessment of the years ahead.

The most radical and simple thing we can do in the face of Jesus' invitation to follow him into this end-time season is to say a wholehearted 'yes'. I wonder what it might look like for a group of churches in a city, or a whole denomination, to say 'yes' to God's invitation to end-time ministry. A corporate embracing of the need of the hour, from church movements and streams, sets in motion the rising up of the church, a church that fixes its gaze on the return of the Son of God to earth and how we must live towards that glorious end. Such a heart response, from many millions of believers, begins the process of the retuning of our hearts, the alignment of our spirit, the renewing of our minds, that is needed to face the approaching storm.

Pause for Thought

- What does Mary's response to the angel's words teach me about being open to God's call and future?

Greater clarity of vision

A book on the church in the end times is not too surprising in the current popular climate of future thinking in the twenty-first century. Yet if our prospection into future scenarios for humanity is truly Christian, it already has a shape, an orientation and a goal. The shape has been set in the great biblical acts of God in Christ that form an arc from the incarnation, through the crucifixion, resurrection and ascension, to their culmination in his second coming. The orientation is towards a final drama in which God defeats evil, vindicates the saints, and brings in his kingdom in its fullness. The goal is union – God living with people, heaven coming to earth, the renewal of all things, the perfection of the age to come.

If we are not soaked in Scripture we can miss seeing the ending that God has in store. The average Christian tends to listen more to contemporary cultural influencers than they do to the word of God, so no wonder our vision is a little dim.

As believers, we need to learn to refocus our gaze on what God has set out as his future for our world and the universe. This takes some effort because we are bombarded with worldly observations on the meaning and purpose of life. Media channels are filled with what current evolutionary atheistic science puts out about future scenarios for the extinction of the world, for finding extraterrestrial life, and for human transcendence through medicine, mind-uploading technologies and artificial intelligence. As followers of Jesus, we need to fix our minds and focus on the future that God has purposed – a future that is brilliantly devised, fully able to accommodate all the twists and turns of human free will and societal decisions, and gracefully yet powerfully drawing everything together in the fullness of time.

This is what Paul means in Ephesians chapter 1 when he says that God will 'bring unity to all things in heaven and on earth under Christ' (1:10).

In a fascinating recent book called *Game Over? Reconsidering Eschatology*, a group of Christian academics discuss the relation of traditional Christian understandings of the 'end' with recent developments in the natural sciences about the inevitable end of the universe. Is there an easy reconciling of the bad news of a cataclysmic end of the known universe with the good news of a Christian view of the eschaton? The editors face this dilemma:

Christians ought to place their trust in a certain vision of the 'end,' but as women and men of the 21st century they might find it difficult to articulate this trust with the picture modern science presents to us. Or perhaps schizophrenia can be avoided, but in such a way that, in the Christian view, modern science only gives us one part of the equation (the finitude of the created order), whereas the Christian faith adds something crucial, namely: the world will indeed end, but God, as creator of the world, will renew it through God's resurrecting power.[1]

The reality in the church is that we don't think biblically about the future very often and we don't envision our future very far ahead. We put in place strategies for the next few years or decade. We plan from inside our current paradigm and we struggle to think out of the box and envisage radically new futures. As Christians we should be better at this than most, for we have the biblical texts of prophetic promise of a renewed world, and a kingdom which is not just vague potential but formed clearly in God's purposes and coming from the future to meet us.

Jesus wants to encourage us as his church to have his glorious return and the coming perfect eschaton as a clear and consistent focal point in our lives because it will help us focus better on what to do here and now. Consider for a moment how people focus a camera. Well, it's easy with phone cameras, because they do it automatically for you. Yet if you held the most expensive camera in the world, a Leica rangefinder, you would have to learn a whole new way of focusing your image. Rangefinder cameras have two small focusing windows when you look through the viewfinder at a scene. You have a clear far image of the scene and you're given a second fuzzy image of the scene, and your goal is to turn the focus ring until the two images match up for the subject you'd like to have in focus. Then you can take your perfect photo!

I think that is a little like focusing on the end times. If we only focus on the near-future view, just the next few years, we may lack the clarity of last-days purpose which Jesus is encouraging us to have. We may also struggle to make sense of turbulent global events. But, if we have a clear end-time view of what God has in store for us, and if we search the Scriptures to understand a biblical, prophetic end-time timeline, then we can adjust our focus on how we live now and run well. When we read the Bible what do we find? We find our destiny is not about living a nice life and being a good Christian until we die. It is about being caught up in God's great mission, the *missio Dei*, and his worldwide plans to demonstrate the kingdom now and to prepare the earth for Jesus' return. In Scripture we find clear indications of a great final harvest, the clash of nations, Satan's great rage against the saints, and a countdown to Jesus' coming on the clouds. Knowing this future as God's people, we can adjust our thinking about life in the years to come. We need to refocus on the end so that we can live well in the present moment.

Pause for Thought

- How could a sharp focus on the end times help me in my walk with God here and now?

Stronger faith stance

One of my favourite animated films is the Pixar movie *Wall-E*. It is a futuristic tale about how life on earth has become

Preparing as the Whole Church

uninhabitable, and the story centres on a cute little robot, Wall-E, the only one left on earth, who is cleaning up the years of human waste. He meets a reconnaissance robot, EVE, and after finding a living plant among the debris, they are transported to a space cruise ship which had evacuated humans seven hundred years previously and is in a forever orbit. The pathetic scene painted shows people riding on hover chairs around this space resort, being fed through straws, entertained to the point of stupidity and, either through fat or bone loss, unable to walk or stand. The endearing plot culminates in the stupefied human captain being helped by the robots to stand up and take responsibility for a rescue mission to earth, and motivating the people on board to return to recolonize the world. The vision in the movie, of people learning to stand and walk again after years of incapacity and lack of exercise, is both hilarious and sobering.

I believe that we will need to learn to stand well in the midst of glory and shaking. Where once Christians were pew sitters or conference consumers, in the future we will have to have a stronger faith stance, train as though preparing for an endurance challenge, and rely deeply on the Holy Spirit's empowerment to navigate the most difficult but awesome global context for Christian living.

In the Luke 21 discourse about the end times, Jesus speaks three times about the need to stand well in the last days. In the midst of persecution, when Christians will be imprisoned, betrayed, put on trial and even martyred, he tells us to 'stand firm, and you will win life' (v. 19). That is an encouragement that we will be enabled by God to stand strong in our faith and witness in the most pressing times. Some people crumble under pressure; others find that it reveals their inner strength. Jesus stood unwavering throughout his passion, leading to the cross, while his disciples crumbled and fled. In later years, leaning on the Holy Spirit, they emulated him in their own response to trouble and persecution and death. We too are promised strength to stand firm in our witness to him, whatever the cost.

Then, in the midst of apocalyptic signs in the heavens, shaking and anxiety on earth, and glorious signs of Jesus' imminent return, the Lord exhorts us to 'stand up and lift up your heads, because your redemption is drawing near' (v. 28). There is an English idiom I like: 'to stand a-tiptoe'. It means to be alive or awake to something exciting, to be full of anticipation; we have all seen small children standing a-tiptoe in great excitement about something they are about to enjoy. I think that is the meaning Jesus is bringing here. He is exhorting us to believe that in the worst of the Tribulation time, we will be given, in contrast, great faith and joyful anticipation of his coming in glory. We will be like children about to be liberated and let out for joyful play.

Then, in the midst of global troubles and turmoil, when people are burying their heads in the sand or being paralysed by fear, Jesus tells us to 'be always on the watch, and pray that you may be able to escape all that is about to happen, and that you may be able to stand before the Son of Man' (v. 36). This is a confident standing while all else is shaking. To 'escape' here doesn't mean to be whisked away out of trouble, but to be carried or sustained through the worst. It is fascinating that what sustains people or communities through crisis times tends to be hope for a better future. Without that hope, communities quickly fall into despair. Christians have a confident hope that, at the end of end-time tribulation, we will stand before the Lord, fully delivered from Satan's attacks and living in God's glory. God wants to inspire us now to watch and pray like never before, to stand and not fail in our faith when everything around is being shaken; for we know the glorious future to which we are heading.

So a challenge to the church in these days is to learn in the Spirit how to stand well – standing firm and resolute in persecution, standing expectantly in glory and last-days signs, standing confidently in the day of trouble. This is the clear biblical call to all Christian believers and communities who find themselves navigating the days of the end times. We start by standing more strongly now – finding deeper trust in God when faced by the personal crises of today, becoming more confident in sharing our faith today, not being over-shaken by a tragic world news report. We are in a training season and we must make the most of the time. There will need to be a much more united standing together as the church in the coming years, oriented around the gospel which unites us, and the coming triumph of God. We can stand stronger when surrounded by fellow believers who are encouraging each other by their commitment of faith and resoluteness of spirit. Jesus' exhortation is for a generational group of believers, and he wants to train us now to stand firm, expectant and confident in him, before the last days become even more challenging.

Pause for Thought

- How well do I stand up for my faith at the moment?
- How can I grow stronger in my Christian convictions?

Preparing as Leaders

A book about the marks of the church in the end times is of interest to anyone who has been stirred to ponder the signs of the times and where we are in an end-time timeline. It will be of particular significance to those who have been called or appointed to leadership in part of God's church, wherever that is in the world. People look to leaders, as they set vision, motivate others to a cause, mobilize teams to achieve great ends, and oversee responsibilities that affect communities and even nations. Christian leaders have a high calling, particularly those who have some level of gifting to oversee the life of the church. They are also required by God to be spiritually aware of the signs of the times.

I have set out a vision of what the church in the end times might look like, one in which the collective body of Christ has been energized by the Spirit to shine like a radiant and resolute bride. In reality, most congregations or church streams do not look like that. So, what is our role in partnering with God as we lead the flock and pioneer in kingdom work in a way that steers us towards the transformation of the people of God? Do we think that God is going to sovereignly renew the lives of millions of believers without our aid, or have we a role to play?

A Word to Church Leaders: What Are You Building?

In the recent post-pandemic years, there has been much angst among church leaders as to how to grow Christian communities and regather congregations. Many felt pastoral heartache in trying to shepherd the flock through difficult times, and many struggled with a mix of both weariness and hope in trying to lead churches into a genuinely new missional opportunity after Covid. Growing a church in this new context has been a contemporary challenge for every leader. Alan Hirsch describes these times of painful transitions as fresh moments of *metanoia*, 'a transformational cleansing of perception, which enables a new, expansive, way of viewing the world'.[1] Refusing to recognize this metanoia shift in perception results in a place where 'we are no longer able to recognize the ever-widening greatness of the living God who has an eternity of revelation to show us'.[2]

Is this eschatologically charged moment one of the great metanoia moments in the life of the worldwide church? Can it help to reframe our noble visions for our churches and communities with God's greater vision for his glory filling the earth? The Lord holds out a future of great hope amid difficulty. Most leaders see locally or regionally; God's vision is for everyone in the global body of Christ to move in his purposes together, and to become radiant and resolute in our walk and witness.

Houses of the Watchful and the Wise

The most wonderful and yet testing time of ministry is upon us as church leaders. A global move of the Spirit is prophesied alongside the shaking of nations in the end times. This means that Holy Spirit anointing, renewal and harvest will be hand in hand with global and local turmoil and spiritual opposition to the gospel. For those who are pastors or teachers, I believe Jesus' teaching on the end times in the synoptic gospels is a relevant tutorial on leadership ministry. In the Olivet discourse of Matthew 24, after speaking about the Tribulation and the coming of the Son of Man, Jesus closes with a call to his followers to live watchful and wise lives. I believe that in this critical hour of history, the Lord wants us to build houses of the watchful and the wise.

House of the watchful

Jesus said: 'Therefore keep watch, because you do not know on what day your Lord will come' (Matt. 24:42). He spoke these words in the context of world trouble and the swiftness of his return. What does a watchful house of God look like? How do you model and equip people to be watchful?

Watchfulness refers to spiritual alertness and to prayer. This is certainly a challenge to the church in more prosperous western nations. In places where the church is enduring persecution, there is certainly more prayer and there is more attentiveness to being strong in the spiritual life. We looked earlier in this book at the letters to the churches in Revelation, in which Jesus constantly called churches to overcome spiritual dullness and compromise, and to respond well to what the Spirit is saying.

Watching before Jesus and watching for Jesus

Leaders need to help their people to both watch *before* Jesus and watch *for* Jesus. To watch *before* Jesus refers to alertness to the biblical signs of the times. If you are a Bible teacher and have not taught on end-time prophecy, now would be a good time to start. Doctrinal differences are not as important as opening the prophetic scriptures and letting people read and hear what the biblical authors were led to write about the last days. The Spirit will increasingly bring discernment as to what is happening in the world as it lines up with prophecy, so that his people can be ready for the intense times that are coming.

To watch before Jesus also refers to intercessory prayer. Seasoned intercessors in the Bible transitioned from cries of help and shopping-list prayers to conversation and partnership. Abraham sought to understand God's judgments against Sodom and Gomorrah. Habakkuk tried to discern why God used apparent evil to bring about his greater good. Daniel waited for God's explanation of end-time visions beyond his generation. If you are teaching about prayer in your church, you will need to touch on these aspects of the church standing in the gap and partnering with heaven in intercession. Watching and praying may mean living in great tension in Tribulation times, but it is the church's privilege to pray in the purposes of God in the end times.

To watch *for* Jesus means encouraging expectancy about his near return. Churches have sometimes been sidetracked from serious teaching on the parousia because of more sensationalized early Rapture doctrines. Now is the opportune time to bolster the core hope of Christian faith among your congregation, namely that we 'wait for the blessed hope – the appearing of the glory of our great God and Saviour, Jesus Christ' (Titus 2:13). Far from the second coming being a distraction to the church's mission, it becomes the great motivator. Knowing that the end of the Christian story is near actually increases our joy and our desire to seed and share the gospel. To watch for Jesus also means vocalizing our longing for his return. Holy love for our bridegroom King is kindled by our realization that he longs for us and longs to return and take us to his side. Even to say in church together '*Maranatha!* Come, Lord Jesus' is powerful; it is a profound phrase, and it draws us into the longing of the church through the ages. It would be good to encourage this expectancy about his return in your own life as well as that of your faith community. Worship leaders in the midst of the coming revival will become less like performers or leaders of liturgy, and more like awestruck worshippers who sense the pull of the end of the age on their spirit. What would it be like to have whole communities of faith across the world sharing the heart of the psalmist: 'I wait for the Lord more than watchmen wait for the morning' (Ps. 130:6)? This expectancy will certainly grow, the closer we move to his return.

Pause for Thought

- Is there a prophetic intercession group in my church or a house of prayer in my city?
- How might that help me to talk and pray about the signs of the times?

House of the wise

Jesus moved on in Matthew 24 to call for houses of the wise: 'Who then is the faithful and wise servant, whom the master has put in charge of the servants in his household to give them their food at the proper time?' (v. 45).

The days are coming when we won't need better, bigger churches but wiser churches – the house of the wise. In the light of the signs of the times, Jesus calls for faithful and wise ministry in the church. Wisdom will be in short supply in the end times, according to Scripture, because of people's pride and because of turmoil. We are tasked with looking after our house and attending to our ministry assignment. Both are important. What is the call of God on your life and ministry? What has he called you specifically to do or concentrate on? You will be responsible for answering to him for that. We are also responsible to God for the life of our spiritual communities. This is not supposed to bring fear into ministry, but instead to cause us to cry out for God's wisdom in discharging our ministry. Jesus here speaks of a direct correlation between disinterest in the signs of the times, forgetfulness about Jesus' return, and a misusing of our leadership responsibilities. If we lose sight of God's overarching salvation narrative, if we lose heart in the gospel hope set in Christ's first and second coming, if we lose our sense of kingdom orientation because the state of the world overwhelms us, we are in danger of missing our ministry mandate in the last days.

The Lord wants us to help lead people into discovering the unexplored terrain of end-time ministry, and for that we need the power of the Spirit and the wisdom of heaven. The end-of-the-age promise in Daniel is that 'those who impart wisdom will shine like the brightness of the heavens, and those who lead many to righteousness, like the stars for ever and ever' (Dan. 12:3). Thankfully, God is a father who longs to give the Holy Spirit to those who ask him, and so he stirs leaders to seek him and find him in all his fullness.

Houses to grow disciples and bring in the harvest

The context of congregational growth may have been difficult in recent years. However, there is soon coming a time when the life of the Spirit will be poured out across every nation in a global opportunity for spiritual harvest before Jesus comes back. Church leaders must endeavour now to build churches that become channels of Holy Spirit anointing and salvation which can be greatly used in a time of future revival. It is like raising our sails in anticipation of the coming wind.

To start with, we can pray that Jesus anoints a whole multitude of evangelists. As Christendom crumbles, a brand-new opportunity to share the gospel in the power of the Spirit will present itself to us. Church planting, already built into the mission strategy of many denominations, will become the major growth point and resource focus of church groups. As a church leader in this mode of being, you will become less the 'do-it-all pastor' and much more a facilitator of lay leadership and witness in the marketplace. Christian leadership may well be more about being a father or mother in the faith, giving permission to enable a multitude of kingdom disciples to seed missional communities in a myriad of places. Even now across the world, the wind of the Spirit seems to be stirring not big churches but creative communities of disciples who make disciples. The size of churches won't matter as much as the multiplication of disciples and kingdom witness in the community. Models of worship service won't be as important as responding to the greatness of God's presence among us. You may spend more time in nurturing people in faith, bringing the word of God into situations, and in overseeing fresh kingdom projects being seeded in every community. Perhaps the whole sense of hierarchy in denominations will fade into the background as spiritual mothers and fathers step forward to model kingdom values and bless sons and daughters to run in end-time ministry. Even in cities and regions, perhaps the Spirit will cause a great coming together of church leaders, throwing us open to new ways of working together in localities and cities for a spiritual harvest in an atmosphere of great faith and pressure.

Houses to equip the saints

Houses of the wise will be marked by an anointing to equip the saints. We will help people to stand strong in shaking times and to stay humble in revival times. Believers will need the full armour of God so that 'when the day of evil comes, you may be able to stand your ground' (Eph. 6:13). The rage of the devil will be unleashed against the church in the Tribulation, but the glory of the Lord will fill his church. Humble yet strong believers will be forged in this mix.

Those who teach and lead should be 'giving food at the proper time' to those in their care. I wonder if the preaching diet we are giving each other in the church is one that will help us stand in the glory and the shaking. Will it help us to withstand the assaults of the devil and the evil that will arise? The prophet Jeremiah stood alone among the leaders of his day, declaring God's word and warnings of trouble on the way, when all other public figures were proclaiming peace. Jeremiah was the only one preparing people well to understand what God was doing.

As a church pastor or teacher, you will find that the increasing global shaking, alongside moves of the Spirit, will force a certain concentration of people's minds to know God's word more. You can train people to be wise in their lifestyle, forgoing the pride and pleasures that our materialistic world chases after, and instead championing sober, focused and joyful discipleship. Pastors of end-time faith communities may deal with profound issues – division in families when some family members find faith; helping people through times of persecution; people problems in the mix of nurturing disciples and training leaders, as numbers of disciples multiply; encouraging faith in the midst of shaking in the nations. As the clash of light and darkness increases, it will become clear that 'the world and its desires pass away, but whoever does the will of God lives for ever' (1 John 2:17). We will encourage people to take a prophetic stance: that we are living for the age to come. Not that earth does not matter – far from it. Earth matters greatly, because the Lord has plans to renew all creation. But the hold that the things of this age have on us will lessen as we pursue his kingdom and righteousness.

As part of the renewing of his church as his radiant and resolute bride, I encourage you to believe that God will greatly anoint spiritual leaders of Christian communities across the world. If you seek him in the seriousness and privilege of these days, you will help build houses of the watchful and the wise, ready for all that is about to come at the close of this age.

Pause for Thought

- How does this encourage me to pray for the leaders in my church?
- If I am a leader, would I describe my church as a house of the watchful and the wise? (Think about your answer.)

A Word to Apostles and Prophets: What Kind of Church Are You Calling Out?

The prophetic call in Isaiah 60:1 to arise and shine is, I believe, a key prophetic scripture for this hour of history. The church is called to rise from slumber or despair, and shine in the reflection of the light of God's glory, and to be a bright presence in the context of great darkness on the earth. This passage spoke initially about the time of Jesus' first coming, and the salvation that he would bring as Israel's Messiah. Yet, as I have already mentioned, it has a fuller prophetic relevance in the time leading to Jesus' second coming, when the people of God are preparing for the great revealing of the Lord and his full kingdom in-breaking.

Apostles and prophets have a key role in helping to call out a radiant and resolute church to rise up in the nations of the earth.

Apostolic

The apostolic gifting is to pioneer and establish the church or an area of kingdom ministry in a particular context and place. As apostles respond to the stirring of the Spirit in these last days, they will be both pioneers and establishers of kingdom life in the coming end-time revival.

I will venture to suggest two key ways in which people with apostolic callings will be a blessing to the church in these days.

Establishing the church

Apostles will help people to stand strong on the foundation of the gospel and to understand and find conviction in the full hope of the gospel. The foundation is the first coming of Jesus, with the salvation revealed in his life, death and resurrection which calls all people to repentance and faith. When this truth is fiercely contested in our world of a multitude of beliefs, the apostles establish clearly the priority of the church to offer the saving grace of God in Christ. Apostles help to keep the main thing the main thing. This of course is not new, but is again critical in the harvest fields of the end times.

Apostles will also help the body of Christ find its full hope in the second coming of Jesus – a coming that redeems his people, defeats evil, renews planet earth and fills the world with the glory of God. They need to help establish the church in confidence in this fuller narrative. Light and darkness is increasing; the Christian story is not just about a saviour who died for our sins; it is also about a king who is coming to bring heaven to earth. This message is very countercultural. It goes against the grain of the popular evolutionary progression of human history, and of people's expectations for the future of our planet. Even the great theodicy of God's dealings with ever-present evil is answered in the fuller presentation of the gospel. Ahead of the Tribulation times, apostles can help the church find its confidence in the fullness of the biblical story and the arc of salvation history. As those with a kingdom focus rather than a local church focus, apostles can bring a clearer view of what God is doing in our days, and equip God's people to rise in brightness. There is a clear anointing on apostolic ministries to help reform the church into the life God is establishing. In the dark days of the end times, God's people will need to be people of conviction. Apostles will help us realize that we have a gospel to proclaim that culminates in the Lord's return to save his people and bring the greatness of his kingdom. Because of this global witness, multitudes of unbelievers will be drawn to faith, to the hope set in the gospel, and to a God who will allow the shaking of everything that can be shaken in order to win the hearts of those who are lost.

Blazing a trail

The second way in which apostles will bless and strengthen the church will be in blazing a trail in navigating the terrain of end-time ministry. The marks of being overshadowed, fervent, anointed, outpoured, cruciform, mature and transfiguring will gradually emerge in the midst of outpourings of the Spirit and the increasing pressure of the global shaking, but they will first be championed by apostolic ministries and individuals. These will help to establish a way of being that is unusual for the body of Christ, and help it to become normative. There is a new church 'architecture' and a last-days kingdom expression that needs pioneering in many spheres, wherever apostles are found. This will be true whether in church planting, in kingdom business initiatives, in working in mercy ministries, in overseeing church streams, or in the political arena, to name a few. Apostles will flow with the power of the Spirit in revival, along with meeting the needs of the world in the midst of shaking, and harnessing their God-given initiatives of bringing kingdom life into certain areas of society or a community, blazing a trail for others to follow. They will help the global church to grow in brightness and in clarity concerning her end-time gospel mandate.

Pause for Thought

- Can I recognize apostolic leaders and ministry in my city or nation?
- Do I value them?

Prophetic

God is also maturing and anointing prophetic ministries across the world. There are new, emerging councils of prophets in different nations, and myriad prophetic voices declaring the word of the Lord online and in social media. While these can be conflicting and confusing in part, I believe that the Spirit will sharpen, refine and use these ministries powerfully in the coming years. As well as heralding what God is doing and bringing prophetic warnings, the core of their message will be increasingly to call out the radiance and resoluteness of the end-time church. Jesus' instruction in the letters of Revelation is to hear what the Spirit is saying to the church. All of those calls to overcome find their ultimate expression in the rising up of the bride of Christ in the last days.

We must not forget that the Bible also warns of the rise of false prophets in the last days. How to discern true from false prophets? Personal character will be a test of true prophetic voices, because, as Jesus said, 'By their fruit you will recognise them' (Matt. 7:16). Accountability to church leadership and to other mature prophetic voices will be another test, as prophets living in strong fellowship will allow their messages to be weighed and discerned. Other tests of godly prophets will be the sincerity of their personal following of Christ as Lord, and how their messages amplify rather than contest the clear teachings of the Bible.

Showing who we are in Jesus' eyes and calling the church into position

In the last days the church's calling and vision are of paramount importance. Prophets will help the church to see who she really is in Jesus' eyes and estimation. They will help to communicate his zeal for his bride to become a mature partner in the end-time harvest, and his challenge to walk a tight, bright path of discipleship. They will explain the meaning of the glorious supernatural ways of God in the midst of revival outpourings. Prophetic voices will also bring a shocking relevance to biblical prophecies as birth pains increase and Tribulation events begin to unfold. In short, they will also help to call the end-time church into her place and identity.

The prophetic anointing will be a great blessing to the individual believer and the local congregation. As the gifts of the Spirit increase in the fires of revival in the coming years, it will be common to experience unerringly accurate prophetic words in communities of faith. Yet the prophets will also call out the apostolic church, in each city or region, to walk in end-time revival and awakening. Wherever churches come together in a common end-time revival purpose, the prophetic anointing to strengthen God's people and bring last-days direction will increase. On a bigger scale, God will use prophets to call each national church into its position in God's redemptive purposes for the end times. The church in every nation has a distinctive gifting that will bring a unique kingdom-expression in their land in order to bless the global body of Christ.

Moreover, in turn the prophets will help each church to call its nation or region to receive the kingdom. As the Lord's return draws nearer, the whole church will become a clear prophetic voice to call the nations to repentance and faith, and will speak into the lives of populations on how to be prepared for the end-time shaking. The destiny of communities and nations will depend on their response to the gospel in the midst of great crisis – how they either line up with kingdom ways or align with the Antichrist system as it comes into existence. God is bringing a measure of his glory upon the earth prior to his Son's return, and then, as he comes, Jesus will overturn all evil and fill the earth with his Father's glory. Every nation will be caught in this clash in the end times. Prophets will gain revelation on all these truths, for the individual believer, local congregations, national churches, and for nations and continents. As they see and hear the purposes of the Lord, they will declare these truths and help reveal his ways. God will draw out the gifts of his prophetic people to enable the church to fully arise and shine.

Pause for Thought

- What prophetic voices or ministries do I value and respect?
- If walking in a prophetic gifting, can I ask God to sharpen my voice to bless the body of Christ?

18

The Personal Challenge

I have spoken about the end-time message as it applies to the church generally and leaders specifically. I close by making a few remarks as to how you and I respond personally. The apostle Paul starts his concluding and practical section of Romans with these words: 'Therefore, I urge you, brothers and sisters, in view of God's mercy, to offer your bodies as a living sacrifice, holy and pleasing to God – this is your true and proper worship' (Rom. 12:1).

God is asking each of us for wholehearted living of our faith, especially as the time is short. How can we make this personal? You and I can learn how to live prayerfully (enjoying day-by-day communion with God), fully (embracing our life destiny), hopefully (sharing the good news) and preparedly (adjusting our priorities).

Live Prayerfully

If I took you to the country of Indonesia, you would find a radical prayer movement in the church that has been growing in the last twenty years. You would discover 5 million intercessors praying in the midst of the most hostile Muslim nation. You would be shown dozens of 24/7 prayer towers in office complexes which have been established for round-the-clock prayer over their nation. You would be told of the children's prayer movement there across 100 cities with 200,000 children. You would find a 12,000-seater World Prayer Centre built for regular mass prayer gatherings. You could move around Asia and find other, similar stories of prayer in the life of the church. You would begin to realize that the global church is waking up to the call to pray like never before.[1]

Jesus encouraged his disciples to 'always pray and not give up' so that when the Son of Man returns he will find people of faith on the earth (Luke 18:1,8). Right now, God is stirring his people to prayer across the world – ordinary Christians seeking God because of the urgency of the times. Choosing a prayerful and God-centred life is the best preparation for the coming years when we will experience both the anointing and the cost of being a disciple.

Christians always live in a state of tension: how much to live in equilibrium within their prevailing culture and how much to stand against the spirit of the age. The Sermon on the Mount reveals a tight, bright path of discipleship that Jesus calls us to walk. At the heart of this demanding yet liberating discipleship teaching, he calls his people into a lifestyle of praying, fasting and giving in the secret place. In the light of this, I think Jesus would encourage you to live closer to him, discover intimacy with him, and seek the Spirit's strength to pray in this hour. Make your times of worship and prayer with God the anchor point of your day. The apostle Paul exhorted his friends to live 'self-controlled, upright and godly lives' as they awaited the Lord's return (Titus 2:11–14). We too must learn to follow Jesus as purely and prayerfully as possible, so that we will receive a 'well done' from the Lord when we stand before him (Matt. 25:23).

In a passage charged with end-time symbolism, the prophet Joel calls for solemn assemblies of prayer in his nation. He sees the trouble coming upon his people as he declares:

> Blow the trumpet in Zion,
>   declare a holy fast,
>   call a sacred assembly.
> Gather the people,
>   consecrate the assembly;
> bring together the elders,
>   gather the children,
>   those nursing at the breast.
> Let the bridegroom leave his room
>   and the bride her chamber.
>
> *Joel 2:15–16*

Maybe the Lord is calling many of us to organize solemn assemblies of prayer to cry out to the Lord for his help and anointing in days of trouble and great opportunity for the gospel. God is taking the prayer meeting out of the back room and into the centre of the life of his church. Prayer is our lungs, our power, our communications centre as an end-time church.

There is a wonderful call for you to discover a deeper life of prayer with the Holy Spirit. He prays with you, is groaning deep within you, and joins your prayers with Jesus who is preparing to come back for you. The Lord is inviting us, as his whole people, to intimately know and walk with him through our lives and through the last days. He wants us all to pray and hopefully never give up in our generation. So may you live prayerfully, and walk as close to the Lord as you can, into the coming storm.

Pause for Thought

- Is my time of prayer the anchor point of my day?
- Can I gather with others to pray for God's help in the shaking that is happening?

Live Fully

At certain points in church history, there have been groups of people who thought the end of the world was near and subsequently went into a kind of *Star Trek* 'Beam me up, Scottie' moment! As an example, take the Millerites in 1843, a group of a few thousand New England residents, led by farmer-cum-preacher William Miller, who sold their possessions ready for a predicted rapture on April 23rd of that year. Many of them took to high ground, expecting to be lifted up into heaven. When Jesus didn't return, they were left embarrassed, and soon the group largely disbanded in frustration. There are a handful of unfortunate stories like that in history. Leaving family and possessions to go up a mountain to await Jesus' return sounds dramatic but not very responsible. The great Reformer Martin Luther reportedly said, 'If I knew that tomorrow was the end of the world, I would plant an apple tree today.' God has a call on your life, and he wants you to walk that out until the day you die or the day Jesus comes again. He would encourage you to fulfil your destiny. In the words of the apostle Peter: 'Each of you should use whatever gift you have received to serve others, as faithful stewards of God's grace in its various forms' (1 Pet. 4:10).

In these last days, therefore, I want to encourage you to take time to listen to God and discern your call and personal

The Personal Challenge 289

destiny. What unique difference can you make in this world in the name of Christ? Then, when you have discerned this, follow through on what the Lord has given you to do. Like the apostle Paul, run your race and receive a crown of righteousness (2 Tim. 4:7–8). Some people think Jesus' second coming is a way of leaving the world's mess behind for the bliss of heaven. We have seen in this book that the biblical story tells us that Jesus is returning to rule over planet earth and renew a spoiled creation. Whether you are a preacher, an environmentalist, a politician, a nurse or a warehouse worker or a student, I want to encourage you to see your life as bringing a unique contribution to preparing the way for the Lord. You prepare his way in your righteous living, in vocation, in service, in demonstrating his love and power, in extending God's kingdom in any sphere of life in which he places you. All of it is relevant, for Jesus wants to save and help people and shine his light through you. He is coming soon to renew our world and to rule righteously along with his saints.

The day of the Lord's return might be a few years off or a couple of generations away. None of us knows for sure. You might have a decade or the span of a whole career to bring your distinctive contribution towards seeing the church rise up, nations touched for Jesus, and transformation in your community. I expect the diet of Christian conferences and church teaching to become much sharper and more discipleship-focused in coming years. As the global church begins to realize that we are living in the final generation or two before the Lord's coming, there will be much more concentrated attention on the essentials of the Christian life and on equipping every believer to be a missionary and minister of the gospel.

What will happen in our world as millions of motivated Christians and an inspired visionary church move and walk with a fresh sense of destiny and great mission urgency? The world will be turned upside down. Your unique life and influence is helping to prepare the way of the Lord. So live fully the destiny God has crafted for your life.

Pause for Thought

- What do I feel God has placed me on this planet to do?
- Do I realize how it contributes to the kingdom of God spreading on earth?

Live Hopefully

In a best-selling book, *Twelve Rules for Life*, the psychologist and philosopher Jordan Peterson speaks about the importance of choosing our attitude to life. He draws attention, bizarrely, to lobsters, a 350-million-year-old species which has perfected a simple dominance hierarchy among its kind. There are victors and losers in lobster battles; the winner takes the spoils and the territory, while the loser lives at the bottom of the pile – and what is more, their simple brains have allowed scientists to see big chemical differences between a winning lobster and a losing lobster. Peterson encourages us to learn from this evolutionary example and to choose our attitude to life; to stand with our shoulders back, and take responsibility for our choice to live either a defeated or a positive life. He writes the following:

> To stand up straight with your shoulders back means building the ark that protects the world from the flood, guiding your people

through the desert after they have escaped tyranny, making your way away from comfortable home and country, and speaking the prophetic word to those who ignore the widows and children. It means shouldering the cross that marks the X, the place where you and Being intersect so terribly.[2]

While that doesn't sound very hopeful, Peterson is deliberately using biblical language to convey powerful messages of choice and transcendence. He calls people to rise up and take responsibility for the huge burden of their life. Many are stuck in the immanent possibilities of life – what we can humanly achieve with our own resources. And we have seen how disastrously that has worked out in western civilization over the last three hundred years, with empire building, world wars, ecological wastefulness and breakdown of community. Millions more are also stuck today, not just in the drudgery of life, but in the paralysing fear that the material world is all there is, that life has no transcendent meaning and that the future is bleak. Christian hope is about the transcendent, about what is beyond our human experience; we know that we are in God's big story and that his kingdom is both here now and coming fully. Indeed, life itself is full of transcendent moments, regardless of faith; our choice is to see them and to be part of the hope-building project of being an image of restored humanity.

Hope for the Christian is the most powerful motivation of all. Your invitation is to face the reality of a troubled world, and to rise up above your situation, suffering or lack of confidence; take your life, put it into God's hands and, together with others, make a huge Christian difference. That is why we are encouraged in Scripture to be 'joyful in hope' (Rom. 12:12). Hope is one of the most potent aspects of living Christianly. Whereas many people around you have no hope or sense of where the future is leading us, your witness, actions and hope shine with the light of heaven.

The apostle Paul gave a great example of this when he wrote to his son in the faith, Timothy, in his last-known letter from prison before his martyr death. In it he wrote powerfully about his hope. He found no shame in his suffering or imprisonment, because he knew the One he had believed in and was convinced 'that he is able to guard what I have entrusted to him until that day' (2 Tim. 1:12). He was not afraid that the time of his departure was drawing near, because he knew 'there is in store for me the crown of righteousness, which the Lord, the righteous Judge, will award to me on that day – and not only to me, but also to all who have longed for his appearing' (4:8).

The early church lived in vibrant hope, and those in the suffering, martyr church down through the centuries have lived and died in great assurance and confidence. Their fearless hope in Christ motivated them to live with transcendent purpose and to change the world person after person, city after city.

So I would encourage you to live hopefully and let your hope burn like a beacon in the world around you. You are part of God's answer to this world; you can find transcendent meaning through your faith. Specifically, let Jesus' coming kingdom be your inspiration to hope. The issues of the meaning of life will be hugely important in the swirl of trouble and revival. You will have many opportunities to tell people your story and tell them the big story, the great acts of God in Christ; share with people around you the hope that burns inside you.

The church will shine brighter as the days grow darker. I pray that Christian communities will become significant hubs of hope and practical action in the midst of their neighbourhoods. History teaches us never to underestimate the power of significant minorities acting with a vision for change in their world. I believe that the church will be the most significant global community in coming years, contributing much that is good for society and also holding a clear, life-affirming faith system.

The apostle Peter reminds us that God 'has given us new birth into a living hope through the resurrection of Jesus Christ from the dead, and into an inheritance that can never perish, spoil or fade' (1 Pet. 1:3–4). Our hope in the vindication of our faith, our hope in the spreading of God's kingdom in these last days – this hope in the gospel for Christians can and must overflow and affect our families, communities and society. God has got a plan. We know the beginning, middle and end of the story of history; evil does not win, but love triumphs! So live with your shoulders back and be a hopeful witness.

Pause for Thought

- If someone asked me to explain why my Christian faith gives me hope, what would I say?

Live Preparedly

I have been reading and rereading the stories of the Desert Fathers in recent years. I am fascinated by these Christian radicals of the second to fifth centuries AD who followed a call to a life of prayer, simplicity and solitude in the deserts of Egypt. In their simple dwellings, called 'cells', the Desert Fathers sought to live holy lives and influence their world through prayer and wise teaching. Their austere discipleship would shock most of us today, not just for their fasting and voluntary poverty, but also for their strict examination of the condition of their souls. They always had an eye on eternity and how they would one day stand before God. Abba Evagrius is a good example of a saint who learned that the fear of the Lord is the beginning of wisdom. He once counselled younger monks in this way:

> Keep in mind the remembrance of these two realities. Weep for the judgement of sinners, afflict yourself for fear lest you too feel those pains. But rejoice and be glad at the lot of the righteous. Strive to obtain those joys but be a stranger to those pains. Whether you are inside or outside your cell, be careful that the remembrance of those things never leaves you, so that, thanks to their remembrance, you may at least flee wrong and harmful thoughts.[3]

Weep for the judgment of sinners, rejoice in the lot of the righteous – in other words, live with eternity in mind. Are we preparing our lives to be rewarded by God on the day we stand before him? I want to encourage you to examine your soul, to prepare yourself for the things that precede Jesus' return – both glory and shaking, revival and persecution – so you can persevere to receive a 'well done' from the Lord. The psalmist said:

> Wait for the LORD;
>   be strong and take heart
> and wait for the LORD.
>
> Ps. 27:14

The apostle Paul called on his followers to realize that 'the night is nearly over; the day is almost here. So let us put aside the deeds of darkness and put on the armour of light' (Rom. 13:12). Isaiah called on us to 'arise, shine, for . . . the glory of the LORD rises upon you' (Isa. 60:1).

Intrinsic to the end-time message in Scripture is the call to holiness – for those who follow God to be wholehearted, to give everything to serve him. We live holy lives as we wait for his coming. We walk in the light, and we shine that into the darkness around us.

As we have seen previously, in Matthew 25 Jesus told a parable about a group of wise and foolish young women to explain the need for wise living while waiting for his return: 'At that time the kingdom of heaven will be like ten virgins who took their lamps and went out to meet the bridegroom. Five of them were foolish and five were wise. The foolish ones took their lamps but did not take any oil with them. The wise ones, however, took oil in jars along with their lamps' (Matt. 25:1–4).

The wisdom of the five wedding attendants was not in their enthusiasm or desire but in the preparedness of their lives before God. They had oil; they had invested in their relationship with the Lord. In the confusion of end-time pressure and difficulty, will we be those who grow weary and become dull or compromised in our Christian lifestyle, or those who stay alert and fully surrendered for God to use us in his purposes? You may well be carried along by waves of revival in coming years, but there is no substitute for personal development through feeding on God's word and times of prayer to help you stay strong in faith. Small groups of disciples, living life together, being real with one another, and encouraging each other in their destiny and faith, will be the core make-up of the church of the future.

The wisdom of the five young women was also in their prophetic stance. They kept their lamps burning so as not to miss the arrival of the bridegroom. It was night-time and all were sleepy, but the wise ones were ready for the midnight cry: 'Here's the bridegroom! Come out to meet him!' (Matt. 25:6). There is so much on the agenda of the church, so many needs, so many calls for our attention, but Jesus asks us to be those who live in the light of the age to come. The kingdom is about to break in fully. How will you walk in a way which shows to a watching world that you are living for the age to come? The closing years of human history will be the best of times and the worst of times. The Lord wants you to stand with a peaceful spirit in shaking times and be able to speak words of wisdom or guidance to those shaken by the coming Tribulation: to neighbours in distress, friends in trouble, even governmental leaders at a loss for what decisions to make. There is a necessary preparation now so we can be used by the Lord in the future.

Many are starting to wonder if the shaking in the recent global pandemic has forced a total reformation of how we are church. God may well be reshaping us at a depth that is uncomfortable so that we can emerge more surrendered, more flexible, more loving and more prophetic for the end times. If that is true, it is because God wants to enable you and me to cope and overcome in the intense pressure of chaos and crisis and evil that could threaten our faith. Our lamps need to be trimmed and ready; in our walk with the Lord we need to be expectant and longing for his return. Now is the time for you to grow in faith and purpose and prayer, so you can navigate the end times well, call others into the kingdom, and not lose focus on the Lord amid the troubles. So live preparedly to journey through the years of glory and crisis, so you can be fully ready when the bridegroom King returns.

Pause for Thought

- How does Jesus' parable about the wise and foolish young women challenge or encourage me in my faith?

Summing Up

How does God ask us to see the church in the future?

When Thomas Edison, the great American inventor who gave us the light bulb and the phonograph, was a child, he came home one day and gave a piece of paper to his mother. He said, 'My teacher gave this paper to me and told me to only give it to my mother.' His mother scanned it through, and became tearful as she read the letter out loud to him: 'Your son is a genius. This school is too small for him and doesn't have enough good teachers for training him. Please teach him yourself.'

Edison went on to become one of the greatest inventors of the early twentieth century. Many years later, after his mother had died, he found himself looking through some old family papers. He came across that old letter from school, picked it up and opened it. On the paper was written the following words: 'Your son is addled [meaning mentally ill]. We won't let him come to school any more.' Edison cried for a long time and then wrote in his diary: 'Thomas Alva Edison was an addled child that, by a hero mother, became the genius of the century.'

The church is the greatest yet the most misunderstood reality, the most beautiful but flawed entity in human history. The world may have sidelined us and marginalized us. The devil may taunt us and put fear into us. Yet God calls out what we are becoming, and he simply asks that we listen to him, believe him, and rise into our destiny – that of being a radiant and resolute church. He will help us to live prayerfully, fully, hopefully and preparedly before him. The bride of Christ is rising up, and she will make herself ready to meet her King!

Coda: Three Visions of the Bride of Christ in the Age to Come (Rev. 19 – 22)

I want to end this book by painting for you a meditative reflection on three visions that we see at the close of the book of Revelation. They depict the church at the end of the age – the people of God that we will one day be – as we are rewarded for our faithfulness and the Lord is celebrated for his triumph. They are: a wedding, a reigning and a dwelling. I have quoted scriptures to anchor these visions, and then provided a devotional reflection on each.

Vision 1: A Wedding

Key Scripture:

> Then I heard what sounded like a great multitude, like the roar of rushing waters and like loud peals of thunder, shouting:
>
> 'Hallelujah!
>   For our Lord God Almighty reigns.
> Let us rejoice and be glad
>   and give him glory!
> For the wedding of the Lamb has come,
>   and his bride has made herself ready.

Fine linen, bright and clean,
  was given her to wear.'

(Fine linen stands for the righteous acts of God's holy people.)

Then the angel said to me, 'Write this: Blessed are those who are invited to the wedding supper of the Lamb!'

Rev. 19:6–9

Additional Scriptures:

I say to you that many will come from the east and the west, and will take their places at the feast with Abraham, Isaac and Jacob in the kingdom of heaven.

Matt. 8:11

The kingdom of heaven is like a king who prepared a wedding banquet for his son.

Matt. 22:2

I tell you, I will not drink from this fruit of the vine from now on until that day when I drink it new with you in my Father's kingdom.

Matt. 26:29

On this mountain the L<small>ORD</small> Almighty will prepare
  a feast of rich food for all peoples,
a banquet of aged wine –
  the best of meats and the finest of wines.
On this mountain he will destroy
  the shroud that enfolds all peoples,
the sheet that covers all nations;
  he will swallow up death forever.

Isa. 25:6–8

Reflection

The saints stand bedazzled by the sights around them. They have found themselves on the heights of the mountain with heavenly vistas stretching as far as one can see. They are all rubbing their eyes; all have been waiting for this moment, but none are truly ready as it happens. Some have come almost fresh from the horror and thrill of the great last battle, where they fought as martyrs and resisters against everything the Antichrist regime stood for; once scorched and bloodied, they are now washed and healed. Some have recently awoken from the long bliss, the idyllic resting place in God's presence of those awaiting resurrection, new life now surging through their veins. Gladness and joy has overtaken them all.

All move about in wonder in their glorified bodies, dressed as wedding guests but more than guests, since they have been allocated seats of honour across the vast banqueting hall. There are new sounds, sights and dimensions to take in without being overwhelmed. The roar of 'Hallelujahs' still resounds around the heavenly chambers, the praise of angels and saints mingling in everlasting joy at what they all knew would come, though they almost didn't dare dream it could be here now.

Jesus is with them, among them, an awesome presence in his majesty and beauty. He is walking around, gazing collectively in love and affection at his people, his precious people; speaking words of affirmation into every spirit; laughing with them at the wonder he has been waiting so long to show them. All eyes are drawn to him, hearts bursting with pride at his magnificence, and gazing on his scarred and glorified body dazzling in light and power. He truly is the conquering lion of Judah and the darling lamb of God.

Angels mingle – serving, honouring, helping to host the beloved church on this most feted day. Their excitement knows no bounds, ministering to and cheering those whom they had helped so faithfully on earth. The Father's glory and grace encompass the whole celebration as he gazes upon his Son and his children; the perfection of this moment which was planned before the foundation of the world cannot be truly comprehended by any but him. The numinous presence of the Spirit is everywhere, flowing through and around the wedding feast. God in his overflowing Trinitarian love has reached out to all creation on earth and has now drawn his holy ones into the glory of fully knowing and being fully known.

The saints find themselves in a company, made up not of strangers, but of people whom they now relate to with instinctive knowledge and perfect love. Wonderful stories are told, testimonies heard everywhere of each person's life of faith and God's work of grace. Joyful wonder accompanies this sharing between all the guests at the banquet – redeemed human beings whose destinies were glimpsed dimly on earth but are now seen crystal clear here in the atmosphere of heaven. This company is many but one, shimmering in glorious splendour, all purified and transformed, revealed to the awe of heaven's multitude as the beautiful bride of Christ. In her dazzling garments of righteousness given and overcoming faith gained, she is led into this eternal moment of intimacy with her Lord, with his fragrant royal robes and fiery eyes of passionate love.

Tumultuous toasts are given to the union of the bride and bridegroom; glasses are raised to the triumph of God and his Messiah. And so the feasting – oh, the richness of this banquet prepared for all who love him, this wedding celebration which will last for a beatified season – so the feasting begins!

Vision 2: A Reigning

Key Scripture:

> I saw thrones on which were seated those who had been given authority to judge. And I saw the souls of those who had been beheaded because of their testimony about Jesus and because of the word of God. They had not worshipped the beast or its image and had not received its mark on their foreheads or their hands. They came to life and reigned with Christ a thousand years.
>
> *Rev. 20:4*

Additional Scriptures:

> In the last days
>
> > the mountain of the Lord's temple will be established
> > > as the highest of the mountains;
> > it will be exalted above the hills,
> > > and all nations will stream to it.
>
> Many peoples will come and say,
>
> 'Come, let us go up to the mountain of the Lord,
> > to the temple of the God of Jacob.
> He will teach us his ways,
> > so that we may walk in his paths.'
> The law will go out from Zion,
> > the word of the Lord from Jerusalem.

He will judge between the nations
  and will settle disputes for many peoples.

Isa. 2:2–4

See, a king will reign in righteousness
  and rulers will rule with justice.
Each one will be like a shelter from the wind
  and a refuge from the storm,
like streams of water in the desert
  and the shadow of a great rock in a thirsty land.

Isa. 32:1–2

But the court will sit, and his power will be taken away and completely destroyed forever. Then the sovereignty, power and greatness of all the kingdoms under heaven will be handed over to the holy people of the Most High. His kingdom will be an everlasting kingdom, and all rulers will worship and obey him.

Dan. 7:26–27

Truly I tell you, at the renewal of all things, when the Son of Man sits on his glorious throne, you who have followed me will also sit on twelve thrones, judging the twelve tribes of Israel.

Matt. 19:28

You are worthy to take the scroll
  and to open its seals,
because you were slain,
  and with your blood you purchased for God
  persons from every tribe and language and people and nation.
You have made them to be a kingdom and priests to serve our God,
  and they will reign on the earth.

Rev. 5:9–10

Reflection

Everything in the world was changing beyond recognition. The great King was on his glorious throne; the long-dreamed-of theocracy had begun. There was a new political centre now around which all life on earth revolved and to which everyone looked – the city of Zion, the millennial Jerusalem. How different life was now! Even the very atmosphere was changed and purified. The Armageddon war trials were long finished; the malevolence and filth of demonic influence were a distant memory. Satan had been bound, evil influences in the world rebuked and no longer prevalent. Sin was still a possibility, of course, for the humans populating the nations, but the curse of the fall over the earth was gone and the liberation of all things was fully in progress. National ruling systems, polluted and once aligned with the Antichrist, were now dismantled. Restorative justice was the theme of the season, as new administrations loyal to the King were in place in every land and sorting out the havoc and devastation of the old age.

Everything was now transforming because Jesus was here. His vast and complete government was being fully established both in heaven and on earth. Saints in their glorified bodies had positions of honour throughout the world. Some, such as the end-time martyrs, had special positions close to the Lord. Also those privileged few who had marked their lives on earth with particular humility and service were now ruling and administering God's edicts in different lands. The Jewish people, who had heralded the Lord's return to their land, now served him in the global worship centre of Jerusalem. Resurrected saints were governing alongside human rulers who had bowed the knee and worshipped as he returned. Angelic forces were now visible everywhere, resplendent in light and engaged with the King's business, instructing people how to live in the kingdom realm. For old paradigms of philosophy, religion and science were submitting to a superior reality. All were being versed in the concepts of the kingdom and the wisdom of the Spirit.

Worship and prayer echoed in homes and in civic life globally, pure and unclouded because there was no spiritual interference now. Even the very air was sweet and fresh. Great highways and transport systems were in place for the massive worship festivals at Jerusalem. And the King's manifesto was being implemented; the Great Renewal Project of planet earth was well under way. Scorched and ravaged ecosystems were slowly being balanced and replenished. The seas were now restored and teeming with life; the climate had been rescued from its dangerous weather extremes. Habitats were flourishing in every animal group, and both nature and people were living at peace and in equality with each other. Heaven's healing touch was felt everywhere; even top-level global summits in the presence of the King brought joy and clarity of thinking, for all dreams for the betterment of all societies and the planet were now possible. Technology, once harnessed to oppressive systems, was now yoked to wisdom to service people's needs and not master them. Even wealth creation with heavenly ingenuity, and wealth redistribution in every society, were becoming a resounding success. None now had too little and none had too much. The old societal transformational enterprises of God's people, untimely interrupted by the Antichrist's machinations, were now being picked up again and finished, better than had ever been hoped.

All this was taking time, of course; it might take the best part of a thousand years. But then that was fine, because lifespans were increasing, and families and communities were becoming multigenerational in walking in the ways of the Lord. God's resurrected people continued to intercede for and give guidance to those leading the task of restoring the various spheres of life to their full potential. The saints were happy beyond measure, living beyond the sting of death; they were kings and priests, living in intimacy with the King, and every day was better than the one before. Everything in the world was changing for the better in the King's Great Renewal Project, and best of all, the new heaven and earth and the new Jerusalem – finally coming to earth – were being prepared for them by the Father as his greatest gift. The best was yet to be.

Vision 3: A Dwelling

Key Scripture:

> One of the seven angels who had the seven bowls full of the seven last plagues came and said to me, 'Come, I will show you the bride, the wife of the Lamb.' And he carried me away in the Spirit to a mountain great and high, and showed me the Holy City, Jerusalem, coming down out of heaven from God. It shone with the glory of God, and its brilliance was like that of a very precious jewel, like a jasper, clear as crystal.
>
> Rev. 21:9–11

Additional Scriptures:

> Then the Lord will create over all of Mount Zion and over those who assemble there a cloud of smoke by day and a glow of flaming

fire by night; over everything the glory will be a canopy. It will be a shelter and shade from the heat of the day, and a refuge and hiding-place from the storm and rain.

Isa. 4:5–6

I did not see a temple in the city, because the Lord God Almighty and the Lamb are its temple. The city does not need the sun or the moon to shine on it, for the glory of God gives it light, and the Lamb is its lamp. The nations will walk by its light, and the kings of the earth will bring their splendour into it.

Rev. 21:22–24

Then the angel showed me the river of the water of life, as clear as crystal, flowing from the throne of God and of the Lamb down the middle of the great street of the city. On each side of the river stood the tree of life, bearing twelve crops of fruit, yielding its fruit every month. And the leaves of the tree are for the healing of the nations. No longer will there be any curse. The throne of God and of the Lamb will be in the city, and his servants will serve him. They will see his face, and his name will be on their foreheads. There will be no more night. They will not need the light of a lamp or the light of the sun, for the Lord God will give them light. And they will reign for ever and ever.

Rev. 22:1–5

Reflection

She walked unhurriedly among the rustling trees beside the flowing river in the freshness of the eternal new morning. She was close to the centre of everything right now; well, 'close' was a relative term in this place. The saint was at home in the great city of God, vast and spacious, intricate and intimate in its dimensions. It had countless layers and cavernous interconnected celestial spaces. She had a new body and new senses to appreciate all that was before her. It was so many things at the same time. It was her wonderful new home, for she had her own perfect space nestled by one high wall; it was a bustling city incredible to behold, full of life and people and movement; it was an idyllic garden, a paradise off the scale in glorious variety, a great vista of all that is beautiful, extending beyond sight; it was a vast realm, a kingdom domain with nothing to fear and everything to explore.

She often took long moments just to sit and experience the life around her and within her. The place shimmered with light; it reverberated with the hum of praise which pulsated through her and every other saint living there. The glory of the Lord's presence was so powerful, not just near the throne, but everywhere she went. In her glorious resurrected body, she had perfect insight, unsullied emotions, freedom from all earthly weights and restraints, and great intimacy with the Lord at all times. She, like everything in the city, was illuminated with the light of his presence. She had unhurried and joyful purpose in every step, whether moving at lightning speed or a walking pace.

Everyone here had purpose, with assignments that brought joy and contributed to the plans of God. Was there a hierarchy? Not that she had been told about. Yes, there was a heavenly pattern, beings with orders of glory, and saints accorded particular honour, but all here were esteemed and nowhere was out of bounds. Harmony, yes, perfect harmony existed between all residents, with time to share, praise, serve, and enjoy all that was prepared for them in heaven's environment. No darkness, no threat, no real need for sleep, but all the time in the world – time for every burst of praise, every kingdom job, every important conversation, every fresh fascination with eternity, every gasp at the beauty which appeared whenever you turned a corner in the paths of this city.

The saint could still see earth from here, for the new Jerusalem was hovering over the planet like a massive jewel, a dazzling celestial object. The new heaven and earth were still being prepared for the full revealing and the glorious extent of the dwelling of God with his creation. There was constant movement between here and earth, through the glory corridor of thunder, bright cloud and fiery light. The coming and going of angels and the people of God to administer his kingdom realm on earth was constant and delightful. There was a united and wonderful reality now of the government of the Lord, both in the heavenly city and in the earthly Jerusalem. The saint was involved, as all were, in the Great Renewal Project of planet earth throughout the Millennium. Even delegations of the redeemed earthly nations were allowed here, sharing in the pulsating life of the heavenly city, aligning everything on earth with the Father's perfect purposes, now fully revealed.

It wasn't right to talk about 'up here and down there' because dimensions in eternity were different. The world was opened now to the life of heaven; spiritual reality was not hidden but fully revealed; the limits of material reality were dissolved and brought into the greater dimensions of kingdom and eternity. The saint often lost track of time, yet it didn't matter, for there was time beyond measure to explore, and treasure this eternal life, so solid and deep, holy and light. All of her best dreams on earth were nothing compared to the life that she had entered into here. Every doorway led to more of the Lord; every fresh hour brought new glimpses of his majesty; and her joy, like that of all the billions of saints, knew no end.

Notes

Prologue: Calling Out the Church

1. Adapted from Isa. 60:1–2.

1 The Coming End Times

1. Martin E.P. Seligman, Peter Railton, Roy F. Baumeister and Chandra Sripada, *Homo Prospectus* (New York, NY: Oxford University Press, 2016), p. 7.
2. See also Zeph. 1:14; Isa. 13:9–11; Ezek. 30:3.
3. See also Dan. 7:23–27; Rev. 19:19–20.
4. Joshua Fields, 'Is Civilisation on the Brink of Collapse?' *Medium* (10 July 2018) https://medium.com/@joshfields/is-civilisation-on-the-verge-of-collapse-14ffa9cac6e4 (accessed 1 May 2024).
5. Alan Hirsch, *Metanoia: How God Radically Transforms People, Churches, and Organizations from the Inside Out* (Cody, WY: 100 Movements Publishing / Movement Leaders Collective, 2023), p. 10.
6. Hirsch, *Metanoia*, p. 10.
7. Jürgen Moltmann, *The Coming of God: Christian Eschatology* (trans. Margaret Kohl; London: SCM Press, 1996), p. 204.
8. Lana Vawser, *I Hear the Lord Say New Era* (Pittensburg, PA: Destiny Image, 2020), p. 11.

⁹ Christopher Rowland, 'Apocalyptic and Mission', in *Dictionary of Mission: Theology, History, Perspectives* (ed. Karl Müller et al.; New York, NY: Orbis, 1997), p. 31.

¹⁰ R.T. France, *The Gospel of Matthew*, New International Commentary on the New Testament (Grand Rapids, MI: Eerdmans, 2007), p. 899.

¹¹ Morna Hooker, *The Gospel According to St Mark*, Black's New Testament Commentaries (London: A & C Black, 1991), p. 306.

2 God Has Got a Plan

¹ See Lausanne Committee for World Evangelization, 'The Two Thirds World Church', *Lausanne Occasional Paper* 44 (produced by the Issue Group on this topic at the 2004 Forum for World Evangelization, 'A New Vision, a New Heart, a Renewed Call', Pattaya, Thailand, 29 September – 5 October 2004).

² See John Robb, 'Prayer as a Strategic Weapon in Frontier Missions', *International Journal of Frontier Missions* 8.1 (1991): pp. 23–31.

³ Harry A. Hahne, 'The Whole Creation Has Been Groaning', in *Christian Reflection: A Series in Faith and Ethics* (Waco, TX: Center for Christian Ethics, Baylor University, 2010), p. 21.

⁴ James D.G. Dunn, *Romans 1–8*, Word Biblical Commentary (Dallas, TX: Word, 1988), p. 472.

⁵ David Barrett, 'The Worldwide Holy Spirit Renewal', in *The Century of the Holy Spirit: 100 Years of Pentecostal and Charismatic Renewal* (ed. Vinson Synan; Nashville, TN: Thomas Nelson, 2001), p. 387.

3 Great Revival, Great Turbulence

¹ Alan Hirsch, *Metanoia: How God Radically Transforms People, Churches, and Organizations from the Inside Out* (Cody, WY: 100 Movements Publishing / Movement Leaders Collective, 2023), p. 8.

² David A. Hubbard, *Joel and Amos*, Tyndale Old Testament Commentaries (Leicester: IVP, 1989), p. 73.
³ Paul E. Leonard, 'Commentary on Joel', in *The International Bible Commentary* (ed. F.F. Bruce; Grand Rapids, MI: Zondervan; London: Marshall & Pickering, rev. edn, 1986), pp. 886–7.
⁴ Hubbard, *Joel and Amos*, p. 71.
⁵ Mike Bickle, *God's Answer to the Growing Crisis: A Bold Call to Action in the End Times* (Lake Mary, FL: Charisma House, 2016), p. 182.
⁶ David Sliker, *The Nations Rage: Prayer, Promise and Power in an Anti-Christian Age* (Bloomington, MN: Chosen Books, 2020), p. 89.
⁷ David F. Payne, 'Commentary on Isaiah', in *The International Bible Commentary* (ed. F.F. Bruce; Grand Rapids, MI: Zondervan; London: Marshall Pickering, rev. edn, 1986), p. 760.
⁸ Payne, 'Commentary on Isaiah', p. 760.
⁹ Tom Brokaw, *The Greatest Generation* (New York, NY: Random House, 1998), pp. xxvii, xxviii.

4 Keeping Our Eyes on the Lord's Return

¹ Larry J. Kreitzer, 'Parousia', in *Dictionary of the Later New Testament and Its Developments* (ed. Ralph Martin and Peter Davids; Leicester: IVP, 1997), p. 856.
² J.C. Ryle, 'Expository Thoughts on Mark – Mark 13:24–31', *Sermon Index* https://www.sermonindex.net/modules/articles/index.php?view=article&aid=32847_ (accessed 1 May 2024).
³ Justin Martyr, 'Dialogue 80', *The Ante-Nicene Fathers*, vol. 1, Christian Classics Ethereal Library https://www.ccel.org/ccel/schaff/anf01.viii.iv.lxxx.html (accessed 1 May 2024).
⁴ See Timothy Weber, 'Millennialism', in *The Oxford Handbook of Eschatology* (ed. Jerry Walls; Oxford: Oxford University Press, 2008), pp. 365–83.
⁵ Jürgen Moltmann, *The Coming of God: Christian Eschatology* (trans. Margaret Kohl; London: SCM Press, 1996), p. 198.
⁶ Moltmann, *Coming of God*, p. 201.

5 A Fresh Look at the Church

1. Brad Harper and Paul Metzger, *Exploring Ecclesiology: An Evangelical and Ecumenical Introduction* (Grand Rapids, MI: Brazos Press, 2009), p. 18.
2. Peter Hocken, *God's Masterplan: Penetrating the Mystery of Christ* (Stoke-on-Trent: Alive Publishing, 2003), p. 130.
3. Other passages that point to Jesus as the Bridegroom God include: Isa. 54:4–12; 62:2–5; Jer. 2:2; 3:14; 31:32; Ezek. 16:13–15,32; 23:1–45; Hos. 1:2; 2:7,14–23; 3:1–5; Matt. 9:15; 22:1–14; 25:1–13; John 3:29; 2 Cor. 11:2; Eph. 5:25–32; Rev. 19:7–9; 21:9; 22:17.
4. See Kim Huff, *The Holy Wedding: Christ and His Bride* (Murrells Inlet, SC: Covenant Books, 2018), introduction.

6 Radiant: Journey into Intimacy in the Song of Songs

1. St Bernard of Clairvaux, *Sermon 1*, VI.II.
2. Sermon, 'A Bundle of Myrrh', in Charles H. Spurgeon, *The Most Holy Place: Sermons on the Song of Solomon* (Ross-shire: Christian Focus, 1996), p. 112.
3. Brian and Candice Simmons, *The Sacred Journey: God's Relentless Pursuit of Our Affection* (Savage, MN: BroadStreet Publishing, 2015), p. 9.
4. Some of the insights below are borrowed from Simmons, *The Sacred Journey*, which I recommend as a lovely commentary on the Song of Songs.
5. Charlie Cleverly, *The Song of Songs: Exploring the Divine Romance* (London: Hodder & Stoughton, 2015), p. 203.

7 Resolute: Glimpses into the End-Time Church in the Book of Revelation

1. Robert Mounce, *The Book of Revelation* (Grand Rapids, MI: Eerdmans, 1977), p. 44.

² This saying is often attributed to the American missionary Jim Elliot, who was killed in South America in the 1950s. However, it may originate in the mid-1660s with Philip Henry, father of the well-known Bible commentator, Matthew Henry.

³ F.F. Bruce, 'Commentary on Revelation', in *The International Bible Commentary* (ed. F.F. Bruce; Grand Rapids, MI: Zondervan; London: Marshall Pickering, rev. edn, 1986), p. 1628.

8 God Will Finish What He Has Started: The Book of Acts and the End-Time Church

¹ Martyn Lloyd-Jones, *The Puritans: Their Origins and Successors* (Edinburgh: Banner of Truth, 1987), pp. 12–13.

² John McGinley, *The Church of Tomorrow: Being a Christ-centred People in a Changing World* (London: SPCK, 2023), p. 42.

³ R.T. Kendall, *Prepare Your Heart for the Midnight Cry* (London: SPCK, 2016), p. 8.

⁴ Douglas Farrow, *Ascension and Ecclesia: On the Significance of the Doctrine of the Ascension for Ecclesiology and Christian Cosmology* (Grand Rapids, MI: Eerdmans, 1999), pp. 16–17.

⁵ See www.call2all.org.

⁶ The 10/40 window is the rectangular area of North Africa, the Middle East and Asia between 10 degrees north and 40 degrees north latitude. It contains the world's four dominant religious blocs and includes most of the world's Muslims, Hindus and Buddhists.

Introduction to Part Three: Marks of the Emerging End-Time Church

¹ C.S. Lewis, *Voyage of the Dawn Treader* (London: Geoffrey Bles, 1952), pp. 353–4.

9 First Mark: Known for the Numinous Presence of the Lord (the Overshadowed Community)

1. Bob Dunnett, *Let God Arise: Making Way for Revival* (London: Marshall Pickering, 1990), p. 150.
2. Frank Macchia, 'The Church of the Latter Rain: The Church and Eschatology in Pentecostal Perspective', in *Towards a Pentecostal Ecclesiology: The Church and the Fivefold Gospel* (ed. John C. Thomas; Cleveland, TN: CTP Press, 2010), p. 254.
3. Andrew White, *Faith under Fire: What the Middle East Conflict Has Taught Me about God* (Oxford: Monarch, 2011), p. 108.

10 Second Mark: Devoted in Love for the Lord and for Each Other (the Fervent Community)

1. Rick Heeren, *Marketplace Miracles: Extraordinary Stories of Marketplace Turnarounds Transforming Businesses, Schools and Communities* (Grand Rapids, MI: Revell/Baker, 2008) p. 139.
2. Julie Brown, *The Mantle of Purity* (Tolworth: Grosvenor House Publishing, 2018), p. 43.
3. Peter Hocken, *Pentecost and Parousia: Charismatic Renewal, Christian Unity, and the Coming Glory* (Eugene, OR: Wipf & Stock, 2013), p. 145.

11 Third Mark: Spreading the Gospel in Word and Spirit (the Anointed Community)

1. Bill Johnson, *Face to Face with God: The Ultimate Quest to Experience His Presence* (Lake Mary, FL: Charisma House, 2007), p. 84.
2. Anecdotal; see 'Smith Wigglesworth's 1947 Prophetic Word', *Pray for Scotland* https://www.prayforscotland.org.uk/smith-wigglesworths-1947-prophetic-word (accessed 1 May 2024).

³ Lou Engle, *The Jesus Fast* (Colorado Springs, CO: Engle House Publishing, 2020), p. 1.
⁴ Kenneth J. Archer, 'The Fivefold Gospel and the Mission of the Church: Ecclesiastical Implications and Opportunities', in *Towards a Pentecostal Ecclesiology: The Church and the Fivefold Gospel* (ed. John C. Thomas; Cleveland, TN: CTP Press, 2010), p. 15.
⁵ Arthur Blessitt, *The Cross* (Colorado Springs, CO: Authentic, 2008), p. 121.
⁶ Alexander Solzhenitsyn, *Warning to the West: Speeches 1975–1976* (London: Vintage / Penguin Random House, 1976), p. 102.

12 Fourth Mark: Expressing God's Heart for the Poor and Broken (the Outpoured Community)

¹ Jackie Pullinger, *Chasing the Dragon* (London: Hodder & Stoughton, 2006).
² Jackie Pullinger, 'Loving the Poor', *Vineyard Churches* (20 August 2012) https://www.vineyardchurches.org.uk/articles/loving-the-poor (accessed 1 May 2024).
³ Guy Chevreau, *Turnings: The Kingdom of God and the Western World* (Tonbridge: Sovereign World, 2004), pp. 76–7.
⁴ Heidi Baker, *Compelled by Love: How to Change the World through the Simple Power of Love in Action* (Lake Mary, FL: Charisma House, 2008), p. 97.
⁵ Walter Wink, *The Powers That Be: Theology for a New Millennium* (New York, NY: Doubleday, 1998), p. 175.
⁶ Richard Stengel, *Nelson Mandela: Portrait of an Extraordinary Man* (London: Virgin Books / Ebury Publishing, 2012), p. 146.

13 Fifth Mark: Refined by Persecution and Falling Away (the Cruciform Community)

¹ Matt Chandler, *Take Heart: Christian Courage in the Age of Unbelief* (Flower Mound, TX: The Village Church, 2018), p. 117.

14 Sixth Mark: Mature in Development, Growth, Influence and Prayer (the Grown-Up Community)

1. Peter Hocken, *The Strategy of the Spirit? Worldwide Renewal and Revival in the Established Church and Modern Movements* (Guildford: Eagle, 1996), p. 245.

15 Seventh Mark: Creating First Fruits of the Coming Eschaton (the Transfiguring Community)

1. J.R.R. Tolkien, *The Lord of the Rings* (London: HarperCollins, 2001), p. 1000. Taken from *The Lord of the Rings* by J.R.R. Tolkien Copyright © 2001. Used by permission of HarperCollins Christian Publishing. www.harpercollinschristian.com.
2. Steve Botham, *His Kingdom, My Business: Partnering with God in the Workplace* (Rickmansworth: Instant Apostle, 2022), p. 278.
3. Ed Silvoso, *Transformation: Change the Marketplace and You Change the World* (Ventura, CA: Regal Books, 2007), p. 233.
4. Silvoso, *Transformation*, p. 203.
5. Justin Wiggins, 'Why Should We Remember Desmond Tutu?' *Christianity* (2023) https://www.christianity.com/wiki/people/desmond-tutu.html (accessed 1 Jan. 2023).
6. J. Richard Middleton, *A New Heaven and a New Earth: Reclaiming Biblical Eschatology* (Grand Rapids, MI: Baker Academic, 2014), p. 70.
7. Middleton, *A New Heaven and a New Earth*, p. 71.

16 Preparing as the Whole Church

1. Christophe Chalamet, Andreas Dettwiler, Mariel Mazzocco and Ghislain Waterlot, eds, *Game Over? Reconsidering Eschatology* (Berlin: De Gruyter, 2017), pp. ix, x.

17 Preparing as Leaders

[1] Alan Hirsch, *Metanoia: How God Radically Transforms People, Churches, and Organizations from the Inside Out* (Cody, WY: 100 Movements Publishing / Movement Leaders Collective, 2023), p. 24.
[2] Hirsch, *Metanoia*, p. 25.

18 The Personal Challenge

[1] Dick Eastman, *Intercessory Worship: Combining Worship and Prayer to Touch the Heart of God* (London: Regal Books, 2012), p. 90.
[2] Jordan Peterson, *Twelve Rules for Life: An Antidote to Chaos* (London: Penguin, 2018), p. 27.
[3] *The Sayings of the Desert Fathers: The Apophthegmata Patrum: The Alphabetical Collection*, Cistercian Studies Series 59 (trans. Benedicta Ward; Trappist, KY: Cistercian Publications, 1975), p. 64.

Bibliography

Archer, Kenneth J. 'The Fivefold Gospel and the Mission of the Church: Ecclesiastical Implications and Opportunities.' Pages 7–43 in *Towards a Pentecostal Ecclesiology: The Church and the Fivefold Gospel* (ed. John C. Thomas; Cleveland, TN: CTP Press, 2010).

Baker, Heidi. *Compelled by Love: How to Change the World through the Simple Power of Love in Action* (Lake Mary, FL: Charisma House, 2008).

Barrett, David. 'The Worldwide Holy Spirit Renewal.' Pages 381–414 in *The Century of the Holy Spirit: 100 Years of Pentecostal and Charismatic Renewal* (ed. Vinson Synan; Nashville, TN: Thomas Nelson, 2001).

Bickle, Mike. *God's Answer to the Growing Crisis: A Bold Call to Action in the End Times* (Lake Mary, FL: Charisma House, 2016).

Blessitt, Arthur. *The Cross* (Colorado Springs, CO: Authentic, 2008).

Botham, Steve. *His Kingdom, My Business: Partnering with God in the Workplace* (Rickmansworth: Instant Apostle, 2022).

Brokaw, Tom. *The Greatest Generation* (New York, NY: Random House, 1998), pp. xxvii, xxviii.

Brown, Julie. *The Mantle of Purity* (Tolworth: Grosvenor House Publishing, 2018).

Bruce, F.F. 'Commentary on Revelation.' Pages 1593–629 in *The International Bible Commentary* (ed. F.F. Bruce; Grand Rapids, MI: Zondervan; London: Marshall Pickering, rev. edn, 1986).

Chalamet, Christophe, Andreas Dettwiler, Mariel Mazzocco and Ghislain Waterlot, eds. *Game Over? Reconsidering Eschatology* (Berlin: De Gruyter, 2017).

Chandler, Matt. *Take Heart: Christian Courage in the Age of Unbelief* (Flower Mound, TX: The Village Church, 2018).

Chevreau, Guy. *Turnings: The Kingdom of God and the Western World* (Tonbridge: Sovereign World, 2004).

Cleverly, Charlie. *The Song of Songs: Exploring the Divine Romance* (London: Hodder & Stoughton, 2015).

Dunn, James D. *Romans 1–8*, Word Biblical Commentary (Dallas, TX: Word, 1988).

Dunnett, Bob. *Let God Arise: Making Way for Revival* (London: Marshall Pickering, 1990).

Eastman, Dick. *Intercessory Worship: Combining Worship and Prayer to Touch the Heart of God* (London: Regal Books, 2012).

Engle, Lou. *The Jesus Fast* (Colorado Springs, CO: Engle House Publishing, 2020).

Farrow, Douglas. *Ascension and Ecclesia: On the Significance of the Doctrine of the Ascension for Ecclesiology and Christian Cosmology* (Grand Rapids, MI: Eerdmans, 1999).

Fields, Joshua. 'Is Civilisation on the Verge of Collapse?' *Medium* (10 July 2018) https://medium.com/@joshfields/is-civilisation-on-the-verge-of-collapse-14ffa9cac6e4 (accessed 1 May 2024).

France, R.T. *The Gospel of Matthew*, New International Commentary on the New Testament (Grand Rapids, MI: Eerdmans, 2007).

Hahne, Harry A. 'The Whole Creation Has Been Groaning.' Pages 19–28 in *Christian Reflection: A Series in Faith and Ethics* (Waco, TX: Center for Christian Ethics, Baylor University, 2010).

Harper, Brad, and Paul Metzger. *Exploring Ecclesiology: An Evangelical and Ecumenical Introduction* (Grand Rapids, MI: Brazos Press, 2009).

Heeren, Rick. *Marketplace Miracles: Extraordinary Stories of Marketplace Turnarounds Transforming Businesses, Schools and Communities* (Grand Rapids, MI: Revell/Baker, 2008).

Hirsch, Alan. *Metanoia: How God Radically Transforms People, Churches, and Organizations from the Inside Out* (Cody, WY: 100 Movements Publishing / Movement Leaders Collective, 2023).

Hocken, Peter. *God's Masterplan: Penetrating the Mystery of Christ* (Stoke-on-Trent: Alive Publishing, 2003).

———. *Pentecost and Parousia: Charismatic Renewal, Christian Unity, and the Coming Glory* (Eugene, OR: Wipf & Stock, 2013).

———. *The Strategy of the Spirit? Worldwide Renewal and Revival in the Established Church and Modern Movements* (Guildford: Eagle, 1996).

Hooker, Morna. *The Gospel According to St Mark*, Black's New Testament Commentaries (London: A & C Black, 1991).

Hubbard, David A. *Joel and Amos*, Tyndale Old Testament Commentaries (Leicester: IVP, 1989).

Huff, Kim. *The Holy Wedding: Christ and His Bride* (Murrells Inlet, SC: Covenant Books, 2018).

Johnson, Bill. *Face to Face with God: The Ultimate Quest to Experience His Presence* (Lake Mary, FL: Charisma House, 2007).

Justin Martyr. 'Dialogue 80.' *The Ante-Nicene Fathers*, vol. 1. Christian Classics Ethereal Library https://www.ccel.org/ccel/schaff/anf01.viii.iv.lxxx.html (accessed 1 May 2024).

Kendall, R.T. *Prepare Your Heart for the Midnight Cry* (London: SPCK, 2016).

Kreitzer, Larry, J. 'Parousia.' Pages 856–75 in *Dictionary of the Later New Testament and Its Developments* (ed. Ralph Martin and Peter Davids; Leicester: IVP, 1997).

Lausanne Committee for World Evangelization. 'The Two Thirds World Church,' *Lausanne Occasional Paper* 44 (produced by the Issue Group on this topic at the 2004 Forum for World Evangelization, 'A New Vision, a New Heart, a Renewed Call', Pattaya, Thailand, 29 September – 5 October 2004).

Leonard, Paul E. 'Commentary on Joel.' Pages 884–91 in *The International Bible Commentary* (ed. F.F. Bruce; Grand Rapids, MI: Zondervan; London: Marshall Pickering, rev. edn, 1986).

Lloyd-Jones, Martyn. *The Puritans: Their Origins and Successors* (Edinburgh: Banner of Truth, 1987).

Macchia, Frank. 'The Church of the Latter Rain: The Church and Eschatology in Pentecostal Perspective.' Pages 248–58 in *Towards a Pentecostal Ecclesiology: The Church and the Fivefold Gospel* (ed. John C. Thomas; Cleveland, TN: CTP Press, 2010).

McGinley, John. *The Church of Tomorrow: Being a Christ-centred People in a Changing World* (London: SPCK, 2023).

Middleton, J. Richard. *A New Heaven and a New Earth: Reclaiming Biblical Eschatology* (Grand Rapids, MI: Baker Academic, 2014).

Moltmann, Jürgen. *The Coming of God: Christian Eschatology* (trans. Margaret Kohl; London: SCM Press, 1996).

Mounce, Robert. *The Book of Revelation* (Grand Rapids, MI: Eerdmans, 1977).

Payne, David F. 'Commentary on Isaiah.' Pages 714–63 in *The International Bible Commentary* (ed. F.F. Bruce; Grand Rapids, MI: Zondervan; London: Marshall Pickering, rev. edn, 1986).

Peterson, Jordan. *Twelve Rules for Life: An Antidote to Chaos* (London: Penguin, 2018).

Pullinger, Jackie. *Chasing the Dragon* (London: Hodder & Stoughton, 2006).

——. 'Loving the Poor,' *Vineyard Churches* (20 August 2012) https://www.vineyardchurches.org.uk/articles/loving-the-poor (accessed 1 May 2024).

Robb, John. 'Prayer as a Strategic Weapon in Frontier Missions.' *International Journal of Frontier Missions* 8.1 (1991): pp. 23–31.

Rowland, Christopher. 'Apocalyptic and Mission.' Pages 30–33 in *Dictionary of Mission: Theology, History, Perspectives* (ed. Karl Müller et al.; New York, NY: Orbis, 1997).

Ryle, J.C. 'Expository Thoughts on Mark – Mark 13:24–31.' *Sermon Index* https://www.sermonindex.net/modules/articles/index.php?view=article&aid=32847_ (accessed 1 May 2024).

The Sayings of the Desert Fathers: The Apophthegmata Patrum: The Alphabetical Collection, Cistercian Studies Series 59 (trans. Benedicta Ward; Trappist, KY: Cistercian Publications, 1975).

Seligman, Martin E.P., Peter Railton, Roy F. Baumeister and Chandra Sripada. *Homo Prospectus* (New York, NY: Oxford University Press, 2016).

Silvoso, Ed. *Transformation: Change the Marketplace and You Change the World* (Ventura, CA: Regal Books, 2007).

Simmons, Brian and Candice. *The Sacred Journey: God's Relentless Pursuit of Our Affection* (Savage, MN: BroadStreet Publishing, 2015).

Sliker, David. *The Nations Rage: Prayer, Promise and Power in an Anti-Christian Age* (Bloomington, MN: Chosen Books, 2020).

Solzhenitsyn, Alexander. *Warning to the West: Speeches 1975–1976* (London: Vintage / Penguin Random House, 1976).

Spurgeon, Charles H. *The Most Holy Place: Sermons on the Song of Solomon* (Ross-shire: Christian Focus, 1996).

Stengel, Richard. *Nelson Mandela: Portrait of an Extraordinary Man* (London: Virgin Books / Ebury Publishing, 2012).

Tolkien, J.R.R. *The Lord of the Rings* (London: HarperCollins, 2001).

Vawser, Lana. *I Hear the Lord Say New Era* (Pittensburg, PA: Destiny Image, 2020).

Walls, Jerry. *The Oxford Handbook of Eschatology* (Oxford: Oxford University Press, 2008).

Weber, Timothy. 'Millennialism.' Pages 365–83 in *The Oxford Handbook of Eschatology* (ed. J. Walls; Oxford: Oxford University Press, 2008).

White, Andrew. *Faith under Fire: What the Middle East Conflict Has Taught Me about God* (Oxford: Monarch, 2011).

Wiggins, Justin. 'Why Should We Remember Desmond Tutu?' *Christianity* (2023) https://www.christianity.com/wiki/people/desmond-tutu.html (accessed 1 January 2023).

Wink, Walter. *The Powers That Be: Theology for a New Millennium* (New York, NY: Doubleday, 1998).

Authentic

We trust you enjoyed reading this book from Authentic. If you want to be informed of any new titles from this author and other releases you can sign up to the Authentic newsletter by scanning below:

Online:
authenticmedia.co.uk

Follow us:

www.ingramcontent.com/pod-product-compliance
Lightning Source LLC
Chambersburg PA
CBHW050551170426
43201CB00011B/1651